The CAROL *of* CHRISTMAS

Life Story of Christmas Carol Kauffman

Marcia Kauffman Clark

D1253219

DIGITAL
LEGEND

Christmas Carol Kauffman

1901–1969

Christmas Carol Kauffman was born on December 25, 1901, in Elkhart, Indiana, the second daughter of Abraham Rohrer and Selena Bell Wade Miller. Carol, as she was known, graduated from Elkhart High School and attended both Hesston and Goshen Colleges. She began writing short stories at Hesston College and continued writing one short story per month for the *Youths Christian Companion*. In total, she wrote more than one hundred short stories.

In 1929 she married Nelson Edward Kauffman. They served together at the Hannibal Mission Church in Missouri for twenty-two years, where Nelson was the pastor. They are parents of four children. While in Hannibal, Carol began writing book-length inspirational true stories that were published by Herald Press.

Lucy Winchester, her first book, was published in 1945. Throughout the next two decades she authored six additional books: *Light from Heaven* (1948), *Dannie of Cedar Cliffs* (1950), *Not Regina* (1954), *Hidden Rainbow* (1957), *For One Moment* (1960), and *Search to Belong* (1963). After her death, two more books were published in 1971: *Little Pete and Other Stories* a collection of thirteen of her short stories, originally written in 1928 and *One Boy's Battle*, written in 1948 and originally titled *Unspoken Love*. All nine of her books continue to be published today.

Christmas Carol Kauffman died on January 30, 1969

To my mother,
Christmas Carol Kauffman,
whose life story becomes an open book

© 2008 Digital Legend Press

All rights reserved. No part of this book may be reproduced in any form or by any means without permission in writing from the publisher, Digital Legend. Send inquiries to:
Digital Legend Publishing
4700 Clover St.
Honeoye Falls, NY 14472
U.S.A.
Visit www.Digitalegend.com/Carol
or write to info@digitalegend.com

Printed in the United States of America
ISBN: 978-1-934537-92-3

Cover and interior design by Anastasia Tyler (King City, Oregon)

Contents

Foreword

Christmas Carol Kauffman was no ordinary person. She embraced enormous faith in God. Yet she was a fully human individual as we all are.

Carol's plan for her future was suddenly interrupted by a tragic loss that changed her life's goals forever. With her childlike faith in God, she gathered strength and was able to accept her loss even though it was wrapped in a blanket of unimaginable suffering.

When the call came for Carol and Nelson to plant themselves in Hannibal, Missouri, to create a Mennonite mission church, she was ready for the challenge. God could be trusted to provide whatever was needed. The story of Carol's life along with her husband's unwavering dedication shows remarkable evidence of God's faithfulness in the most trying circumstances.

Marcia Kauffman Clark's ability to write takes us into Carol's life of commitment to God through extreme adversities and great triumphs. Romance, tragedy, and serious illness are woven together to make up the fabric of Carol's life. Here is an example of faith in a loving God who is able to sustain us in the best of times and the worst of times. In this story, we are compelled to face the questions: Is my faith commitment to the will of God able to survive what Carol experienced? Is there a significant part of my life that I hold back for myself? This dramatic story includes such an incident. It plagued

Carol with a deep sense of guilt for a long while afterwards.

This is a remarkable story of a young couple who planted a mission church in Hannibal, Missouri, during the great economic depression of the 1930s. Their faith was often tested as they were forced to cope with what seemed to be insurmountable choices.

For me, reading this story was like living again in those years of Carol and Nelson's work in Hannibal. Summer Bible School and young people's monthly literary gatherings were a great contribution to my adolescent and teenage development. I will never forget the hilarious laughter that was often characteristic of those literary gatherings. Carol and Nelson were creative and fun-loving personalities.

I loved Nelson and Carol and was dedicated to serve and support them in any way that I could. One day, probably in the early part of 1950, Nelson stopped by where I was farming with my father near Palmyra, a few miles from Hannibal. I was surprised when he asked me if I ever felt God calling me to be a minister of the Gospel. In response to his query, I told Nelson that when I was a small child, my mother told me that her prayer was that I might be a minister some day. My mother's prayer and Nelson's question convinced me that this was God's call to me personally. To resist the Lord's call could result in a guilt too heavy to bear. On September 3, 1950, I was ordained to assist Nelson in pastoral ministry.

Carol was also a writer. Thousands of people here and abroad have read her books and have been inspired to a fuller commitment to the will and purpose of God in their lives. This story of Christmas Carol is both intriguing and convincing. To view her life so close up is a rare privilege. Marcia's story of her mother's life is capable of touching one's emotions on many levels. When you begin to read this humble story, you will not wish to lay it aside until you are finished.

Thank you, Marcia, for allowing me the pleasure of living again those years when our lives were so intertwined.

HAROLD KREIDER

Preface

When I decided to write the life story of my mother, Christmas Carol Kauffman, my heart immediately turned to feelings of deep gratitude for the valuable lessons she taught me. Her example of faith and commitment shines throughout her entire life. I am honored to have this privilege. Many who read these forthcoming pages will be those who have already read my mother's books. I am grateful her books are still being published and read by a new generation of readers.

Generations before us have a tremendous influence upon our lives. Mother's faith and commitment derived largely from the influence of her righteous, faithful parents. To know our heritage is to know those from whom we come and consequently who we are.

Within her deep commitment to our Lord and Savior, my mother shared her testimony daily by word and deed. Jesus Christ truly was the Lord of her life. I wish to thank my Heavenly Father for the privilege of being born to such a valiant and faithful woman. As you read about Mother's life experiences, you will see a strong thread of hope and faith running through them all.

I am very grateful for the kind interest and assistance from Dennis Stoesz, archivist, and John Lapp of the Mennonite Church USA Historical Committee at Goshen College, Goshen, Indiana. Preserved files, cassette tapes of Mother sharing her life story, a cassette tape of her funeral service, and perfectly preserved files containing her writing correspondence were of great value to me. Thanks to my parents for keeping such detailed files, such as the Hannibal Mission Church Scrapbooks, which also served well.

The mission statement of the Historical Committee is "God calls us to preserve our heritage, to interpret our faith stories, and to proclaim God's work among us." Since my mother had such a strong testimony of Our Lord and Savior Jesus Christ, in writing this, as the author I share mine.

It is my sincere desire that through its pages this story will touch your heart deeply. I hope you will experience Carol's virtue, pain, joy, sacrifice, courage, tears, honor, sickness, angels, unity, endurance, testimony, grief, humility, death, obedience, trials, acceptance, compassion, strength, suffering, patience, gratitude, respect, miracles, calmness, faith, hope, and love.

We learn from our own experiences and the experiences of others. Mother learned to reign victorious through her life's trials and tests of faith. I have come to love and appreciate Mother and Father even more as I discovered details about their lives that I never knew.

I express appreciation to Mother's parents, who kept the priceless letters that she wrote. These letters provide many details, serving as a journal, with interesting facts about her life and also a glimpse into Mother's delightful personality.

Special thanks to my sister Ma Donna and my aunt Nellie. In 1968, Mother's sister Nellie wrote a long letter to Ma Donna, recalling fond memories and unusual family experiences. Also, several years before her death in early 1977, Ma Donna took a writing course and wrote a short story of Mother's life. I have drawn from both of these sources extensively.

I am indebted to my cousins David Mann and Dorothy Jean Horst, Nellie's children, for the time and effort they took to keep family history alive through preserved letters and a cassette-taped interview with Mother's father, Abraham Rohrer Miller, when he was ninety-four.

Another Mennonite author, Robert Baker, wrote two articles about Mother. Before his death, he graciously gave me permission to add them to this story. He had a remarkable gift in writing.

Thanks to Mary Histand, Mother's roommate at Hesston College, Hesston, Kansas, who kept the letters she received from Mother. Mary was ninety years old when she sent copies of these letters to my niece, Yvonne Kauffman Boettger, in December 1995. Thank you, Yvonne, for passing them on to me.

I could not have provided this endearing story without the help of my husband, Stephen. His help with the computer was most valuable.

I am grateful for my family and friends Ben and Martha Eberly, Stephen J. Clark, Sharon Porter, and Sandra Morris who helped with proofreading.

My editor, Anastasia Tyler, provided much personal interest, professional help, and advice. Without her expertise, this story would not be what it is today. My publisher, Boyd J. Tuttle, gave me wonderful encouragement and support. He is the reason you are holding this powerful book in your hands and have the opportunity to read about Mother's remarkable life. Thank you both, Anastasia and Boyd, for your confidence in me.

And lastly, I wish to thank both my parents, Christmas Carol Miller and Nelson Edward Kauffman, for the example they provided throughout my life and for teaching me what real dedication to the Lord is all about. I honor my mother and father, who together devoted their lives to the service of others and in doing so expressed the true measure of their testimony of Our Lord and Savior Jesus Christ.

Chapter 1

Faith of My Father

M ama! Mama!"
   "What is it Nellie?"

It was only two weeks before Christmas, and five-year-old Nellie Miller bounced down the stairs so fast she had to grab onto the railing to keep from falling. Her soft curls bounced even harder as she pushed on her mother's legs.

Even though Nellie had weighed just five pounds when she was born, her mother, Selena, nearly died during childbirth. Since that day five years ago, Selena had to stay in bed most of the time because her body was so weak. Selena and her husband, Abraham, hired someone to come into the home and do the housework and help attend precious little Nellie.

Together they prayed for the Lord's hand in their lives and sought advice from their family physician. He advised Selena to eat a special diet and exercise as much as she could physically withstand. A second pregnancy, he said, would either take her life or greatly improve her health. Abraham and Selena Miller knew they wanted more children and together decided they would deal with whatever came their way.

They were very excited as they anticipated the new baby's arrival to bless their home—and at the same time were deeply concerned, since Selena might actually leave their new baby and priceless little Nellie motherless.

Nellie almost pushed her mother over. Selena was barely five feet tall, and the baby she was carrying was due near the end of January. She had to grab hold of the Indiana Cupboard to keep from falling.

"Little Darlin', calm down! Calm down! What is it?" questioned Selena. "Can you see the new fallen snow outside?"

Selena knew Nellie was excited about getting the house decorated for Christmas. And the newly fallen snow, the first of what promised to be a typical harsh and long northern Indiana winter, was another reminder that Christmas was just a few weeks away.

"Mama, Mama, when is Papa coming home?" Nellie asked.

"Not until tomorrow night. Remember, Papa is singing again this weekend with the men's chorus."

Nellie pulled on Selena's apron. "Mama, I had this dream. Please sit over here and listen to my happy dream!"

Selena's husband, Abraham "Abe" Rohrer Miller, was born to Amos Buckwalter Miller and Esther Habbegger Rohrer, on August 8, 1868, near Millersville, Pennsylvania, in Lancaster County. He was the oldest of three children.

One morning, three-and-a-half-year-old Abe and his older sister, Ida, woke up to commotion in their mother and father's bedroom. Abe saw his mother lying in the bed. His father ran out of room and the house in a panic then rode on horseback to get the doctor.

"What's wrong with Mama? What's wrong with our Mama?" sobbed little Abe.

Before their daddy and the doctor returned, their sweet mama was gone. Esther had passed away just a month after giving birth to another baby boy, Ephraim. She was not yet twenty-seven.

"Papa, where are they taking my mama?" Little Abe clung to Ida and sobbed uncontrollably as they carried away his tender mother. "Where are they taking my mama?"

Abe, as an innocent little child, not only had to face the unforgettable reality of seeing his primary source of love, hope, and tenderness die a painful death in front of his very eyes, but watch as unknown strange men carried his mama down the stairs, out of the house, and into a cold, dark grave.

Abe never forgot this tragic day. A few unforgettable days later, Abe's uncle held him up so he could see down the deep, dark hole in the ground at the cemetery.

"Look Abe, see down there in that big deep hole?" he asked. "That's where your mama is now."

Abe had no understanding of what was going on. He probably had seen a favorite cat or puppy covered up with dirt in a shallow grave. That was sad enough, but no, never, not his mama! Back in those days feelings weren't openly expressed. No child psychologist tried to come to his rescue. He had no television or videos to keep his mind occupied.

His father, Amos, not knowing how else to cope with his wife's passing, sold the farm and went to live with his father. Abe and his baby brother, Ephraim, were immediately whisked off to live with his grandparents on his mother's side, his Grandma Rohrer. He not only had to face the pain of his mama's death but felt shoved into a home he hardly recognized, with a grandma he barely knew. Suddenly he was living in unfamiliar surroundings.

To make matters even worse, his loving little sister Ida was taken away to live with his grandmother's sister, Mrs. Havaker. So Abe had only his new baby brother close to his side at Grandma Rohrer's as he adjusted to the loss of his precious mother, life without a daddy nearby, and Ida too far away to see very often.

Grandma Rohrer, dealing with the loss of her daughter and witnessing the grief of tenderhearted little Abe, had problems of her own. She was left grasping for inner comfort and peace within herself, as she clung to her new little grandson, Ephraim, and watched over Abe. Caring for her newborn grandchild brought loving memories to Grandma Rohrer of holding her baby daughter Esther, who was now lying in a grave a short distance away.

The days were scary and uncertain for Abe. Years later, Abe said he was very, very sad as a young boy. His parents' farm was the only life he knew. Abe spent many a night crying himself to sleep, knowing his mama was never coming back and that he'd seldom see Ida.

Young Abe felt abandoned, rejected, forgotten, fearful, resentful, and alone. He had never even heard of these grown-up words; even so, he knew inside the reality of these undeniable feelings. At the same time he felt guilty for feeling angry and hurt. Good little Christian boys weren't supposed to get angry. Yet, as the days passed, he felt the constant love and protection of a loving Heavenly Father. His grandma did the best she could under the circumstances, caring for her precious little motherless grandchildren.

Uncle Jacob, father Amos's brother, lost his wife that same year. Amos moved in with Jacob, and the two started farming together on a farm located near the town of Danville, Pennsylvania. Abe said the town was made up of a small country store and a few other buildings. Down the hill from the house flowed a creek, with a large mill built on it, and a bridge.

A year later, Jacob married, and Amos purchased another farm in the southern part of the county near Quarryville, Pennsylvania, with a stone house and a small barn. Abe said that the soil was so poor and barren that an old black crow wouldn't even want to fly over it or try landing on the property.

Amos married Barbara Stickler. It proved to be far too soon for Abe to adjust to a new woman taking over his father's life. After they set up housekeeping, Amos came to retrieve the boys from Grandma and Grandpa Rohrer's place—just as Abe and Ephraim were finally settling in to their new home. Grandma Rohrer absolutely refused to let Barbara and Amos take Ephraim. As a result, Abe and his baby brother never grew up together, another major loss Abe never forgot.

Grandma and Grandpa Rohrer did not take kindly to Amos marrying Barbara Stickler, which had a negative effect upon Abe's attitude towards his stepmother. He was already certain that he did not like her and would never want her to be a part of his life. Poor Ida could hardly stand it, either. They shed many tears together about this strange woman coming into their home and taking over their mother's belongings.

Father Amos built a new, large barn on his Quarryville farm. The neighbors said, "Amos, you'll never get that barn full!" But they soon changed their minds about Amos and began saying he was the best farmer in town. Despite having purchased a farm with poor soil, he grew more crops on his one-hundred acres than other farmers in the area grew on one-hundred-sixty acres. He fertilized the ground with huge piles of manure provided by his many steer. The big barn had four stalls for the cattle, paddocks for seven horses, and a place for twelve cows. It even had eleven stalls for young cattle. The livestock produced a generous amount of good manure!

The north side of the barn included a hog pen for fourteen hogs. There was a chicken house, and a windmill to pump the water. Amos built a big tank that held one hundred barrels of water piped to the stables, so the cows could have a drink whenever they wanted. It was very modern for the times.

Abe kept busy doing chores around the house since he was the oldest in the family. He had to work in the kitchen, split and saw the wood to keep the kitchen's wood box full, feed the chickens, hunt for the eggs, and churn the butter. They produced enough butter to ship surplus to New York, where it could be sold for twice the price they could get at home. The butter was put in wooden molds. Abraham would deliver butter in a box at the Fulton House railroad station, about four miles from his home.

Father Amos was a very fine Christian man. He was not well educated and couldn't speak very good English, but he knew how to run a farm.

Abe wasn't able to attend school on a regular basis. When he was old enough to help on the farm, he worked on their homestead and often as a hired hand for neighboring farmers. Even though he had little formal schooling, he loved to read.

Ida died at the age of seventeen. Abe didn't remember how or why, but he did remember that one morning right after breakfast his father said, "You need to go up to Ida's room."

He went up to Ida's room, and she said, "Oh my Abe, I saw the Lord my Savior last night!" She pined away and passed out. Just before she died, Abe was in her room again, and she quietly said, "Oh my, I saw paradise, and it was the most beautiful thing I ever saw!"

Ida's passing was yet another anguish for Abe, his father, and grandparents to withstand. The knowledge of eternal life helped pull them through the untimely separations from those they so deeply loved.

When he was growing up, Abe's family didn't have family worship, and he heard his father pray aloud only twice. The family always said morning grace at the table, but in silence. Grandma Rohrer's family was raised Mennonite and came from a rich devout heritage. Her family kept true to the Mennonite faith.

Before Abe was a teenager, he started running around with rowdy boys. Amos hired older teenage boys to help with the chores on the farm that brought a negative influence into Abe's life. When Abe was twelve years old, a Methodist church about three miles from their home was having special revival services for a week. The family farm was the farthest away from the church, so Abe would go from farm to farm and pick up two or three young folk. "There was quite a bunch of us when we finally got to the church where the revival meetings was held," recalled Abe.

Abe didn't remember much of what the minister had to say that evening because he was up in the balcony with a bunch of row-dies. One day when he was nineteen, he was pondering his life and his feelings about religion. He was busy feeding and harnessing the horses when he had an overwhelming feeling of being spiritually lost. He wanted to go back to the altar at church, but his father didn't want him to.

"Those altars and conversions, don't very many of them hold to it," Amos declared. "There are a lot of them out there, but they never did stick with anyone I've ever known."

Amos and Barbara hired a Christian girl who belonged to the church just a few miles from their farm, where Abe attended the revivals seven years earlier. She became interested in Abe and was a very positive influence in his life. He struggled spiritually and just couldn't find inner peace and desired an experience like his sister Ida. She had a vision of the Lord, and Abe wanted a vision of the Lord also. The only thing he thought that could teach him and help him would be an experience like that.

The Christian girl talked to Abe about Thomas who doubted and had a hard time believing until he placed his hand in the palms of the Savior. She helped him recall John 20:29: "Blessed are they that have not seen, and yet have believed."

On the strength of that, combined with fervent prayer, Abe finally felt peace. It took him about a week to feel like he was reconciled. A man who worked on the family farm came by the farm's line fence one sunny day. Abe called out, "Oh Sam, I'm saved, I feel like I am saved!" "Well," the man responded, "that's wonderful. I hope you hold out."

Chapter 2

Letters of Love

Selena Belle Wade was born May 5, 1866, near Quarryville, Lancaster County, Pennsylvania, to Amos Wade and Mary Keene. She had six sisters and three brothers. Selena was the only one of the ten children who attended school beyond the eighth grade.

Selena came from a very wealthy family. Her father, Amos, was a prosperous tobacco farmer. She attended Millersville State School in Millersville, Pennsylvania, and became a schoolteacher when she was just seventeen years old. She taught in the town of Buck, near her home. The Mechanics Grove School, a one-room schoolhouse, became her life for eleven years.

Selena was very fashionable with gorgeous clothes adorned with beads and lace. Her ears were pierced, and she was bedecked with beautiful jewelry. She was a tiny woman with a waistline measuring twenty-two inches; she stood barely five feet tall. Her daughter Christmas Carol Kauffman, in a talk she gave to a group of women at Kokomo, Indiana, described Selena as a "proud little peacock of a woman."

When Abe Miller was finally able to get away from the farm, he had a desire to learn more and attend school, working toward an eighth grade diploma. He attended the school where Selena taught. Selena was Abe's eighth grade schoolteacher! She was only two years older than her newfound friend. Selena boarded at the neighbors, just west of their family farm.

A young man down the road from the farm was giving music lessons. He went around to the neighborhood farms to get pupils to sign up for a course study of thirteen music lessons. Abe was interested because he loved to sing. The man told him that the girls at the farm adjacent wanted to take music lessons too. One of the girls was Abe's schoolteacher, Selena Wade. Abe had a very nice buggy with fringe on top, so it was up to him to give the girls rides to the music lessons, and since he really wanted to go too, it was a good thing.

One evening when Abe drove his buggy over to pick up the girls, the family's hired man, John Goff, walked up to him and said, "Abe, you know that new little schoolteacher? She thinks you're a pretty nice fellow."

Selena was beautiful, smart, and just the right height—both Selena and Abe were barely five feet tall. Abe got up enough courage to ask her for a date. After he graduated from eighth grade, Abe got a job as the janitor in the one-room schoolhouse where Selena taught. He saw a lot of his wonderful new friend. It didn't take Abe very long to fall in love with this sweet young lady.

He invited Selena to accompany him to church, where she learned about the Mennonite beliefs. Selena was so impressed with the messages of the evangelist that they went every night the revival meetings were held. The messages that the preacher gave were enlightening to her and different from anything she had ever heard before.

Selena went home and, one by one, shed her jewelry. As soon as she could sew some new clothes, she changed from her fashionable clothing and shoes to clothes that were very neat, but unquestionably austere and plain. She wore her hair pulled back under the typical Mennonite white, net hair-covering with wide white ribbons and the traditional black bonnet.

Selena told her family that she was becoming a Mennonite. Her entire family strenuously objected. Her brothers and sisters said that she would be making a fool of herself. She insisted that she had found something that satisfied her heart.

Even though the Methodist church had taken her in, Selena had never known what an "experience" was (feeling the Spirit and making a public confession of her beliefs). She grew up under Christian teachings from her Methodist upbringing. Her parents and family were very fine, honorable Christian citizens of the community.

Selena found within herself a desire to not only make an inward commitment for her newfound beliefs, but she was also more than willing to tell the world through her complete change of dress and lifestyle that she had found what she was looking for.

Abe went to the bishop of the Mennonite church at Millersville and applied for church membership. All the bishops went into the anteroom and stayed a long time with the door closed and came out and told him that they had never received in the church a lad as young as twenty and "he couldn't be knowin' what such a step would be." It was not an ordinary practice to baptize and receive unmarried members. He told them that he had purchased a Bible after listening to John F. Kauffman preach, and he had diligently read the Bible again and felt like he knew what it meant to be saved.

Abe went home and studied some more and went back a month later and begged them to accept him into the church by water baptism. Again, the preachers went to the anteroom to discuss this issue. They came out and asked him some point-blank questions from the Word of God. He was able to answer all their questions, to their utter amazement, with scripture because he studied the Bible daily.

He was then baptized, being the youngest member of that particular congregation ever to have been received into the church. The honorable, righteous character of her valiant sweetheart provided the encouragement for Selena to make the change. They spent many hours discussing the courage and commitment of the early Anabaptists who literally gave their lives in defense of their devotion to the truths they found for themselves. Selena was able to convince the preachers of her testimony and conviction of what she found for herself and was soon baptized as well.

One might wonder how many of us have within our hearts that same kind of assurance and conviction of our Lord and Savior Jesus Christ and have the knowledge required within our souls to be willing to sacrifice our own lives if necessary in building up and defending the kingdom of God.

Selena became a lifetime member of the Mennonite church. She didn't do as her brothers and sisters feared she would do: she didn't try it out for a few weeks or months and then go back to her old ways.

While still courting Selena, Abe went to Mount Joy, Pennsylvania, to work on the farm of his Uncle Joe Charles Miller. Later a friend invited him to move to Leola, Pennsylvania, to learn the sheet metal and heating business. He spent three years learning the tinner's trade and getting his apprenticeship. He found that his small stature proved to be a real asset to his future business.

During this time away from each other, Abe and Selena corresponded by letters—thirty-five in total. Abe addressed Selena as his "Esteemed Friend." They wrote about their daily lives, shared scriptures that illustrated the depth of their faith, and expressed love for each other. Their letters illustrate the kind of unshakable faith and testimony that Abe and Selena would pass on to their children, including Christmas Carol.

One such example is a poem written in Selena's handwriting and possibly sent to her loving friend in early April 1890:

We met, we loved, and we parted near
A corner of life's way;
And ever since we have been sad
  Though seeming blithe and gay.

Our weeping eye, our whitened cheek
And wildly throbbing heart,
Constrained us both in soul to say,
  "Tis hard, Tis hard to Part."
We've parted now, and yet we're joined
By love's mysterious power;
We speak not, but our soul's commune
  Through many a thoughtful hour.
Mysterious fate! We're doomed to live
Asunder and forlorn
Though Heaven decreed that we should love,
  Ere ever we were born.
To Thee, O darling of my heart!
My first love has been given;
But loved one thou wilt surely be
  Both mine and Christ's in Heaven.

One theme touched on in many of their letters centered around Abe's stomach condition. One extremely hot day when Abe was working at a neighboring farm as a hired hand, he became overheated and drank too much cold water. As a result, he suffered from severe damage to his stomach and was able to eat only very small portions at a time for the rest of his life.

"Thanks to God for all things. Everything is for the good of them that love Him," wrote Abe in late December 1894. "Could I but more fully confide in Him? I am so weak and unworthy. Pray for me, loving sister in faith. . . . I haven't eaten anything yet out side of milk but sucked part of an orange. I am getting very weak. I don't feel like working and I think I ought to see the Dr. anyway. I think I have something else to contend with now."

Selena wrote to him within the week:

I received your letter on New Year evening. I was longing to hear from you and tried to think you were better because it was so long coming. Last night, New Year evening, I was the last one to leave the room, and I was feeling very much depressed and thought I would pray there. As I was about to kneel, the scene of one week previous, when we knelt together there came to my mind. And a sudden gush of tears was a great relief to me. You say you need words of comfort. Yes, I too. I wish I knew words to comfort you. I think it would be well for us to try to comfort each other, in the Lord. Jesus says, 'I will not leave you comfortless; I will come to you.' And the Father has promised to send us the Comforter, which is the Holy Ghost, with the promise that he will teach all things.

Dear Friend, let us take him at His word. Let us believe that He doeth all things well. "He does not afflict willingly, nor grieve the children of men." "Happy is the man whom the Lord corrected, therefore despise not the chastening of the Almighty for He maketh sore and bindeth up; he woundeth and his hands make whole."

Jesus says, "call upon me in the day of trouble and I will deliver you." Surely this is the day of trouble and I have called upon Him, and shall continue calling and I am waiting for deliverance.

This is what I have decided to do. Each day, about 4:30 o'clock to withdraw from all persons and work and pray unto God especially for your pardon and restoration. And I think if we could send up a joint petition it would be a greater blessing to us both. "For if two agree on earth as touching anything that they shall ask, it shall be done for them by my Father which is in heaven."

Abe welcomed the kind admonishing letters from Selena. Her words brought relief and comfort to his soul. He did improve slowly and mentioned that it was because of a kind, loving Heavenly Father who heard his pleas for added strength. He was very grateful for her consoling words of comfort. He always spoke of the blessings of Jesus Christ, believing that they could be "truly united, walking hand in hand in the fear of the Lord." Abe returned a letter to Selena:

Last night father wrote a letter to Dr. Hartman of Columbus Ohio, about my case thinking he may be able to do something for me. It seems as though Dr. Keene's medicine isn't doing me very much good anymore. But I have my faith to believe His promises, for He says, "What things so ever ye desire, when ye pray, believe that ye receive them, and ye shall have them."

And I know that God cannot lie and that His promises are as firm today as the day He spoke them, for the Apostle Paul speaks of Jesus Christ being the same yesterday, today and forever. And again, in my case to me it seems almost impossible, but Jesus says "But with God all things are possible."

I hope the Lord will have mercy upon me for doubting it. I am so weak in that point. Let us endeavor to help one another to be steadfast in the Lord.

"It seems so long between letters receiving," wrote Abe to his fond sweetheart while he was spending time in Columbus, Ohio, in March 1895. "I think every morning I ought to get a letter but it has been some time already since I received the last letter. So I thought to satisfy myself, I would write one to you."

In June 1895, Abe reported in a letter to Selena that his pay was going to be raised by a dollar a week, bringing his monthly salary from eight dollars to twelve. Also in June 1895 the couple decided to be married, but it would be almost a year before the marriage took place.

After nine precious years of courtship, Selena Belle Wade and Abraham Rohrer Miller married on March 19, 1896, at the home of Selena's parents in Lancaster County, Pennsylvania. Thus they began a new life as Mr. and Mrs. Abraham Rohrer Miller.

Abe received his apprenticeship before their marriage and continued working in the tinner's trade with his good friend. Selena began calling her new husband Abram, a personal, endearing name especially chosen by her.

Abram always had a desire to go and see the West. Selena had relatives in southern Illinois, so they decided to go there, but John Brubaker said that they should stop off at Elkhart, Indiana.

Abram and Selena got such a royal reception from all the folks at the church there that they decided not to go any farther West.

On the way to Elkhart, both Abram and Selena prayed that they might locate somewhere where they could raise children in the Mennonite faith. Selena had saved one thousand dollars throughout her years of teaching, so they rented a house for six dollars a month and started looking around for property.

A real estate man took them around to see the available properties to purchase, and they soon found a house with enough property to build a second house. Because of the passing of Selena's grandfather and Abram's grandfather, they both got some inheritance money and were able to build a second house next door.

Abram got the money out of the bank the day before the bank failed. They could have lost everything! That was a testimony to both of them that the Lord watches over those who pay a full tithe.

When Selena and Abram arrived in Elkhart, he was not able to get a steady job in the tinner's trade. There just wasn't anything in Elkhart that he could do in his chosen profession, so he got a job for a few weeks with Keen Brothers and also worked at the railroad shop.

Nellie Marie Miller, Abram and Selena's first child, was born on March 27, 1897, weighing barely five pounds. Selena nearly died during the delivery, which left her unable to do the housework and care for Nellie.

Abram purchased a canary to help cheer her up and keep her company since many weekends he traveled with the church's Men's Chorus. To their disappointment, the bird never sang one note.

Four-and-a-half years later, with only two weeks before Christmas 1901, Selena was in the eighth month of her second pregnancy. She felt exceptionally well and cheerful, despite the warnings she'd received about her health.

Chapter 3

A Child's Faith

Mama, Mama, when is Papa coming home?" Five-year-old Nellie could hardly contain her excitement. "Mama, I had this dream. Please sit over here and listen to my happy dream! Mama, I am going to have a baby sister on Christmas morning! I had this dream last night, and Jesus told me so!"

"No, no, you are just too anxious, Nellie darling," replied Selena, trying to calm Nellie, "we don't know what our baby is going to be, and this little bundle of joy is not going to come to our home until after Christmas. You will have to wait just a few more weeks."

For three mornings in a row, Nellie came running down the stairs with the same excited message. All the while, Selena was continually praying for the strength to go through what might be a disaster for their family. She trembled as she vividly remembered how difficult her delivery was with her darling little Nellie and the months after Nellie's birth without strength to even care for her beautiful little girl. The doctor warned of the possibility of losing her life with the second birthing experience. The thought of leaving her Nellie motherless was almost more than she could bear.

Selena and Abram had prayed fervently for the Lord's direction in their lives since they first met. They knew the possibility of losing

16

both mother and baby with the second delivery. Still, they felt that they would accept whatever came their way. In spite of the grave concerns for Selena's health and the baby's life, they felt deep peace in knowing that they would accept Heavenly Father's will for their lives. They clung to the doctor's promise that the second birth could restore Selena to the health they repeatedly prayed for.

Selena was so grateful that she had found such hope and trust in her loving Heavenly Father. How blessed she was to have a caring compassionate companion in Abram. She was ever so blessed to have a healthy, beautiful five-year-old to keep her company and give her yet another reason for living.

Abram's choir was asked to sing at the Prairie Street Mennonite Church's annual Christmas Eve service. Selena felt quite well and made plans to attend, knowing how much Nellie would love to see and hear her Papa sing. Selena even felt strong enough to walk the few blocks to the church.

Sitting in the church full of happy worshippers, Selena felt better than she had in years. She was so pleased to see all of her good friends and their families. Nellie sat wide-eyed as the children's Sunday School classes recited their Christmas selections. Nellie was even more excited to hear her Papa's "O Holy Night" solo.

Just after six on Christmas morning, Selena had a feeling that she was in paradise. Nellie's dream did come true. She did have a baby sister on Christmas morning.

After the delivery of a nine-pound baby girl, Selena immediately felt a wave of healing sweep over her frail body. As soon as the healthy baby started to cry, the song-less canary started to warble the most beautiful bird song.

"What a glorious sound!" Selena exclaimed. "My baby crying and at the very same time the canary is singing! Abram, the name Gertrude just doesn't seem to fit our new little baby girl."

"I was thinking the exact same thing, Selena! This is Christmas morning and our bird is singing his Christmas carols. How about calling our new baby Carol?"

"That's a wonderful idea, sweetheart," replied Selena.

"Yes, yes, I know what we should call her," said Abram. "Why not name her Christmas Carol. She'll become our very own Carol of Christmas!"

So it was. Christmas Carol Miller was born on Christmas morning of 1901.

Selena made steady progress with her health after Carol's birth, gaining strength daily. Before long she was able to be up, caring for her beautiful baby girl and attending to her lively five-year-old. She had experienced a miracle, a direct answer to prayer.

Christmas Carol Miller at age three months, 1902.

Abram purchased a baby carriage as long as two oval wash baskets put end to end and sixteen inches deep. The inside was upholstered with variegated brown and tan sateen. The bottom was covered with two thick pillows. This luxurious basket-carriage rested on four marvelous springs that kept the baby almost floating in the air. Nellie loved pushing her baby sister around the house.

"See Mama, you believe me now," exclaimed Nellie. "I knew my baby sister was coming on Christmas morning just like Jesus told me!"

Abram and Selena were blessed with two more little girls: Mary Esther, born February 24, 1906, and Helena Wade, born October 21, 1907. In the evening after supper, Abram often romped with the girls while Selena relaxed in her favorite rocking chair near the grandfather clock.

Life in 1901

- More than 95 percent of all births took place in the home.
- The average life expectancy was forty-seven.
- Only 14 percent of U.S. homes had bathtubs.
- 8 percent of the homes in the United States had telephones.
- 18 percent of all the households in the United States had at least one full-time servant or domestic.
- One in ten U.S. residents could not read or write.
- Only 6 percent of all Americans graduated from high school.
- The speed limit in most cities was ten miles per hour.
- The average U.S. worker made between two- and four-hundred dollars a year. Averaged, that is roughly twenty-five dollars a month, about one-dollar a day.
- Sugar cost four cents a pound, eggs fourteen cents a dozen, and coffee fifteen cents a pound.
- Most women washed their hair only once a week with either egg yolks or borax.
- McCalls patterns cost fifteen cents.
- A train ride from New York to Chicago set a record time of twenty hours.
- Postage from the United States to Europe cost two cents.
- The leading causes of U.S. deaths were pneumonia, influenza, tuberculosis, diarrhea, heart disease, and stroke.

"More. Do it again, Papa," Carol begged in her sweet way. Amid hilarious shouting and laughter, Papa got down on all fours and crawled around the house, prancing and bucking, while the girls hung on for dear life. Around and around they went on their "daddy horse" through the dining room, living room, parlor, bedroom, kitchen, and back again to the parlor. Not only did Carol's birth bring new strength to Selena, but also the entire family enjoyed more fun and laughter.

As a child, Carol lacked only one thing: an abundant head of hair.

"You sure have a cute little boy there, Mrs. Miller. What's his name?"

Selena thought that Carol would never grow enough hair to curl or braid. Finally, at the age of five, Carol had enough hair to make one little braid on the top of her head. Around the back it was very short and uneven.

"Maybe if it is cut the same length all around it would all grow out a lot nicer," Selena said. "Abram, I don't have enough time to take Carol to the barber, will you do it for me?"

Reluctantly he agreed. There was a barber near his tin shop, so he left Carol there while he ran over to check on some of his business. Hurriedly he gave the barber instructions and left.

When Abram and Carol came home, Selena gave Carol one look and screamed out in horror. "Papa, what have you done!?"

"Here's my braid, Mama!" Carol sang out, gleefully waving something in her hand. "Here's my braid!"

It was no laughing matter to Selena. *Oh no! What will all our friends think?* thought Selena.

"That stupid barber made Carol look more like a boy than ever!" she cried.

One fine summer, Carol and two other little girls were sitting in the carriage on the porch playing and shouting with glee as they bounced up and down. Suddenly the lock gave way, and the carriage flew down the five porch steps onto the lawn. With another springing leap, it rushed down over the high grassy bank and landed upside down beyond the sidewalk. The girls' yells for help brought Mama running from the kitchen in the back of the house. Nellie reached the carriage first but was too frightened to look. Mama found the girls smothered in soft cushions but, thankfully, uninjured.

Before Carol was old enough to go to school, she was giving recitations at church. She learned to sew by piecing a comforter top and doing simple embroidery. She had a natural creative talent that surprised even Papa and Mama. Soon she was making all kinds of doll clothes for herself, her sisters, and the neighbor children, including fancy hats and accessories. This gift was exceptional for a child so young—a gift that would prove extremely useful throughout her life.

Carol said that as a child, she wished for only two things: First, to have another special day as a birthday. Having a birthday on the twenty-fifth day of December never gave her a special birthday just for her since it was always Christmas day. Second, for a different name. When it came time for Carol to start public school, she was reluctant to tell her teacher her full name in front of all the other children.

"What if all the children call me Christmas Tree or Merry Christmas or Christmas Present?" she cried to her Mama. "I don't want to go to school and tell the teacher my name is Christmas Carol. Other children have pretty names like Elizabeth and Martha. I don't want anyone to call me Halloween or Easter."

Carol thought her name was ridiculous. She crawled under the dining room table kicking and screaming, "I hate my name! I hate it! I hate Christmas! My name is utterly stupid. How could you have done this to me?"

Selena, disappointment in her voice, looked at Carol and said, "Some day, I hope that you won't be ashamed of your special name."

Selena then sat down beside Carol and told her about her birth, how they prayed for her to come straight from heaven and why they chose her unusual name. After she found out what it meant to her parents to call her Christmas Carol, she begged them to forgive her. From that point on, Carol never was ashamed of her special one-of-a-kind name.

The first day of school finally rolled around. And when Carol spoke her name to the teacher, her entire class started to snicker. But to her delight, no one ever called her those other names. They did ask if Christmas really was her real name.

The Bunkers were the Miller family's next-door neighbors. They had one grown son and a parrot named Polly. If Polly was in her cage on the porch when Carol passed by, the parrot would call out, "Hello Carol, Hello Carol, Hello Carol." Grandma Bunker also lived with the family and loved to come over and visit with Selena and her beautiful girls and chat about old times.

One day Carol announced to her friends, "Let's have a band and all dress up!"

All the neighbor children agreed. Carol found some old clothes, hats, lace curtains, and shoes. They gathered things up from everyone's houses and armed themselves with lids, pots, pans, spoons, and sticks. They began to march in their parade—up the street, down the alley, between the houses (which were very close together). Polly was on the front porch. The commotion of the children shouting, singing, and beating the pans frightened Polly so fiercely that she flew forcefully against the side of her cage. She knocked it over and flapped out into the middle of Indiana Avenue. Selena and Mrs. Bunker came running out of their houses.

"Oh, my poor little Polly," shouted Mrs. Bunker. "She'll kill herself!"

"Oh, my soul and body!" screamed Grandma Bunker.

When Polly was finally coaxed back into her cage, Carol received a scolding from Mrs. Bunker like she had never had before.

Later, the Bunkers went on vacation and surprisingly asked the Millers to take care of Polly. One evening after cottage prayer meeting, the children gathered around Polly's cage trying to get her to talk. Finally the bird burst out with the surprising words, "Go home! Go home! Go home!"

Every Christmas, some friends gave the Miller family a big turkey. Mama fixed it up with all the trimmings. Papa proudly sat at the head of the table to carve the turkey for each hungry little girl, always serving his bride first. Carol ate and ate till she couldn't eat any more and had to lie down on the settee in the parlor. After a short rest she would always come back to the table and ask for more.

In the springtime, Carol liked to go to the huckleberry patch several miles out of town. Mama always packed her lunch in a syrup bucket. One afternoon, just before leaving for the patch, she noticed a baby rabbit. She quickly caught it and put it in her lunch bucket. She persuaded Mama to let her keep the rabbit in an old bird cage, the one that had held the yellow canary whose beautiful song announced Carol's birth.

This home for the rabbit worked very nicely until it grew big enough to open the cage and hop out. One night when everyone was sound asleep, strange noises came from the parlor. Startled, Papa got up out of bed to investigate. It was only the rabbit, Hoppy, running back and forth on the keys of the piano. After Hoppy chewed up the bottoms of the lace curtains in the parlor, Mama told Carol that the rabbit would have to go!

Carol's hair did finally grow thick and long enough to pull back with a beautiful bow. That is how she wore her hair on Sundays. The other days of the week she had it up on top of her head in braids. During the summers, Carol was a regular tomboy. With her hair pulled up on top of her head, it wouldn't get in the way when she was climbing trees, playing ball with the neighbor boys, or crawling around in the small barn behind the house.

One summer a family of skunks took up residence under the woodshed in the back. Every night they came out and played on the front lawn under the streetlight, while Carol's family fretted over how to get rid of them. Selena called the police, who obediently drove by, looked at the skunks, and then drove on.

Eventually one got into the basement. Apparently he must have burrowed under the back porch and came in through an open basement window under the kitchen. Selena appealed to a neighbor, who responded with his rifle and shot the poor creature. But what a stench! It permeated every nook and cranny. The horrible smell seemed to last forever!

Mama scrubbed the basement floor with lye. She poured gasoline and burned it. Still, the horrible odor remained. She tried everything the neighbors and friends recommended, but the odor still overtook the place. Selena even wrote to the agricultural department at Purdue University requesting a solution. Their suggestions proved useless.

Even after a year went by, the odor could be detected on damp days, all too common occurrences in northern Indiana. Finally, everyone in the household was able to breathe freely! The Miller's found out later that a young man in the neighborhood happened to be sprayed on graduation night with his good suit on. They buried all of his clothes in a deep hole in the backyard, and it took two weeks to finally get rid of the odor; an experience the family never forgot.

Carol enjoyed being in the middle of all the action, which at times turned into near tragedy, like the day she and her little sister Helena were having such a great time sticking their tongues out at each other while playing on the front porch. Carol was on the inside of the house in the living room, and Helena was outside on the front porch. The girls darted back and forth from the window to the screen door, full of giggles and excitement. Each one tried to outdo the other by making funny faces.

Carol pushed the screen door as wide open as it would go in a darting manner while the girls played with glee. Helena quickly stuck her tongue out at Carol through the crack on the backside of the screen door. Accidentally, Carol let go of the door because she was laughing so hard, and the door slammed closed on Helena's little tongue! Blood began to gush from Helena's mouth. Carol, taking one horrified look, ran into the house and crawled under the dining room table screaming, "Mama, I've killed her! I've killed her!"

Helena could barely cry because she was stuck. Mama came running to their rescue. Poor little Helena was in shock. Mama quickly got a wet towel and held it to the bleeding tongue. The doctor was called and came immediately. The end of Helena's tongue was nearly cut off. It was just dangling by a thread.

"I'm sorry, I can't make stitches on the tongue," the doctor shook his head and said. "The only things that you can try is take drops of warm milk and put in on the cut and hope and pray that it will heal back together. We need to make sure that Helena stays very still."

For hours, Selena held Helena, rocking her wrapped in her favorite blanket, comforting her, and praying aloud for a miracle.

By the next morning, Helena's injured tongue was knitting back together with only a little pain. Helena's tongue healed perfectly, leaving her with no speech defect. This again had a lasting impression on the entire family of a watchful Heavenly Father who hears and answers prayers.

One day two Sioux Indians on horseback stopped at the Miller home and wondered if they could stay with the family and rest for several days. They were on their way to a special meeting in Washington, D.C. Red Fox and Black Hawk had such a good time with the family, telling them tales of the West and learning to eat the food of the white folk, that both the Millers and the Indians would remember their instant friendship for years. Red Fox and Black Hawk called their home "House of Many Laughters."

Carol earned her spending money as a young girl by picking plums and selling them in the neighborhood. She helped Papa paint the barn and, when she was old enough, would baby-sit for the neighbor lady for twenty-five cents a week.

Carol never knew her mother to be frail. She was stout and very jolly and always sociable. She was the most wonderful Sunday School

Carol on the back of Montana, the horse belonging to Red Fox and Black Hawk.

teacher that Carol ever had. In fact, Carol advanced to each new class with her mother. Selena was Carol's Sunday School teacher for seven consecutive years.

Carol and her three sisters were brought up in a family of faith. Very early in life, they were taught to memorize scriptures. Every Sunday night, the four girls would stand up in front of the blackboard where Selena had jotted down the scriptures that they were supposed to have learned that week. When they could say them correctly, she would give each daughter a prize, perhaps an orange or a little thing that she knew they would like, especially candy of some sort.

Abram worked at the railroad shop for seven years. On the way home one day, he stopped at the hardware store where a man named Nolan approached him.

"I'd like to start my own business," Nolan began. "I'm sick of this place here, and I would like to have a partner, and I don't know of anyone else I'd like to have outside of you."

"I already have a good steady job with the railroad," Abram replied. "I feel no need to do anything else right now."

However, they discussed the idea of starting a new business for over an hour. Nolan was sure that together they could make a go of it.

"You go home and pray over it and let me know," said Nolan.

Abram turned to Russ Culp, a man he had confidence in, for advice.

"Well, I think that is a pretty good thing," Mr. Culp responded.

Selena wasn't as certain it would be a good thing. She pondered the idea.

"You know, you already have a pretty good steady job with the railroad," she said. "Why make a change now when things are going good for us? We need to make this a matter of prayer. I need to know we have Heavenly Father's blessing. This is a major decision we cannot make by ourselves alone."

In 1905, Abram and Nolan started a company together. Abram and Selena had received their answer. Both men pooled their little money, but even then they had to borrow money to start their venture. Abram went to a man he knew in the community and asked to borrow some money to get started in the tinner's business. That community man had so much confidence in Abram and Nolan that they were able to borrow money without a note.

They found a little room on Temple Court in Elkhart. They decided that they each could draw out seven dollars a week for themselves. It really wasn't much money, even for 1905, but they were able make it stretch.

They did all kinds of general tin work: roofing, spouting, and furnace work. The big industries that were being built gave them a lot of work, including skylights and ventilators, but mostly furnace work. Abram and Nolan also made elbow spouting and gutters for houses by hand. By the second year they had to buy tin by the railroad carload. They put in about two hundred furnaces a year, an average of four a week.

Before Abram went into business with Nolan, he did all kinds of tin work. When young folks got married, he would make household kitchen items like utensils, pots and pans, buckets and shovels. Once he went into partnership, Abram no longer made pans and ladles.

Once, Papa invited Carol to go with him to Michigan to install a furnace in a farmhouse. This was a special treat for both of them to spend one-on-one time together. After they arrived, however, she had trouble entertaining herself during the long job. But as usual, her resourcefulness rescued her from boredom. Carol found a large stock tank by the barn with some big goldfish in it. She searched around the barn and found a long stick, some binder twine, and an old safety pin (which she bent into a hook). What fun it was to watch the goldfish go for the hook and get caught.

When the lady of the house found out what Carol was up to, she was extremely upset. Poor Carol was almost too frightened to eat any dinner. No one had ever gotten angry with her before this fun day. Both Papa and Mama were soft spoken. On the way home Papa laughed and laughed and said he thought she was very clever to catch the fish and find something fun to do all on her own.

When Carol was seven years old, she and Esther, who was three, contracted typhoid fever. Abram had already lost his loving mother and sister in his childhood and youth. Now the thought of losing his precious little girls was almost more than he could bear!

Typhoid fever usually begins with headache, nosebleeds, nausea, vomiting, constipation, or diarrhea. But as the illness advances, fevers can reach as high as 104 and 105 degrees. The person or child infected with this horrible illness needs to be isolated, their bed linens and dishes continually sterilized. Toilets or commodes need to be carefully disinfected after each use, and the patient needs to be bathed daily.

It is hard to imagine taking care of two very ill little girls, ages three and seven, back in 1909. In the twenty-first century, it would be difficult enough with all the modern conveniences in our homes: automatic washing machines, dishwashers that sanitize, modern medicine, and indoor plumbing. Carol's childhood home had only one bathroom, and it was downstairs off the kitchen. The very sick little girls slept in upstairs bedrooms.

Carol and Esther also developed inflammatory rheumatism, a disease of the muscles and tendons, joints, bones, and nerves that results in tremendous pain. It would often leave those affected completely helpless. Both little girls were wrapped in cotton from their toes to their hips in some kind of powder.

With these two most horrible illnesses, Selena spent endless nights and days holding her precious little girls, her own strength depleted from lack of sleep and tremendous worry. The little girls were almost too sick to even whimper, and Selena wept so much that the tears wouldn't come any more.

On top of typhoid fever and inflammatory rheumatism, three-year-old Esther got diphtheria. Diphtheria was one of the most feared childhood diseases of that time, because it was extremely contagious.

It would begin with a fever, headache, and sore throat. If the illness continued beyond three or four weeks, severe complications would develop in the heart, lungs, kidneys, and nervous systems.

How could this possibly be happening? Three deadly dreaded illnesses all at the same time. How much more could a mother endure, seeing her little girls so near death's door, not knowing from one hour to the next if they would slip away and die? She was also caring for the normal demands of Nellie and Helena, the baby.

After work each night, Papa would come into Carol and Esther's bedroom and pray for each precious daughter. He would go over to Esther's bed, hold his arms heavenward, and plead for the Lord to bring a miracle and make her whole. Then he would come to Carol's bed and do the same for her. Night after night, he and Selena prayed for their two precious little girls.

Carol vividly remembered hearing her mama and papa pray out loud for them. Realizing not only the caring tender love they had for all their girls, but also the faith they had in the Lord to heal them. It forever stuck in her mind. "Hearing my parents pray out loud as they sobbed and cried for us is one of the things on my horizon," Carol later said. "Your horizon is where you look out and heaven and earth come together."

Selena didn't take off her dress for six weeks. When Esther got diphtheria, the doctor said that Carol needed be quarantined in the bedroom upstairs. Nellie, now twelve years old and very responsible, was taken out of school to take care of Carol. She tenderly took very good care of Carol, passing the time each day by reading and pretending. They told each other stories that each one made up. As Carol gained strength, the days became much brighter.

Nellie and Carol were taught how to pray by both of their parents and learned by example to believe that Jesus would help them no matter what would happen to Esther. Nellie and Carol cried together whenever they heard Esther cry because she hurt so badly. Carol and Nellie cried a lot together because they missed seeing and playing with Esther. The girls loved to play house together. Nellie pretended to be the daddy, Carol the mommy, and Esther and Helena the babies.

One evening when Esther was still suffering from diphtheria, Abram came up to give Carol and Nellie their dinner and announced that Esther now had polio.

Polio is an inflammation of the spinal cord and brain, which leads to paralysis. Spasms of the arms, neck, and thighs leave the patient severely weak. If the muscles are not exercised, they will wither and shrink from lack of use. Many polio victims became permanent cripples as a result of the virus. When the respiratory muscles were affected, patients had their breathing supported through an iron lung. "How could this be," Carol wrote years later, "that our little sister could be any sicker than she already was and live!"

The days for Selena and Abram were filled with continual fervent prayers for the healing powers of heaven to intercede in behalf of their precious little girls, but especially Esther.

Carol and Nellie prayed too: "Oh sweet Jesus, please make our little sister well!"

Chapter 4

Sweet Sixteen

Early in her life, Carol heard her mother and father talk to God in intimate terms. They went to Him for everything. Carol and her sisters all heard their individual names mentioned to God every morning in family worship. There never was a single day that their father would go off to work that he didn't kiss each of his darling girls goodbye.

"Mother," he would say, "you know, we never know whether I will ever come back home again."

Carol always remembered her father's tender loving care for each of them and especially his love and devotion to their mother. That gave them all such great comfort and peace, knowing that Papa was so devoted to taking care of them, tenderly loving and working so hard to provide a good life, giving them all the things that they ever needed.

Before Carol got sick, she found a gold ring in the path between their house and the house next door. It was a little signet ring with the initial R on it. She always wanted a ring and never had one, except for those she got with a penny stick of candy.

"It's going to bring me good luck, and I am going to wear it," Carol told her mother when she found it.

"Well," Selena replied, "it must belong to the little boy next door; his name is Reginald. You go over and ask his mother if he didn't lose that ring."

Carol knew the boy's name. It was Reginald Roosevelt Vanderbelt Dunn, but everyone called him Regie, for short. Everyone, that is, except his mother, who shouted at the top of her lungs when she was angry: "Reginald Roosevelt Vanderbelt Dunn, come here this instant!" Just hearing Regie's mother scream made Carol tremble.

Regardless, Carol went over to the Dunn's house and asked, hoping that the ring didn't belong to Regie. Sure enough, it didn't!

But Selena wasn't ready to give in.

"It must belong to Richard across the street," she said, "you go over there and see if it belongs to him." So Carol begrudgingly asked his mama, hoping again that it didn't belong to Richard. And it didn't!

Selena tried to think of all the children in the neighborhood, living within six or eight blocks, whose name began with an R. She ran out of names.

"Oh," Carol shouted, "Glory Hallelujah! This ring is *mine!* I am going to wear it!"

"Well, you can play with it," Selena cautioned, "but I would rather you didn't wear it to school. Don't you remember the story in the Bible about everyone bringing all their jewelry and melting it into making a golden calf?"

Carol was completely determined. "Here is something that is not going to be melted to make any kind of golden calf!" It was the first time Carol could remember that she purposely disobeyed her mother.

Carol secretly hid the ring in her pinafore pocket and always wore it in school, but for some reason or other, she never forgot to take it off before she entered the house. Carol knew her mother didn't want her to wear it.

When Carol was quarantined in her upstairs bedroom, she thought of little sister Esther downstairs. Carol was afraid that Esther would not live—unless a miracle happened.

"If you have a sin in your heart," Papa always said, "you can't get close to God." Carol was old enough to know that, even though she was only seven.

It was a moonlit night, and the window blinds were up. Carol started to twist the little gold ring on her finger. *Mama said that I could play with it in bed,* she thought. *My daddy let me wear his vest jacket to his suit. I love to wear it because of the little pocket in front. I will keep the ring in the little right pocket.*

"I will take this here ring off my finger," Carol prayed in her childish way, "I know that I have disobeyed my mother. God, if you send me a real angel to see, then I will take it all the way off."

She worked the ring up to the first knuckle, waited, and then took it clear off.

Carol often told her life story to women's church groups, especially near Mother's Day. "You can take this story for what it is worth," she'd say. "It's just my personal story, and if you want to laugh about it, well that's all right. But it's my true story." She continued:

I took it off and hid it under the pillow. And I said, "Oh Lord, my little sister is so sick, much sicker than me. Won't you please heal her? I have confessed my sins, I have disobeyed my mother, and I don't know what else to do to get right with you."

The clouds opened up, and a light came down, and an angel actually came to my window and looked at me and smiled. And right away I forgot that there was a bath towel hanging in the stairway, saturated with formaldehyde to keep the germs away. I forgot that it was nighttime and that my daddy would have to come up the ladder in the dark. Even so, I called to him as loud as I could.

"Papa, Papa, come quick!"

He ran up the steps as fast as he could. He passed by the soaked up bath towel and ran into my room yelling,

"What's wrong? What's wrong?"

"There's an angel at my window, there's an angel at my window!"

Papa opened the door and looked around and said,

"I don't see an angel."

"Well, there was one and as soon as you came into the room it disappeared."

"That's strange. Are you awake?"

"Yes I am awake, Papa. I asked it to come and it did! You always told me that I can pray to God and He will answer my prayer, so I did, and now He did."

Well, he went back downstairs and I called the angels to come back to the window, and sure enough they came again, only this time there were little baby angels who smiled at me.

"Here they are again!"

And, as soon as he came into the room they disappeared again.

"I don't know what to make of it," Papa questioned.

"It really was so. I saw them. I really saw them, Papa!"

So, the next night I prayed again and this time three angels came and smiled at me through the window and I was so thrilled. I called him again to come quick, and the same thing happened. Again. And on the third night there were more than three angels. And each time he stepped into the room they disappeared. Some would go on the right side of the window and some would go on the left of the window.

"I just don't know what to think," questioned Papa. Then my daddy cried so hard.

Papa said, "I know that you are telling the truth and that you really saw an angel. I believe you. I just don't think I have a pure enough heart to be able to see an angel like you."

I never felt like I needed to ask to see the angels again, and I never have. The next morning our daddy brought us breakfast.

"I wonder if the angels are going to come and take your little sister," he wondered.

"I don't think so, Papa, I prayed and asked God to make my little sister well, and if God can send me angels if I ask Him, then I know that he can heal my little sister if I ask him to."

"Oh, the faith of a little child; it's so strong and so pure. If I only had that much faith myself," Papa cried.

Well, my little sister did get well. I did too. Oh, she was so sick! She has been in the audience a number of times and has heard me tell this true story. You can believe it if you want to. It really did happen to me. I cannot look at her when I am telling it, because of the tears rolling down her cheeks. I cannot look at my father either, when I tell it, because it is such a precious experience to all three of us.

When Carol had children of her own, she told them of her experience in seeing angels. During more than one family get together at Grandpa Abram's house, Carol's children would start talking to their mother about her visitation of angels. They would go up to that very room and want to see the actual window where this miracle happened. It did happen. An innocent seven-year-old child with much faith had her prayers answered so perfectly. Carol was a little girl brave enough to ask for a visitation of angels and have it actually happen.

It wasn't surprising that when only ten years old, Carol was under conviction when the evangelist came to their church. She knew she needed to accept Jesus as her Savior. The evening she went forward and shook the evangelist's hand was etched in her memory.

"You know sometimes today the evangelists just ask people to raise their hand," Carol later said, "but it means so much more if you have to get up on your feet and go forward in front of the crowd of people and shake the evangelist's hand, and stand there and have some of the older people come up and greet you and say 'God Bless You.' And when my parents came forward and when my father took me into his arms and told me again, 'We gave you to God before you were born, and we want you to grow up to be a blessing to many people.' That did something to me that I could never shake off."

Carol loved to sing. She spent her childhood singing. Selena called her "my precious little Christmas song." At age ten, Carol was accomplished at playing the piano. Papa made sure that all his daughters had an opportunity to develop any talent they were interested in. Carol took piano, voice, and public-speaking lessons. From a very young age, she enjoyed being the center of attention, even though she thought she was rather shy. She memorized very quickly and soon gave readings to audiences of all ages, at school and at church functions. She had the unique ability to make listeners laugh and cry almost within the same minute.

Even as a small child, Carol possessed a fantastic imagination for storytelling. While Esther and Helena rested on the settee in the dining room, Carol made up stories about people in China who did everything backwards. Soon the girls and Mama were rolling in laughter.

She loved school and excelled in anything that required creativity. When it was her turn to read aloud, she captured her classmates' attention because she was able to put so much drama and interest into the stories. She enjoyed making up her own stories and kept the class spellbound with the unexpected suspense that always delighted her friends. She loved to pretend she was a Sunday School teacher, keeping Esther and Helena occupied on Sunday afternoons.

In July 1918, when Carol was fifteen, Papa bought a Rio Car and fixed it up so the family could take a trip to Niagara Falls. A friend suggested to Abram to write to the Firestone Tire Company and tell them about their trip plans. He heard from an acquaintance that Firestone would send maps complete with route directions with the approximate travel time each day.

As promised, the Firestone Tire Company sent information that helped them plan out their route to Niagara Falls. Papa made a rack to fit on the back of the car to carry their big family trunk. They left Elkhart, Indiana, on a Saturday and drove first to Toledo, Ohio, then to Cleveland, and on to Erie, Pennsylvania.

There were no motels back then, so they packed a big tarp with poles so they could set up a makeshift tent each night. Army cots were just what they needed to have a place to sleep. When they wanted to rest for the night, the family would ask people at farmhouses along the way for permission to camp for the night. "Some even invited us to come into their homes to eat," Abram recalled.

The Miller family—Nellie, Selena, Helena, Esther (sitting in the car), Abram, and Carol—with car, around the time of their trip to Niagara Falls, ca. 1918.

They were near Erie, approaching a crossroads blocked by unusually tall corn.

"Watch out!" Carol shouted.

A large tractor-trailer, with a full load of hay, was coming down towards them, taking up half of their side of the road. Papa swerved just in the nick of time onto a bank on the side of the road.

Without Carol's warning, they could have easily all been killed.

It took them three days to get to the falls. They found an appropriate place and set up camp. While they were there, they met two couples they knew from Lancaster. These friends suggested that they ship the huge trunk by express mail to Buffalo. It made their journey a little more comfortable, and they knew that it saved gas because of less weight.

In her early teenage years, Carol found the love of her life—Norman Hostetler. She wrote:

We were fourteen when Norman and I saw each other for the first time on the sixteenth day of the month. In church, right after prayer, our eyes met. He sat right behind me. Norman's family had just moved to Elkhart from Rush Lake, Ontario. Very soon, his family of five and mine numbering six, spent many a Sunday and holiday together. We sang, played, boated, hiked, fished, visited parks for picnics, and went on excursions and church programs together.

Our smiling parents told us from the start, "It's OK to like each other, but no thought of marriage until you're twenty-one." We never once considered disregarding this restriction. Instead we determined to do our utmost to honor and please them, and work hard towards that glad,

Carol Miller as a teenager, ca. 1917.

glad day. It would be without question on the sixteenth day of the month.

We had our first date on the sixteenth of September, the year we were both sixteen. For two years we had been admitting our growing fondness of each other as we walked together sixteen blocks every day to and from High School. Our approving parents said, "It's OK, but no dating until you're sixteen." And that was that. We never argued though we could scarcely wait.

The occasion was Young People's Literary Society, and I gave a reading: the first chapter of Pollyanna (The Glad Game). On our way home we agreed no two sixteen-year-olds had ever been, or ever could be, happier or more deeply in love.

"Carol dear," said Norman, "Let's make sixteen our special day and number from this night on."

"Let's do," I answered, "and we'll play the glad, glad game together on it."

"We will," echoed Norman in my ear.

The Miller family *(left to right)*: Helena, Selena, Carol (standing in front), Abram, and Esther, ca. 1918. Photograph was likely taken by Nellie Miller.

For years, the couple celebrated the sixteenth of each month with "extra special" love letters and a special gift from Norman. These gifts were candy bars or trinkets at first, but Carol kept every "glad sixteen" wrapper and treasure, which became more exquisite and precious each year, in a special "love" box.

Carol continued her voice and piano lessons; Norman took violin lessons. They spent romantic hours making up love songs and singing them to each other.

After graduation they both took clerk jobs—Carol in a large department store on Main Street, Norman in a hardware store right across the street. *Was it luck or the hand of God that was making our path in life so bright, so thrilling, and so promising?* Carol wondered.

Every payday Carol deposited money into her savings account. As a clerk, she received a discount on any item in the store, so she also took home an item for her hope chest. In two years, she'd collected almost every household item a bride could want—pictures, vases, and furniture, both large and small.

"I was proud of my collection!" remembered Carol.

But there was just one tiny thing holding Carol back from absolute happiness: Norman wanted to go to India as a missionary someday. He spoke of it often, and invariably Carol tried to change the subject. Carol wanted a nice home in Elkhart, Indiana, not a jungle in India. She said:

> The first time I heard him mention India was in a Sunday evening Junior Meeting. I concluded he was just saying the nice sounding words he was supposed to say. When my name was called I said, "I have no ambitions to be a foreign missionary, but I'd like to be a seamstress someday, and sew for poor orphans and needy people."
>
> I can point to the spot along the rail-road tracks east of the depot where Norman and I were walking on our way home

Carol Miller around the time she graduated from high school, ca. 1918.

from school two years later, when he stopped, looked down into my face and asked with a tender pleading tone I shall never forget.

"Carol, wouldn't you be willing to go to India with me if God should call me? Well, I remember what you said in Junior Meeting. You know, long ago. You really didn't mean it the way it sounded, did you?"

My warm cheeks got hot. "Oh yes, I did mean what I said," I chuckled nervously. "I still mean it."

"But Carol, dear, listen. If God calls me, and we're truly meant for each other, well, you know what I mean. If we're always going to do things together, He'll call you, too. Won't He? Wouldn't you?" His voice faltered. "Wouldn't you go with me?"

Something unpleasant quivered in the pit of my stomach. I tried desperately to laugh. Instead I gulped.

"If I ever go to India," I said, "I'll go just to be with you. Because I do love you. For keeps. I do Norman, I do."

There was unmistakable disappointment in his reply. "I love you for keeps too, Carol, dear, but, I, well, I thought God would—."

I knew full well the sum of his unfinished sentence. The rest of the way home and on into the sleepless night there raced through the stream of my consciousness vivid, live tormenting thoughts. Facts. Fact thoughts:

My Christian home. My God-fearing parents. Family worship. My name mentioned to God every morning in Papa's prayers. My conversion at ten. My baptismal vows. But still more piercing, the things my parents had repeatedly told me concerning my birth. How I was conceived as a direct answer to prayer. How my birth brought back, after five years, health to my semi-invalid mother. How my name was changed from Gertrude to Christmas Carol when I came unexpectedly on Christmas morning, a month before I was due. How they dedicated me to God then and there.

Oh, that startling trick of memory for one still in my tender teens! I relived the hugs and the kisses my parents gave me the night I went forward and shook the evangelist's hand. I heard again and again my father's tender words in my right ear, "My child, God brought you into this life for a special purpose." I could feel his glad warm tears on my cheek again, just remembering.

I saw again those real angels that came to my window on three different nights while I was praying for my younger sister, Esther, who lay critical with four different terribly serious illnesses, including deadly Polio. Each time I called out "Papa come quick," the angels disappeared when he entered the room. "Child, I'm not pure enough to look on them," he wept the third time.

My godly father not pure enough? He was the best, the purest person I knew, besides my mother. That night I felt it was me who needed purification of some sort; for as surely as my name was Christmas Carol, I knew the hand of God was upon my life. The pressure of it had never left me since the day I learned I had been dedicated.

Yet, I tried to reason with my conscience. If I never missed a church service except for sickness, attended prayer-meeting, Bible class, sang in chorus, taught a Sunday School class, gave my tithe, helped fill missionary boxes, attended church conventions, obeyed my parents, read a chapter in my Bible every night, what more could be expected of me? What more? India? Surely not that hot, snaky, dusty, heathen, mud-hutted, awful place!

My savings grew. So did the contents of my hope chest. No, hope *chests*. I was advanced from button clerk to cashier, where, from the overhanging office, I could view all of the breath-taking merchandise on the first floor. We would have a cozy, attractive home of our own some glorious sixteenth. We would!

About the time I thought Norman had dismissed the idea, another missionary on furlough from India would speak in church and get him re-concerned. He persuaded me to quit my good job, buy a used Ford coupe in partnership with him and enroll at Goshen College.

"I want to prepare myself," he reasoned.

"For what?" I knew what he meant.

"I can't feature myself always selling screws, shovels, wire and bolts. I feel called of God for service. Definite service. I must get some college."

At the end of the first semester, Norman's father got smallpox and [Norman] had to discontinue school to drive his father's bread truck. Thereupon I quit too, and got a job in a doctor's office. With renewed eagerness I added little things, and big things, to my collection for our "glad sixteen" dream home.

Our love grew daily, even though we didn't agree on the India question. What lovers do agree on every minute detail?

I continually remembered Norman giving a talk in Junior Meeting one Sunday night in which he told everyone that he wanted to go to India as a missionary some day. I continued being so troubled remembering, saying to myself, it's way too hot over there, and there are wild beasts that we would have to contend with. I just can't do it!!

Anyway, when he got done giving his talk, right after he sat down, I keep remembering how I got up and I said, "I don't have any conviction that I will ever go to India. But, I will do anything else that the Lord wants me to do for him, I really will, anything else with Norman, when I get a conviction to." It haunted me all the time. I just couldn't bring myself to do such a thing, even though I felt I was as dedicated to the Lord's will as he was. I just couldn't and didn't want to believe what he was saying to me and asking me and trying to convince me into doing!

"Must it be India?" I put it to Norman one day. "Can't we be missionaries right here at home? Doesn't God just as truly call some to work hard to support someone on the field? Or several? Three or four would accomplish more than two of us. Anyhow, I doubt if I'd live very long in India. I'm not the big, strong husky type; I'm only four feet, eleven inches. You'd be a widower in no time!"

Carol Miller and Norman Hostetler, ca. 1920.

"Oh, no! You think?"

I nodded.

"Then," Norman exclaimed, clasping me close to his arms, "I'll work hard and support a couple. Maybe three. I will. I will."

"Oh, Norman. That makes me very happy."

Even if he couldn't go to India, Norman decided that he wanted to know all he could about the Bible. So they began a Bible and a Hebrew correspondence course. They did everything they were asked to at church: attended prayer meetings and Bible study class, taught Sunday School and Summer Bible School, sang in quartets and choirs, visited sick people and old people on Sunday afternoons.

"I actually thought I was the happiest engaged girl in the entire world," said Carol. "Norman carved the word 'sixteen' on more than one tree, wrote it in the sand of more than one beach. His love letters were signed sixteen times sixteen kisses, and many a Saturday night he would bring me sixteen stalks of the most gorgeous gladiolas anyone ever saw! He shared his love to me on the violin and I expressed my love to him on the piano. The whole town knew that we were lovers."

Their engagement announcement appeared in the *Elkhart Truth*, the local paper, on the sixteenth day of April one year before the wedding:

The marriage of Miss Carol Miller, daughter of Mr. and Mrs. A. R. Miller of 145 Indiana Avenue, to Norman Hostetler, whose engagement was announced in September, will take place Wednesday evening, April 16. The secret was revealed at a party last evening at the Miller home by the bride elect in honor of her sister, Miss Nellie Marie Miller, who recently returned from Beirut, Syria, where she spent two years in the service of the Near East Relief. During the serving of refreshments, each guest was presented a rose, and in the petals were hidden tiny envelopes containing the date of the wedding. The guests were Mrs. Henry Aman, Mrs. Virgil Roland, Miss Vera Silvers, Miss Edith Weiss, Miss Esther Seilon and Mrs. Herman Snavley.

Chapter 5

"My Bride that Is to Be"

Carol cherished the book *Riley Love-Lyrics* by James Whitcomb Riley, a special sixteenth-day-of-the-month gift to her from Norman. She affectionately glued precious photographs of her and Norman on selected pages throughout the 190-page, leather-bound book. The pictures document their childhood years, their courtship, and their lives as newlyweds. It was a prized possession that she kept throughout her life.

Carol placed a photograph of her and Norman, taken just prior to their wedding day, directly above Norman's favorite poem, "My Bride that Is to Be."

My Bride That Is To Be

O Soul of mine, look out and see
My bride, my bride that is to be!
Reach out with mad impatient hands,
And draw aside futurity
As one might draw a veil aside---
And so unveil her where she stands
Madonna-like and glorified—
The queen of undiscovered lands
Of love, to where she beckons me—

. . .

Nay-foolish heat and blinded eyes!
My bride hath need of no disguise.
But rather let her come to me
In such a form as bent above
My pillow when in infancy
I knew not anything but love-
O let her come from out the lands
Of Womanhood—not fairy isles,
And let her come with Woman's hands
And Woman's eyes of tears and smiles,
With Woman's hopefulness and grace
Of patience lighting up her face:
And let her diadem be wrought
Of kindly deed and prayerful thought,
That ever over all distress
May beam the light of cheerfulness.
And let her feet be brave to fare
The labyrinths of doubt and care,
That, following, my own may find
The path to Heaven God designed.
O let her come like this to me
My bride—my bride that is to be.

With Carol's creative story-telling talents, it's no surprise that she wrote poems and verse as well as read them. One particular poem titled "I Admire a Boy" shows all the reasons she dearly loved Norman. The poem's original, on aged paper with water stains, has been carefully preserved in the Goshen College Archives.

I Admire a Boy

Who is gentle, but not feminine.
Who is brave, but never reckless.
Who is fair in all his play.
Who has a keen sense of humor.

Who saves and spends money carefully.
Who appreciates good music.
Who does not hold a grudge.
Who likes little children.
Who is quick to learn from observation.
Who is concerned about his personal appearance.
Who has the moral courage to say, "No."
Who is not easily embarrassed.
Who needs to be called but once in the morning.
Who takes an interest in beautifying the home.
Who ignores a brazen girl.
Who isn't ashamed to be seen on Main Street with his mother,
   Even though she may be old and stooped and deaf.
Who has a businesslike walk.
Who has a hearty appetite.
Who takes no pleasure in making sport of another.
Who can make animals love him.
Who is eager to become a man.
Who makes the home happier the minute he steps in.
Who is interested in current events.
Who makes a big hole in his Sunday school class
   when he is absent.
Who would not intentionally distress his father.
Who is willing to do more than what he is paid for.
Who isn't perfect, but will admit it when he makes a mistake.
Who dreams a little now and then.
Who takes delight in preparing his schoolwork.
Who isn't always seen on the back seat of the church.
Who does his part to protect the family name.
Who makes friends among older folks.
Who confides in his father.
I admire a boy who isn't ashamed to be seen shedding
   an honest tear.
Who gets permission from parents to go to places.

Who would delight in a personal sacrifice in order to remember his
mother and father at Christmas.

Who would take off his own coat to warm his brother.

Who can stand it to be called a fool for the sake of right.

Who never stoops to uncleanness.

Who is a prince in spite of poverty.

Who would risk his own life to save a life.

Who would jump at the chance to earn his own way
through school.

Who would never under any circumstances, defend a lie.

Who remembers kindnesses done for him.

Who tells it by his face that he is worthy of confidence.

Who believes he can do things.

Who would not make for himself a name by running
down another.

Who is slow to sound his own praises.

Who is out and out for Jesus Christ.

Norman Gingerich Hostetler and Christmas Carol Miller were married on the evening of April 16, 1924. Carol was twenty-two; Norman twenty-one. For years, throughout high school and college,
they had been best friends and love birds. They'd known, without a
doubt, they were foreordained to be together the day their eyes met
at church. They held their parents' love and respect and showed by
their actions that they loved the Lord with all their heart, mind, and
soul.

"The night couldn't have been more perfect," Carol said. "We had
a love and devotion for each other no two married persons would or
could ever surpass."

Norman and Carol rented the seven-room house that Abram
had built next door to his and Selena's home. Over the years, Carol
had purchased enough furniture to furnish the entire house. In the
yearlong wait between their engagement and wedding day, she'd
bought all that she wanted and ever dreamed of having. She was

a meticulous housekeeper, taking pride in her home and keeping it spotlessly clean. She even swept the garden paths!

Norman purchased a baby grand piano for her birthday, their first Christmas together after their marriage. Carol never dreamed that any two married people could have such a perfect life.

They continued their productive, dedicated lives. They always went to midweek prayer meetings at church and never missed morning worship in their home each day right after breakfast. In short, Norman and Carol oc-

Carol and Norman Hostetler on their "Sweet Sixteen" wedding day, April 16, 1924, Elkhart, Indiana.

cupied themselves as devoted members of the Prairie Street Mennonite congregation.

Norman was soon busy in his radio shop, trying to make ends meet, provide enough money to support missionaries in India, and make payments towards the loan for the prized piano.

He was also helping to pay for their correspondence courses. After a few months, however, they dropped their Hebrew class. She hadn't wanted to take Hebrew, Carol admitted; to her it was a waste of time. After all, Carol got involved only to satisfy Norman's interest. She was more interested in spending one-on-one time with him, than learning anything she never intended to use in her lifetime.

Carol was secretly quite distressed when she found Norman's Sunday School lesson helps marked up with numbers and calculations instead of his usual comments. Similar figures appeared on the top and along the edges of the daily newspapers and *Saturday Evening Posts*. Norman was tangling himself in the division-and-subtraction forest of personal finance. Carol knew it; she could see it. They were making monthly payments to satisfy her wants over his, for the best of everything.

In an effort to calm Norman's mind, Carol put beautiful, soothing records on the phonograph and played happy tunes on the baby grand piano. Carol knew that nothing, absolutely nothing, dare mar their complete happiness. She showered him and bathed him with love and affection.

Norman ended up buying out the radio/battery shop and when business boomed he asked Cleo Mann, Nellie's husband, to join. Cleo quit his bread route and went to work with Norman. The two men installed the newest radios in their homes and experimented with "the crook necked horn kind" to get the best possible reception. They also tested where and how to install aerials (radio antennas) to receive the least interference.

Not to her inmost friends would Carol have whispered the tinge of uneasiness she felt. Yet at unexpected moments it screamed at her with sudden frightening closeness. Like the night she awoke suddenly and thought, for a second, that Norman had been taken. Like the dream where she was at heaven's gate, and an angel showed her not a mansion but a dilapidated old hut, with cobwebs and broken furniture. But who hasn't had startling moments? Who hasn't dreamed silly, ridiculous dreams? She tried to dismiss it all.

As June 16, 1926, approached, they looked forward to celebrating twenty-six months of married bliss.

"Carol, my darling," said Norman one evening. "What shall I get you this time on the sixteenth?"

"Oh," Carol cried, "just give me your love."

"But you have that. You know you do."

"I want nothing more, Norman. Just you!"

"And I meant it," Carol later said. "My mixed emotions of love and the panic feeling of love and a strange, new fear was almost more than I could conceal. I bit my lip and looked away. He dashed off in his Willys Nite. I had the other car. By this time he was way up to his neck in the radio business, selling radios, having several men working for him. He sold automobile parts too, trying ever so hard to keep his generous pledges to support India missionaries."

June 16 was a million-splendored day, one of the most beautiful days Carol could remember in northern Indiana. Norman ate lunch at home with Carol, as he almost always did. They kissed each other goodbye.

"I'm looking forward to my strawberry shortcake for supper," he called back, his usual jovial self, as he entered his car.

Norman headed back to his radio shop; Carol went to Nellie's home, just a few blocks away, to help scrub her front porch. It was a big job as the winter's coal soot stuck tenaciously to the house.

Nellie, three months pregnant with her first child, daughter Dorothy Jean, stood on a six-foot ladder washing the ceiling. Carol washed the banisters. The air was hot and still, not a breath of wind stirred the leaves on the trees.

Suddenly the silence was broken by the shrill piercing sound of a siren. Despite the strange and startling sound, Nellie and Carol kept working in silence. They listened as the siren proceeded from the downtown station. The siren's sound told them the ambulance was headed down Main Street.

"I wonder who that's going after," Carol finally said to Nellie.

It wasn't very long until they both found out. That day would forever be etched in Carol's memory:

My father came to break the news to me. I saw him coming across the street, and he had a handkerchief across his face, and I thought, What's wrong Papa? I hollered to my sister.

"There's something the matter!"

Then Papa told me that I needed to come quick because something terrible happened to Norman and we needed to go to the hospital right away, that Norman was hurt real bad.

I dropped my brush in terror screaming at the top of my lungs, "Not my Norman!"

We were frightfully dirty from scrubbing soot. They took me home to clean up. Never in my life did I clean up and change clothes so fast. We went back and picked up Nellie. When I arrived back at Nellie's house, Stanley Miller, one of Norman's helpers, ran up to the house and delivered the sad message, "Norman is dead!"

You can imagine how he hated to say those words. He was just a young teenager. The shock was numbing, unbelievable, inconceivable, bewildering, and too deep for tears.

Carol mechanically returned home again and quickly changed into another dress. As she hurried blindly down the steps a second time, a policeman was waiting for her. He caught her arm, asked where she was going, and again announced the horrible news.

Norman had been installing a radio for a family out on South Main Street in Elkhart, where people often experienced noisy interference on their radios. He decided to experiment and see if attaching the aerial to the high-tension pole offered improved reception.

"I'll be careful. I'm not afraid," Norman said, smiling and confident, when the lady of the house pleaded with him not to climb the pole. Her brother, a lineman, had been electrocuted a year previous.

The men threw a rope over the pole holding the high-tension line. One man stood on the chicken coop, pulling the rope, while Norman, who climbed up the pole, pulled the aerial wire. Suddenly the man on the chicken coop felt the rope stop. Turning around, he saw Norman, head fallen back, smoke pouring out of his mouth.

Now with nowhere to go, nothing to see, no one to awaken her out of her nightmarish dream, Carol numbly turned back toward the house. Carol later remembered:

When I entered the house everything turned to mud and ashes before my eyes. The rugs, the drapes, the phonograph, the overstuffed chairs, everything! Things I'd worked so hard for meant absolutely nothing to me. I almost hated the sight of the new piano. What is a seven-room house without the one I loved? All, all I wanted was taken from me! And this is our day! Oh God, I can't take it! It isn't real! I won't believe it!

Everything that I worked so hard to buy looked like nothing to me, just anthills and mud. I must confess that God did something real to me that day. Because even though I didn't do it, and I wasn't on the verge of losing my mind, I could have just so easily taken a hatchet and chopped up everything. And I hated the things that I loved, because I knew just as sure as anything, all these things of this earth stand between me and my God.

Then a still small voice within me whispered, "Not your day Child. All your days have been my days, because you have always belonged to me. This is my day!" I knew that was the voice of truth.

As the news of Norman's death spread through Elkhart like wild-fire, "Carol stopped screaming and started planning the funeral," said Nellie. "I never saw anyone become so completely transformed in such a short time."

"I want Norman brought home as soon as possible," Carol instructed the undertaker. "This afternoon. This evening."

"I want him here as soon as possible!" She demanded when they said he wouldn't be ready for viewing so soon. The undertaker acquiesced and promised to bring him on a cot with a velvet drape.

Before they brought him home, Carol and church chorister Enos Mumaw chose the hymns.

"We always said every sixteenth was our day," Carol later said. "Now it was God's day. We don't have the right to call any days our own. And God told me so that day. Because that's the day He took him from me."

Walley Funeral Home carried Norman's body in a wicker basket and carefully, silently placed it in the music room beside the piano—his Christmas gift to Carol that she would never want to touch again.

Dropping to her knees beside him she cried out in anguish of soul, "Oh Norman, my Norman, my darling, if I had you back I'd gladly go to India with you. Oh, if I only had you back, I'd be happy to live in a mud hut. I'd sleep on a grass mat. I'd give up all this, and go with you. I would. Oh, God! A thousand times I would!"

She meant every word of it. She had set her affections on things of highest value. No one needed to tell her that night.

The front page of the next morning's newspaper told the story in bold type, next to his picture: "Young businessman of unusually high character electrocuted yesterday afternoon, June 16, while installing a radio. His wife, Christmas Carol Miller Hostetler, to whom he was married on April 16, 1924, survives him."

Carol struggled with the reality of being a widow at age twenty-four. "It's not fair!" she thought, in an internal conversation she likely held many times. She blamed herself for refusing to go to India, for her selfishness, for her focus on material things. "But it is fair! I deserve it! It's not right! I'm not right! I was wrong! Wrong! Wrong, to think that way. If I could only turn back time just a few fleeting hours. NO! NO! This is a nightmare! I know I am being punished for my selfishness. I know this wouldn't have happened if I would have been willing to serve with Norman in the forsaken place of India! I can't get him back no matter how hard I pray. I would give anything to have him back. It's too late! It's too late! Only if I would have! Only if! Oh God have mercy on my soul!"

That night the house was swarming with people who came to console Carol, but she couldn't be consoled. One lady came up to Carol and said, "Now let's just forget about everything and smile a bit."

She felt like slapping the lady in the face, not smiling. All Carol wanted to do was pray and ask God to forgive her for her selfish heart. She could see in front of her hundreds of thousands of people, who wanted to know about Christ perhaps, and she felt like she stood in the way.

She was certain that she heard the clock strike twelve midnight twice that night. The reality of it all did happen. Carol woke up and hoped it was gone. The grief was too real. Grief so overwhelming that it caused literal physical pain, not just emotional pain. Then she couldn't sleep. She was too exhausted to bring sleep. Then she sobbed and cried out to God to be able to sleep, hoping she could find any kind of relief from the bitter truth.

Norman's funeral was held June 19, 1926, at the Prairie Street Mennonite Church. She had wanted a private funeral at home, just family and close friends. But Norman was so well known and so many people wanted to offer their condolences that Carol decided to hold it at the church. Six hundred people attended.

Carol wished to have a record play "Still, Still With Thee," one of Norman's favorite songs. A record playing at a funeral, an impersonal action never before seen in their circles, was stoutly objected to by Norman's parents, the Hostetlers. But Carol could think of no tribute so tenderly suitable. The record was played.

She didn't want to live! Really, truly Carol didn't. The doctor had her so heavily doped at the funeral, that she couldn't even feel her hands. She felt like she was dead too.

The service was much too long for Carol's fainting spirit. She had cried so hard since Norman's death, she said, that her tears were like concrete inside her. After the congregation viewed Norman, Carol's family accompanied her to the casket. In front of everyone, Carol knelt beside the casket and silently committed Norman to the Lord and asked for strength to carry on. It was an unusual procedure. She supposed some of the people thought she was crazy, but Carol knew she wasn't.

At the cemetery, after most of the attendees had left, Carol asked the undertaker to open the casket so she could have one last look at her beloved Norman. Impressed with her complete self-control and moved by her pleading voice, he agreed. As the undertaker raised the lid, the clouds parted, and a bright ray of sunshine streamed down on Norman's face. It was a blessed experience. The undertaker afterward told Abram and Selena that they had never taken care of a body that had so impressed them with purity as Norman's, and they never had charge of such a touching service.

The June 20 newspaper write up included the following:

HOSTETLER—Norman Gingerich, son of Levi S. and Nancy Gingerich Hostetler, was born at Elkhart, Indiana, December 1, 1902. In 1906, he moved with his parents to Rush Lake, Saskatchewan, and in 1908 to Preston, Ontario, where at the age of 13 years he publicly confessed Christ. In 1915, the family returned to Elkhart, and on Easter Sunday, 1917, he, with his brother and sister and a number of others, was received into church fellowship by baptism, and he has since been a faithful member of the Prairie Street congregation. He graduated from Elkhart High School in 1920, and attended Goshen College in 1922. On April 16, 1924 he was joined in holy wedlock to Sister Carol Miller of Elkhart, who graduated from High School in the same class and also attended Goshen College with him. Their short wedded life was a happy one. Bro. Norman was a great reader, a good student of the Scriptures and greatly interested in the Lord's return. He often expressed himself as ready to go when God called. He died on June 16, 1926 at Elkhart, Indiana, as a result of coming in contact with a high-tension wire and his death was almost instantaneous. He was aged twenty-three years, six months, fifteen days. He leaves his beloved wife, his parents, a brother Leroy, a sister Sylvia, and a host of relatives and friends. Funeral services were conducted at the Prairie Street Mennonite Church June 19, by J. S. Hartzler and Jacob K. Bixler, from the text, I Samuel 20:3. Interment in the Prairie Street Cemetery. The funeral service was especially well attended, his sudden death making a deep impression on the community. While our brother lived a consistent life, this should be a clear warning to the many who are not fully consecrated or who have never confessed Jesus Christ as their Savior.

I Samuel 20:3 reads "And David swore moreover, and said, Thy father certainly knoweth that I have found grace in thine eyes; and he saith, Let not Jonathan know this, lest ye be grieved: but truly as the Lord liveth, and as thy soul liveth, there is a step between me and death."

For days Carol existed in a state of a daze. All she could hear were her own words pounding on the walls of her mind: "If I only had you now." That phrase held sixteen letters, she counted.

Nellie and Cleo stayed two weeks with Carol. During that time she made plans to dispose of her possessions, deciding to sell all but enough furniture to furnish two rooms. Carol's father and brother-in-law helped her with a private sale.

"I don't care about any thing," she cried, "just get rid of the junk."

She didn't want to know who bought her things, and she shed no tears as her possessions were hauled away.

Carol couldn't go back into their house. Nellie invited Carol to live with her and Cleo. She thought that living with them and taking an interest in their new baby would be comforting. Many an evening Carol wrote page after page, giving expressions of her crushed and bleeding heart. No one ever read what she wrote; she tore it to shreds. "More than once I thought I would die of grief in my sleep," Carol later wrote. "But death rarely comes that easily." Years passed before she stepped foot in her and Norman's house again.

Norman's death was a catalyst in Carol's life. She viewed his death as punishment for her selfishness in not wanting to go to India and in having a heart set on treasures of the world. But she turned to Jesus Christ for comfort, healing, and forgiveness. Without a shadow of a doubt, the Lord gave Carol strength beyond her own. Some how, some way, our Lord steps in and gives us incomprehensible inner strength. Even so, it seemed almost unbearable: unbearable to our human understanding, but bearable with God's.

The scriptures clearly say, "With his stripes we are healed." The atonements healing balm purifies our hearts, cleanses our souls, and lifts our burdens.

No pain that we suffer, no trial that we experience is wasted, *if* we keep close to the Lord and seek His divine help. All of our experiences, especially those tragic life-changing trials, can, because of the Savior's atonement's healing balm, develop within us such qualities as patience, faith, fortitude, and humility.

All that we suffer or endure, especially when we plead for strength beyond our own, and when we plead for strength to endure it patiently, builds up our characters, purifies our hearts, expands our souls, and makes us more tender and charitable.

It is through suffering, toil and tribulation, grief and sorrow, that we gain a very personal understanding and testimony of the incomprehensible love of our Lord and Savior Jesus Christ. He is there to help pull us through. Suffering draws us even closer to Him when we invite Him into our hearts and minds. Through this entire faith promoting process, the Holy Ghost inspires us, enlightens our minds, heals our deep wounds, and whispers peace to our souls, sanctifies our hearts, renews our spirits, and teaches us truth.

We still experience overwhelming grief and pain, because we are human, but at the exact same time, the Holy Ghost creates within us a calming peace that passes all human understanding; an assurance that "all will be well" in spite of the circumstances.

The grief. The pain. It is real. The overwhelming peace brought to us through the Holy Ghost is real. Thank God, we *know* our Lord and Savior Jesus Christ cares about and completely understands us. Carol most assuredly experienced and testified of His healing power in her life. Years later she taught her children how to understand this principle as well, both by her example and in the words of a favorite song:

I must tell Jesus all of my trials: I cannot bear
these burdens alone.
In my distress he kindly will help me: He ever loves and
cares for his own.
I must tell Jesus all of my troubles; He is a kind,
compassionate friend.
If I but ask Him, He will deliver: Make of my troubles,
quickly to end.

Carol likely found solace in Christ's words: "He hath sent me to heal the broken-hearted, to preach deliverance to the captives, and recovering of sight to the blind, to set at liberty them that are bruised" (Luke 4:18). When life brings experiences that cause overwhelming trials and sorrow, we survive through hope and faith in the Lord Jesus Christ. Jesus Christ is the one who went through incomprehensible suffering in Gethsemane. He alone understands the depth of our grief, our emotional pains, and our need to feel understood. The Savior promises us in Matthew 5:4 that when we mourn we shall be comforted. He is waiting with open arms to bring us comfort and peace. We cannot learn to appreciate great joy to its fullest extent without experiencing tremendous sorrow.

Jesus Christ is a healer, a friend, a counselor, and a good shepherd. Because of this we can lay any kind of burden at his feet. We do not learn faith unless it is required of us. We cannot learn joy and calmness of spirit and hope for the future unless we have experiences in life that require that desire. Sorrow, grief and pain are all part of our earthly journey. It teaches us to rely upon our Lord and Savior to carry our heavy load.

Friends and family who are in tune with the spirit are inspired to also bring us comfort. The Lord always sends others to help us heal when we plead for His help. We find tremendous healing within, as we love and serve others and pray as mightily for others as we do for ourselves. *Burdens are lifted at Calvary.* We can truly feel a healing balm within our souls because of His redeeming sacrifice.

"Come, ye disconsolate, where ere ye languish," states a favorite hymn of Carol's, penned by Thomas Moore. "Come to the mercy seat fervently kneel; Here bring your wounded hearts; here tell your anguish; Earth hath no sorrow that heaven cannot heal."

Truly Carol was disconsolate as she dealt with Norman's death. But she did kneel before Jesus Christ, offering her wounds and anguish. And she came to know that her Lord and Savior Jesus Christ cared for and completely understood her pains and her needs.

On December 1, 1926, Carol wrote to her family and friends:

Dear Circle Letter Readers,

Today is my Norman's birthday. It is almost six months since he was promoted to his Heavenly Home. One hundred and sixty one days have passed since he went away, but during this time he has come back and talked with me ten times. He is always with me, but I have actually seen him ten times, and Oh! I wish I could describe to you the sunshine and the joy on his sweet face; but I cannot. You would have to see it for yourself.

I believe today I feel my loss more keenly than at any time yet, but beneath my burdened heart, I have a sweeter peace and understanding and a deeper joy than I ever experienced before in my life, for I know today that Norman (the glory and joy of my heart) is enjoying a more wonderful celebration on this his birthday than he ever could have on this earth. And though he has a thousand birthdays, his new life has no more than just begun.

I praise the Lord with all my soul. In spite of my grief I am stronger and healthier now than I ever was. That perhaps seems strange to you. But I am so happy for Norman, because he is so happy. I would not change a thing. My life is in the hands of God and everything is all right. Norman is always watching over me. He never leaves my side. We were very, very happy, and my memory of him could not be sweeter than it is. Few people knew how good and wonderful he was. I only trust my little message will remind everyone of you to prepare for the great change, for it will not escape one of us.

Norman's devoted wife,

Carol

One day shortly after Norman's death, Carol saw an ad in the paper: the Singer Sewing Machine Shop wanted a hem stitcher. She applied for the job and was very excited to get it. Carol always liked to work with thread and material. Working in that shop, Carol found herself becoming involved again with the beautiful things of this world.

Right after high school, when she had a job at the big department store, Carol worked in the cashier's booth, which was an overhanging room between the first and second floors. Carol could look out over the whole store, with all its pretty items displayed before her. It was while she was working there that she became so fascinated with the desire to possess everything she saw.

Now she worked in a Singer Sewing Machine Shop, dressing mannequins and making other pretty decorations for the shop-window displays.

During one Christmas season, she made seventy-five fancy pillows with organdy flowers stitched on them. She often worked nights to finish all the orders. She needed to keep busy, hoping work would help her forget her grief. It was good for her to be so busy. Carol sewed feverishly. She made fancy aprons, ran out yards and yards of ruffling, even made nine tooling skirts for tightrope walkers.

Two years dragged by. Working overtime kept her occupied, helping her through her grief. When one has too much time on her hands, it's easier for depression to creep in and take over. Carol had enough of that already.

"Oh God, I ask you to forgive me for being so selfish!" she asked again and again. "I don't want to be sitting here in this store, spending the rest of my broken hearted life running off these frivolous, foolish organdy ruffles! Not the rest of my life."

It was a bitter, cold January 1, 1928. Outside the temperature hovered around twenty below zero, with drifts of new fallen snow piled high around the house and huge icicles the size of arms hanging off the eaves. Being the holidays, they decided to make ice cream. Nellie prepared the ice cream and Cleo the ice, but they soon discovered they didn't have any salt.

Carol offered to go retrieve some from their parents' house. So she bundled up and braved the drifts. In the meantime, Nellie got dinner ready, but Carol did not come home. They didn't have a telephone, so they couldn't call to see what the delay was. In the middle of the afternoon, when dusk was already approaching, Carol returned without the salt.

"Guess what!" she shouted. "I'm going to Hesston, Kansas!"

Chapter 6

Assignment to Write

Just the day before, Carol received a phone call at work. Bishop Bixler of the Prairie Street Mennonite church invited Carol to join him on a trip to Hesston Mennonite College in Hesston, Kansas, where he would be an instructor during the six-week winter Bible term.

"Oh my," responded Carol. "Yes, I would love to go along, but I might lose my job, and anyway, I am not sure. I couldn't afford to go because I haven't been saving up my money."

"Well, I just thought I would ask," stated Bishop Bixler. "I will be leaving on Monday morning. You can make your final decision this weekend."

Maybe this would be a good thing for me to consider! thought Carol. *I have been praying for the Lord's guidance in my life, and this just might be the right answer.*

As soon as the shop closed for the day, she hurriedly drove to her parents' to discuss the unexpected opportunity with her mother. To her surprise, Carol found out that she did have money.

"When we had the sale for you right after the funeral, you lost interest in everything you owned," said Selena. "We sold your washing machine, your garden hose, your lawn mower, and many other things. You do have the money to go. It is right here for you!"

"But Mother," Carol persisted, "I don't think my boss will let me go away for six weeks, and anyway, I might lose my job!" Carol was bombarded with doubts and worry.

She picked up the phone and nervously called her boss.

"Carol, you have worked very hard at your job, you have gone the extra mile for me," he declared to her amazement. "I will be happy to give you a short vacation. The other girl can take over for you since business always slows down right after Christmas. We usually don't

Carol Miller Hostetler during the time she attended Hesston Mennonite College in Hesston, Kansas, ca. 1928.

have very many customers needing machines demonstrated, and the orders for sewing always slow down after the holidays. I am sure she can handle both the office work and customer service too."

Beyond just a six-week trip, this invitation opened the door to an amazing educational opportunity for Carol. If she decided to enroll at Hesston Mennonite College for the winter term, she might decide she wanted to stay for an entire semester and not go home to Indiana until the summer.

When Carol got back to Nellie's house on New Year's Day, she forgot what she went to her parents' house for—salt for the ice cream. Instead she'd made the decision to actually go west and start a new life for herself.

"It seemed like I got ready over night," Carol later wrote. "I just took about three dresses. And here I was going out to 'No Man's

Land.' I had never been out west before. I didn't know where I was going. I knew I was going with a good man, and if I didn't like it, I would be back in six weeks with my job back, doing what I love to do. Create beautiful things."

Still, "working at the store, there's no future for me there," she had told her mother.

This touched her mother's heart, and she said, "If you want to go to Hesston, I'll help pay the way."

They called Bishop Bixler to see if Carol could still accompany him to Hesston. And when the train pulled out of the station on Monday morning, there was a happy girl on board beginning an adventure into the future. It was bitter cold, and the train's heating system was frozen. Carol, who wasn't dressed warmly, took her suitcase to the restroom and put on layers of stockings, slips, and sweaters. She was still cold.

Carol soon found herself plunged into the school's atmosphere and activities. It made her forget all the dull weariness she had experienced. She began to once again feel life surging through her veins. She loved being with young people who shared her Christian values, and she attended the religious services on campus.

"I found myself in a strange new world of study, lectures, wholesome entertainment, and Christian fellowship," said Carol. "Hungrily I attended every spiritual activity, including the early morning Missionary Band. Long before the six-week Bible term was over I had determined to prepare myself for definite Christian service. Sincerely. Completely. Where He could use me now, it did not matter. I told Him I'd go to the back sticks, the mountains, and the jungles of Africa, yes India, or even to an old people's home close by. If nothing more, I told Him I'd get down on my knees and scrub spit and urine for His glory. Just to KNOW I was forgiven. Forgiven for my selfish, obstinate attitude, and still be accepted for some service was all I wanted. I presented myself a cracked, worthless vessel to be mended. I knew I'd go alone—alone with God that was."

Among her new acquaintances was Mary Histand, a native of Doylestown, Pennsylvania. In Mary, Carol found a true friend, someone with whom she could share the innermost feelings of her heart. "I think God sent her there just at that time," said Carol.

In her first letter home, Carol stated that it was warm in Kansas, warm enough to go without a coat. "I appreciate more every day the blessing of being born to Christian parents and Mennonites," she said in that same letter. "A privilege I, however, did not always cherish as I do now."

Further letters home soon indicated that Carol was happier than she'd been for two years. She reported joining a quartet to sing at a hospital and a jail. Among the group were eighteen young men, "some of them very handsome and none of them bad looking." It was work Carol felt blessed to be part of, work she said she would choose to do all the time.

"If you want to continue your college, I'll pay the bill," Abram wrote in a letter to his daughter. He continued with words Carol would never forget. "I would gladly sell all I have and die a pauper, if necessary, to help you prepare for Christian service. I would be willing to sell my business, my trucks, everything I have, to send you through school, if you have a conviction to be a missionary, and if that would make you happy. Remember we dedicated you to God long before you were born."

Remember? How could she forget that she'd been dedicated to God? Her father hadn't needed to remind her of that. At the end of the Winter Bible School, Carol enrolled for another semester. She notified her boss in Elkhart—she would not be returning.

"I want you to know of my continual appreciation for making it possible for me to be here to prepare myself for something greater," Carol wrote in another letter home. "I hope I shall someday be able to pay back in some way this manifestation of your love and confidence in me. Not of myself will I ever be able to accomplish anything, but God has blessed me already in many ways."

Life for Carol was blossoming again, yet she still felt emptiness in her heart. "I can never be real happy anywhere without Norman," she wrote in one of her first letters home from Kansas. "Everything reminds me of him."

Still, she continued moving forward and soon received a very un-expected assignment to write. Her English teacher was impressed with a short story Carol had written for the class. She asked Carol's permission to submit it to a weekly youth magazine called the *Youth's Christian Companion*.

To Carol's further astonishment, she received a letter from the editor stating that she had unusual writing ability and asking if she'd be willing to write one short story a month. Carol never thought her writing talents great, but this class and magazine together marked the beginning of her writing career. In total, Carol would go on to write more than one hundred published short stories.

Among her many new-found pursuits, Carol decided she wanted to join the Volunteer Foreign Missionary Band, a sort of club for indi-viduals interested in full-time missionary work. Those interested in joining needed to show their determination and commitment to be and do what the Lord wanted. Timidly, she approached Paul Bender, president of the Volunteer Foreign Missionary Band.

"I would like to make an application to join this band," she said.

"Well, I'll tell ya," he replied. "You go first and talk to the pres-ident of the school, because you have to have a real good reason to join this band. This band of volunteers is just for a select group."

"All right," Carol said, "I will go talk to him!"

And with shaking knees, trembling body, and hot face, Carol told the president she wanted to join the foreign band.

"Could you tell me why you have made this decision?" he asked her.

She told him of her absolute dedication to serve the Lord how and wherever he needed her. When she finished, the president reached out his hand. "God bless you. Would you be willing to give that testimony to the students the next time we meet?"

"Yes I would," replied an elated Carol. "I am so in earnest about it that I wouldn't care if it was the headline of the Chicago Tribune."

"All right, you tell it then."

So Carol did. At the next meeting of the Volunteer Foreign Missionary Band, Carol stood in front of the group and offered her testimony. "Oh, I was so scared!" Carol remembered of that event. "I know I was just shaking when I told it and I didn't dare look at any of the students who would maybe make fun of me, so I looked straight back at the room, like a lot of people do when they don't know where else to look." She told the group that she "wanted to serve the Lord, anywhere, no matter what or where."

In the audience that night was a young man Carol hardly knew— Nelson Kauffman.

Shortly after that evening, some fellow students invited Carol on an Audubon hike, which, she found out later, was a group of students studying bird life. Carol wasn't interested in birds, but agreed to go when the girls said, "Wouldn't you like to go along just for the hike?" Among the group's members was Nelson, an ardent birdwatcher.

Carol found herself hiking alongside Nelson, or perhaps he was walking beside her. He explained the different kinds of birdcalls and then asked about the testimony she'd given in the missionary band meeting.

"Well, I can't tell these things to just anybody!" she responded.

"We hadn't walked together for more than half a mile and I found out that he wasn't just anybody!" remembered Carol of that hike. "That is one of the first things that convinced me that Nelson was a real gentleman; so sincere, so Christian like. He listened to my story and never made fun or belittled my re-consecration."

"I think we should finish taking this walk after supper tonight," Nelson suggested when they returned to the college.

Carol agreed, and they soon found themselves sharing their convictions with each other. It was quite unexpected for Carol. "I never, never dreamed that I could love anybody else again, like I did Norman," she later said. "And, I didn't think that anybody would ever love me. I had been quite disobedient."

Nelson Edward Kauffman was born in Garden City, Missouri, on October 5, 1904—making him almost three years younger than Carol. He was the second of David Gideon Kauffman and Mary E. King's six children. When Nelson was ten, the Kauffmans moved to Minot, North Dakota, where they owned and operated a large dairy farm.

While working during his teen years in the field one day, Nelson felt the promptings of the Lord leading him to someday be involved in full-time church service. He later told his children that right then and there he personally made a commitment to give his life to the Lord, thus yearning to prepare himself in every way possible to realize the fulfillment of that motivating aspiration.

He wished to obtain a higher education and sent for a Hesston College catalogue. Nelson went to high school in Minot then finished his junior and senior high school years at Hesston High School in Hesston, Kansas. He then attended Hesston College, where he was majoring in education and taking as many Bible classes as he could fit into his busy school schedule when he met Carol.

Carol brought the Hesston annual home with her to Elkhart in June 1928. Carol was sitting with Nellie and Cleo at their kitchen table browsing over the pictures and making comments about them. Carol quickly turned to the page with Nelson Kauffman's picture.

"Now that's a nice looking fellow!" Nellie observed.

At that Carol quickly jumped up and gave a little scream clapping her hands over her mouth. "Isn't he absolutely handsome!"

"Now that young man must really truly be a somebody!" Nellie responded.

That was the sure signal that Carol must have needed to confirm many special reasons for thinking so too. Next fall Carol excitedly rode the train, which traveled much too slow, back to Hesston. She could not wait to really come to know this wonderfully dedicated, faithful, one-of-a-kind new friend. Carol wrote:

Three months later the very gates of heaven opened up to me when Nelson (who had often reminded me, so much, of Norman that

I had to look away) took me to a concert in Lindsborg. He told me again with tenderness how my testimony had interested and thrilled him, (little did I imagine that), how he had purchased two tickets for the concert and prayed over them (for two weeks) with me in mind. What? Me? A poor widow? I was completely surprised.

In the months following, every browning blade of grass on the campus looked green and alive. Every star in the heavens helped God tell me I was forgiven and accepted, and that all I had buried was coming to life again. Only this was a richer, sweeter, more meaningful life. I was ready to serve. I was finally humbled enough to serve the Lord wherever he wanted me to go. Just for Him, not me. Oh, to be loved again! To be wanted! To have a pure, God-loving someone who wanted my kind of love poured out on him.

They believed alike. His convictions were her convictions. And they agreed on everything . . . except butter and cheese. Nelson didn't like either. "Who cares about such cheesy differences?" Carol wrote. "We were in love!"

"You know one time, Enoch was walking with God and they went home together. Can we go home together sometime?" Nelson asked during one evening's walk. He was proposing. By "go home together" he meant being married and having a home of their own. "I am just a poor boy; I could never give you all the things you gave up."

"We'll have a few pieces of second hand furniture," Carol replied, "but I love you so much I could live in a tent, and we could live on crackers and cheese."

They laughed as Nelson reminded her that he didn't like cheese.

"Would you be happy with somebody secondhand?" Carol asked Nelson.

"You're not secondhand to me," he replied.

During the next several months, Nelson and Carol each wrote letters to Carol's parents. Abram and Selena kept every letter, placing them back in the envelopes in which they were sent. For us today, the simple act of returning the letters to their envelope is especially important because Carol never put a date on her letters. Their letters express firsthand their individual personalities.

In February 1929 Nelson wrote a letter to Carol's parents asking for her hand in marriage:

It is with the greatest of pleasure that I write to you this first letter. Although I have never seen more of you than your picture and your wonderful daughter, I feel that I know you and want to learn to know you better.

I have wished very much already that I could bring Carol home and visit with you, but since that seems impossible now, we will wait God's time for that happy experience.

I certainly appreciate your interest and concern for me because of my friendship and engagement to Carol. I can never express my thanks to God for the way he has ordered and led my life, that I have been counted worthy of the love of one with such a beautiful character as your daughter Carol. I never knew God in his beauty and fullness before, and I am convinced now that He has led us in a most remarkable way and our lives are completely in His hands.

I feel unworthy of the confidence and trust that she places in me when she has told me of the one God took from her, but I ask Him to continually make me the kind of man I ought to be, and that by His grace I will live a life that will be useful to God and that will make her happy, for she has done so much for me already.

I have very dear parents, they are so good to me, but I know that I will love you too, for Carol's sake, and because I can't help doing it.

Our friendship is unusual, it is intense and I am sure divinely ordered and guided. Although, I do not feel worthy, I wish to ask for your confidence and permission to come to your home as soon as the Lord will open the way. I do not know just definitely what He wants me to do, but I have implicit confidence in Him and that He will bring me to my work at the right time.

Carol has promised to give me her heart and hand for life and I wish to ask for permission to have her. In my weakness I shall always endeavor to make her as happy as she ever was and lead a life of manhood and service to God and the church that will be worthy of her love and devotion.

I consider myself highly favored of God for being able to consider you and your husband among my best friends and to share my appreciation in words, but will endeavor to, by how I conduct my life. I need your interest, prayers, advice and spiritual support for the responsibilities that are mine.

The same day, Carol wrote to her parents also, expressing her love for Nelson, their plans on moving near Nelson's parents in Minot, North Dakota, and Nelson's plans to become a minister:

First of all, let me assure you that he speaks very highly of Norman, very respectful, and I can speak of Norman to him whenever I want to, and he knows he's ideal in my mind, and he often says he wants to be like him. . . .

I must try hard to be a minister's wife. Nelson can certainly preach. His life is most wondrously beautiful. We may always work in the church at Minot, North Dakota. We do not know how, but where the Lord leads we're going. Perhaps, I do not know, Nelson might teach on the faculty here. We never know. . . .

I want to do people good. I want to be a real missionary. We are learning some duets. Oh, you'll adore him. He is a music director. Beautiful voice. He loves you all already, I know. He can hardly wait till he sees you. Can this happiness last? He is so very affectionate and sweet to me. Just like Norman. Wonderful. Pray for us. God is so good to me.

A month later Carol wrote to her parents on their thirty-third anniversary:

Thirty-three years! My! All I can think of is how glad I am I can write to you both! And you both seem so young to me yet. I believe younger than several years ago. At least it seems you enter into my life more. At least I know I never appreciated you more.

I wrote another letter to Nelson's folks. . . . You can't imagine how our love affair has affected their family. Nelson seems to be the leader and his three brothers all think he is so different, and he is. . . .

Oh, it seems like a dream to me! Will I ever get there and be a happy wife again?

. . . No, no, I never knew any one sweeter. He is Norman's equal in every respect. In fact, he is a better public speaker. . . .

And I never saw a man so handy in the kitchen. Whenever we get ready for a social here, Nelson goes right ahead with everything. He can do everything. He just reminds me a lot of Papa all the time. If I ever got sick, I wouldn't need to worry about the work getting done. He knows twice as much as most girls do. . . .

There will be a lot of talk when school is out about what Nelson and I will do, but we don't get teased as much as we did. Everybody seems to think we are meant for each other, and many people tell me they think it is God's will.

Carol wrote to her father:

I surely am having some happy times now. You will not be disap-pointed in Nelson. I am sure you will think every bit as much of him as you did Norman. Our romance is far superior to my other one in every way because we are older, I guess, and then too, because we both have a wonderful Christian experience.

I never knew this happiness before, ever. In the letter Nelson got from his mother yesterday, she says they are about to buy that little old place close to them. Then we would have a home right away. Oh, they take such an interest in us. That's the kind of folks-in-law I always wanted. It seems too good to be true so soon; I should find my true mate. But no, I did not find him; God found us for each other.

The way Nelson proposed is so sweet. We were coming back from a walk. We sat down on the bridge and read the Bible with a flashlight and had such a wonderful time, and as we were coming up from the steps, Nelson said, "You know Enoch walked with God and one day he walked home with him. Shall we just go walking home some day?"

Now, wasn't that a beautiful way to say it? Then we kissed each other and were married by the angels in heaven. Oh, life seems so different. But I have been going through some hard trials, very hard. But through it all God seems very close and real to me.

During spring break 1929, Nelson traveled to Colorado with a men's quartet. They performed with the local congregation at two musical programs and gave much voluntary service with the church members. Carol and Nelson corresponded during his absence.

"My Dearest Sweetheart," Nelson began in a letter dated March 29, 1929, from La Junta, Colorado.

I am so nervous I can hardly write. We drove all night in mud, and I never slept and drove most of the way, so my nerves are not very steady. Honey, this morning at 6:30 I was trying to sleep, and all at once I woke up and was thinking about you and how beautiful you were Wednesday. Oh, how I loved you, your face was so beautiful and sweet. I wanted to get this letter mailed at Dodge City, but couldn't, but you will get this tomorrow. . . .

I can't forget how beautiful, sweet, lovely, pure, kind and dear you looked when I left you. . . .

Sweetheart, it is so beautiful to think that at Hesston there is the dearest and best little girl in all the world thinking and praying for me and she really cares an awful lot for me. It is very wonderful to me, and I just thought, how empty the other boys' lives must be, to have no one. How empty mine was before I knew you. . . .

My beautiful one, God bless and keep you till we meet again
Your Loving Lover, Nelson

Carol wrote this reply back to Nelson immediately after coming home from a May 1 Missionary Band meeting. She couldn't pick up her pencil fast enough. She wished she were an eagle and could glide through the air with the greatest of speed and get it into Nelson's loving hands more quickly than the postmaster general.

Oh how I thank Sweet Jesus tonight for bringing me to this place when he did. Oh, how I love our church and her principles. Oh, how I thank God for you, Nelson, who will help me live true to her. Oh, how glad I am that I made the outward change to prove my inward love for God.

Why was it a struggle? Did I ever lay awake at night and weigh the matter before God? Just ahead of me, far out of my reach, I knew there was something, some grand wonderful surprise, if I but gave up. Why?

Now it is plain to me. Oh, my soul was stirred tonight. It burned in my breast and I wanted to testify. I felt the Spirit with me, but we had to close the meeting.

Loving you more each day,
Tenderly, Carol

Chapter 7

Life with Nelson

Christmas Carol Miller Hostetler married Nelson Edward Kauff-man on June 10, 1929, in Nellie's living room. Carol was twen-ty-seven; he was twenty-four. "It was a simple but lovely wedding," Carol wrote. Paul Erb officiated, Norman's sister Sylvia played the piano, Carol's friend and college roommate Mary Histand was the maid of honor, and Nelson's friend David Alderfer was the best man. It was a small gathering.

Nelson and Carol's desire to serve the Lord brought a unity to their lives that would create a deeper love for each other and greater power and dedication to the Lord. "For where two or three are gath-ered together in my name, there I am in the midst of them," Mat-thew 18:20 reads. "Fulfill ye my joy, that ye be likeminded, having the same love, being of one accord, of one mind," describes Philip-pians 2:2 further. Nelson and Carol found such shared commitment from the very beginning of their acquaintance.

They set up housekeeping, for the summer, in Minot, North Da-kota, next door to Nelson's parents, in the home they had prepared for the young couple. Carol reported that she and "Mother K," her mother-in-law, were planning to knot a comforter. Mother K also gave them a "dandy big kettle," which may have prompted Carol to ask her parents, "What is it you put in a pan to keep things from

Carol and Nelson's wedding day, June 10, 1929, at Nellie's home in Elkhart, Indiana. From left to right: Mary Histand, Carol's roommate and best friend; Carol's sister Esther, Carol, Nelson, Nelson's brother Harold, and David Alderfer, Norman's friend and Mary Histand's future husband.

boiling over? I heard someone say once, but I can't remember. I made scalloped potatoes but they boiled over half a dozen times." Nelson made Carol a beautiful buffet out of orange crates and some boards.

Nelson and Carol worked on the farm, they learned new songs ("We have twenty-four duets now that we sing together," Carol reported, "and he can play the organ better every day."), they cared for each other when sick, and they supported the local congregations. "Never did I once dream anyone as sad as I could be so happy again; and happy without things, and things," Carol said.

Just twelve days after their wedding, Nelson wrote to Abram and Selena about a conference they attended in Kenmore, about fifty miles northwest of Minot. "We certainly enjoyed ourselves at the conference—that is, the meetings were wonderful," he reported. "We feel that the conference has done a great deal in helping our people. At the consecration meeting yesterday evening at four o'clock, at the close of the church conference, twelve young people dedicated their lives to God to be used of Him in any way He chooses."

"I am on for a children's meeting at Bloomfield Sunday," Carol informed her parents a month later. "Nelson is to have two talks too. Last Sunday Nelson poured the oil while Isaac Mast anointed a Mr. Hostetler from Oregon. He's up and around all the time but says his health is failing. All the time the people respected Nelson as if he was the minister, but he isn't ordained yet.

". . . In a way I wouldn't be surprised if we would be stationed there some day. It sure would be like going out in the wild, but as you know, we've promised the Lord to go anywhere, and I'd rather go there than to India, unless God wants me to go to India."

In fall 1929, Nelson and Carol moved back to Kansas. For the next two years, they skimped, stretched, and worked while Nelson finished school. "Nelson carried mail, ran the school laundry, dug ditches, hauled coal, and sold Christmas cards, repaired latches or anything to earn a dollar or less," Carol remembered. "I took in sewing and babysat. We ate a lot of dandelions."

On one occasion a rabbit jumped out of the furnace, and Nelson caught it. Carol soaked it overnight in salt water, steamed it, baked it, and served it with gravy.

As Nelson finished his last year of school, they began looking to the future. They looked at two possibilities—Nelson teaching school or finding a Mennonite mission where they could serve. Carol mentioned their searches in a October 1929 letter to her parents:

We wrote a letter yesterday about finding a place in the spring. We have to know where we're going before time to apply for schools. Burkhart told Nelson someone was needed at the Wichita Mission. If we'd go there, we could move everything without wrapping everything again—dishes and all. Nelson says he dreads to think of wrapping everything up again.

We are really stepping out like all the other couples tonight to hear America's Famous Quartette at Newton. We are taking two other couples with us, so Nelson will have to hold me and have another man drive, as it is against rules here to go double deck. Ha ha. I don't care.

[Carol means that the car would be so full that ladies would have to sit on their husband's laps. It was apparently "against the rules" because it was publicly unacceptable, rather than against the law.]

Today I finished out some things to send to Canada to the Russians. An old coat too small for Nelson, a vest, two pairs of underwear, a petticoat, one pair of pants, one apron, one dress, and those old suede slippers. We will never miss them, as we never wore them. I suppose you will send things too. . . .

I must get to my story. I wrote part of it yesterday. But the radio keeps me from study so much; such beautiful music all day. I must get to writing. It is nearly four o'clock. . . .

[Nelson] takes such an interest in everything. Not many men are like him. He still helps me with the dishes, and on washday, dusting and everything, yet is so busy and does so much work. It is never hard for a good worker to find a job. Everyone calls on Nelson K. He has sold over $50.00 worth of cards, now with 40% commission, and he does it all in spare minutes.

In May 1930, Carol wrote to Nellie, congratulating her sister on the birth of her son David. In the letter, Carol refers to the short stories she is continuing to write for the *Youth's Christian Companion* and mentions that they will be heading again to North Dakota for the summer.

In closing she talks about how many people she and Nelson have invited into their home for dinner, a remarkable feat considering that monies were so scarce in 1930. As a young bride, Carol was developing the kindness and capacity to cook for, feed, and entertain large groups of people—a talent that she would soon be called on to share in an even greater way. Carol wrote:

I do not have any story that I sent to you that you did not type. I had reference to "Dale's Diary" but I know now that is in. I just received recognition of it last week. If my oration takes first place I will send that in with a few changes. If not I will write a story soon. . . .

Four more Sundays and we will be in N. Dakota. Nelson's mother is quite poorly on her feet and legs. She can hardly work so I have a

busy summer awaiting me . . .
last summer I was as busy as I
could be. . . .

I counted up in our record
book yesterday and in eight
months we've been here we've
had 95 people to our house to
eat. Is that very much? Just one,
two, and four people at a time.
Only three times we had more
than four. So I think we've done
our share of entertaining this
year. Never let it be said of us we
don't try to be sociable."

Nelson and Carol in their home in
Halstead, Kansas. Taken in 1931.

When the 1932 school year began, Nelson had an assignment
to teach in a small one-room
school near Halstead, Kansas, in a rural community. He taught elev-
en pupils. Nelson and Carol both felt they needed to earn the money
to pay back his father for the loan he gave them so Nelson could
finish college. They rented a tiny house on a farm owned by one of
the members of the schoolboard. Carol joined Nelson at the school
every Friday to teach the girls a class in Home Economics.

September 1931 was a hot month, especially for a pregnant Carol, who was in her eighth month with her and Nelson's first child.
"It has been so terribly hot here for two weeks," wrote Carol to her
college roommate and friend Mary. "Such hot winds and dust. Some
afternoons I can hardly stand it."

Despite the uncomfortable heat, Carol was enjoying pregnancy.
"I feel so full of pep now and everything goes better," she wrote in
the same letter. "I am perfectly happy to do my work and sew and
sew and feel the cool breeze." She created several items in preparation for her baby: a little kimono with pink snowflakes and a silk

bonnet trimmed in velvet. Mary sent her a baby blanket so wonderful that Carol was "sure no baby at the hospital will have one like it or half so pretty."

Mrs. Erb offered Carol and Nelson her bed, basket, or cart for their baby. Mrs. Bylers gave them her baby basket. "It doesn't quite suit me for a bed [for the baby]," Carol told Mary. "I can't fix it up pretty enough with ruffles, but it fits exactly in the car."

Nelson continued teaching at the school. "Nelson feels so good since he is teaching," Carol said. "He is always rested in the morning and feels so full of pep." Ever the careful husband, he always made time on Saturdays to help Carol around the house, cleaning the attic or garden or the cellar. They were happy and, of course, active in the church.

"I read such a beautiful poem the other day," Carol shared with Mary, "and it said how happy the woman was when her 'holy pains' began that would make her a mother. I never heard that expression before, but it gave me new faith in God.

"Oh Mary, I am so glad what you said about my mother. I know she is rather forgetful, but I can't detect anything in her letters. [Selena was about sixty-five at this time and apparently beginning to become forgetful.] She told me she saw you, and that you were even neater and prettier than ever. She always notices all the little things and takes such an interest. She told me you said that I thought a lot of my parents and it made her so happy."

As the Thanksgiving delivery date drew closer, Carol, at just four feet eleven inches, seemed to be quite uncomfortable in the last two months of her pregnancy. "The last two times we drove to church we had to stop and let me get out and stand up for a while," she wrote to Mary in October 1931. "It gave me so much pain and I had to get up and leave before church was over and I don't want to do that again.

"If I keep quiet and just go about my work, I am all right except that I often get sudden pains and I am awake at night a lot. I do not worry. I am just trusting in God. I do not feel afraid; in fact I am anxious for the time to come. Nelson does the sweeping now and works the bread for me. He says he just loves to do it."

The church revival meeting had been going on for more than a week, but neither Nelson nor Carol attended. Carol was too pregnant and Nelson refused to leave her, even when a friend offered to stay with Carol during the evening. They stayed at home, reading and singing to each other.

Carol expected to deliver before Thanksgiving. "Oh, that God and his angels will give it a safe delivery," she wrote to Mary, "that we may be able to see our dreams come true." Carol hoped for a girl; Nelson thought they'd have a boy. They'd chosen names for both: Ma Donna Lee if the baby was a girl, James De Von if a boy.

Chapter 8

"Our Sweet Little Dolly"

Nelson and Carol Kauffman's baby daughter—Ma Donna Lee— was born on November 13, 1931, at four fifteen. The couple arrived at the hospital at about ten o'clock, and the doctor examined Carol at one o'clock, sending her to the delivery room. At three o'clock the doctor examined her again and called for another doctor, who gave Carol ether. "So what I remember wasn't so bad," Carol wrote to her parents. She was later told the details of what the doctor described as a "hard delivery":

The Doctor didn't want to use instruments so he turned the baby and used a towel around her legs. Her right arm was badly twisted and they had it in a sling for three days, and took an X-Ray of her shoulder to see if anything was broken, and it wasn't.

Nelson said it made him awful nervous. He thought that it would kill me or tear the baby in two. I began to realize I had gone through something and I said, "What in the world did they do to me?" I had something to put me to sleep all but one night, and frequently had medicine for the pain. The doctor said I could never have a big baby. He broke the bag of water. He was very kind to me.

"The labor pains were not worse than I had expected and the time went fast and everyone was so nice to me," Carol wrote. "I was

Life in 1930s America

- The population of the United States was 122.7 million.
- The average life expectancy for men was fifty-eight and sixty-one for women.
- In October 1930, President Herbert Hoover established a committee to address unemployment relief.
- By December 1930 many banks closed their doors.
- The average salary was $1,368 a year, $114 a month, $28.50 a week, or $5.70 a day.
- In 1933, President Franklin D. Roosevelt unveiled a new program to feed and clothe the nation's needy. Seventy-five million dollars of surplus food was provided to feed the needy.
- At the local market, hamburger was fifteen cents a pound, butter twenty-nine cents a pound, potatoes twenty cents a peck, flour was fifty pounds for three dollars, and light bulbs were three for twenty-five cents.
- A new car cost between $900 and $1400; gas prices were between seven and ten cents a gallon.
- Simple, modest print dresses with waistlines and longer lengths were available in the stores. All well-dressed men wore hats.

not afraid at all. God seemed very close to me, and it seemed an angel hung above me." "God gave Carol unusual calm and strength for the hour," said Nelson.

Ma Donna had a fair complexion with blue eyes and golden blond hair. She weighed six pounds, two and a half ounces, and gained two and a half ounces the first week. "She is a very good baby, seldom cries at all and we think she is just a little doll," wrote Carol. "The sweetest little baby I ever saw. . . . I just love to watch her and hold her. It is the easiest thing in the world for me to fuss over her." "It pleased me when the doctor said he liked the name," Carol wrote further. "Not every one does, but I didn't expect that."

At least thirty-two people visited Carol during her hospital stay, and she "read four books through." Every day, cards and letters and presents arrived for little Ma Donna: a pair of white shoes and silk hose, a comb and brush set, money, a bunting, even a baby book. Nelson visited his wife and daughter almost every night, spending all of Sunday and Thanksgiving Day by their side. "The nurse would tell me how different my husband was from lots of others," said Carol. "And I just thanked God. I don't know when I've shed so many tears of joy as I did there. I am not worthy of it all. God has been so good to us. Oh, so good!"

On November 22, 1931, while Carol was still in the hospital, they held a beautiful, impressive dedication service for little Ma Donna Lee. "We offered prayers in her behalf and we feel sure that God has had His way so far and that He has a service for her to fulfill," Nelson wrote. "It is our prayer that we may be used of Him to bring her up to that service. Carol looks rather pale and thin, but she is doing very well for such a hard time as she had. This has been a beautiful endearing experience. It draws us together with words of love never known to us."

Their hospital bill totaled sixty-eight dollars and their doctor bill forty dollars.

Edith Roupp, a good friend and nurse, helped take care of Carol, the baby, and the home for several weeks while Carol recovered. Carol had hoped her sister Esther would come, but she wasn't able to. Carol longed to be up and doing things. "I know I must be careful for several weeks yet," she wrote to her parents. "I have lots of ambition and pep, but I tire so easily."

"Oh, it doesn't seem possible that she is ours and here to stay," wrote Carol as she settled into motherhood. Nelson and Carol called their new baby "our sweet little dolly." Carol fretted over a red spot on Ma Donna's forehead. The doctor told her it was caused by pressure and would fade. It did fade, but perhaps a bit too slowly for the new mother.

Carol reported that the baby had broken out in a rash. At the hospital, Ma Donna had been clothed in cotton, but Carol had only wool at home. The wool made the poor baby too hot, so Carol bought cotton bands and shirts. After three days of olive oil and powder, the rash was gone. "I am so surprised how warm blooded she is," admitted Carol. "I must always be careful not to get her too warm, and I thought it would be the other way around."

During this time, Carol took a month's absence from writing for the magazine. Rightfully so, her baby came before her writing.

On Christmas Eve, Nelson and Carol drove into Hesston for the annual Christmas Eve program at church. It was their first trip with the baby. Everyone crowded around to see Ma Donna dressed in her little wooly suit lying in her pink basket.

Everybody took packages for the poor, which were distributed afterwards. Ma Donna even got some presents too: two pairs of hose and a little rubber dog. Carol received a sewing bag, eight Jell-O molds, a vase, and a towel. Nelson got a box of stationary, three handkerchiefs, one pair of garters, a cedar box, and socks.

They received forty-five greeting cards for the holidays. Nelson's folks sent a nice box with a chicken, oranges, apples, candy, jelly, butter, and a doll for the baby. For their Christmas dinner they feasted on chicken, dressing, gravy, sweet and Irish potatoes, cheese, pickles, coffee, plums, and cookies.

On a Monday morning near Christmas, Carol received a box of presents from all of her family in Elkhart. "I could hardly keep from opening it before Nelson came home," she told her family. But she refrained. That night they hurried through the dishes then opened the box. "I wanted to open it, and Nelson did," reported Carol. "He said I should hold the baby and just sit down and relax and let him open it. . . . I said he should hold the baby and let me do it. So we compromised and he opened half and I opened the other half."

The box contained gifts "done up fit for the president": Seventeen for Carol, twelve for Nelson, and six for the baby. They stacked all the presents on the table then opened them all: a dress, socks, a scarf, incense, combs, a casserole dish, thread, a glass cheese plate, a pencil sharpener, perfume, a flashlight, tea towels, a slicer, a bib, a rattle, and a vase made by Carol's niece Dorothy Jean in kindergarten.

The gifts touched the young couple's hearts. "It made me feel so unworthy when I saw and realized the effort and money spent to prepare the gifts you sent," wrote Nelson to Carol's family. "I told Carol that she said too much when you asked what we needed." Carol's thanks were no less grateful; she and Nelson wrote separate letters home, thanking each of the nine gift givers in turn for their generosity. "We certainly feel grateful to God for such good parents," said Nelson. "I hope we may always try to live and work in a way that we may be an honor to you."

"The most wonderful present in the whole box was the bill for the baby's bank account," wrote Carol to her parents, "Now, that nearly took me right off my feet! I never dreamed of such a thing, Father." In the midst of the economic downturn that would be known as the Great Depression, both Nelson and Carol hoped they could find a bank where Ma Donna's money would be safe. "I have to wonder if any money anywhere will be safe in the future," Nelson wrote in his letter. "I am anxious each day to see the paper, for I rather expect some awful things to take place. The world seems ripe for a Universal Dictator, as the Anti-Christ will be."

"I hope, dear Father," continued Carol, "our little girl grows up to tell you herself, 'thank you,' and also to be an honor to you and Grandma too. There is no doubt in our minds, but that she will love you both dearly when she sees you. Already she is beginning to show affection, and she sure loves to be caressed."

As Christmas and Carol's thirtieth birthday passed, Carol and Nelson were truly settling into parenthood. "When Nelson feeds her she always holds on to the top of his shirt pocket with one hand and puts her other hand on the bottle," wrote Carol. "When I hold her, she holds on my dress neck."

"My, but he surely is a dear husband and a sweet father," she continued in the same letter. "He can bathe and dress the baby like a nurse. He never calls me at night unless the baby's nose needs cleaning. I have learned to sleep right through now if she cries. I know it gives me the rest that I need and I surely do need it too."

Indeed, Carol's family must have rejoiced also in Carol's good faithful husband when they read more of his letter to them:

"We can hardly express the feelings of gratitude that surged through our hearts when the large box came. . . .It made me appreciate more than ever before the great gift of God to the world. The greatness of His gift to us has impressed me more this time than ever before.

I had to think many times of the millions over the world who once enjoyed a happy cheerful Christmas with enough to eat and wear, with few gifts, who this Christmas, may have enough only for a bare existence. How I wish they might all accept the great free gift of God, which can be had without money or station in life.

I have had a keen interest in watching editorials on charity and giving this Christmas season. Many are giving selfishly; many are pretending to give charity benefits, as for instance ball games, movies, etc, when at the bottom of it there is a greater lust for money than a desire to give. I am sorry that we have not been able to give more. I feel ashamed, and yet it seems we have not had it to give. I wonder sometimes if we would be justified in giving at the expense of our creditors."

Becoming a mother herself further deepened her gratitude for her parents. Carol apparently wrote an article that included praise for both Abram and Selena. She told her parents: "As for my article, I am sure it was written in all sincerity. I think my parents are worthy of honorable mention, and I'd rather express myself so, where thousands can read it now, than after you are gone. I do appreciate all you have done for me and meant to me, sacrificed for me, taught me, and lived before me. All I am today I owe to God and you, so why should I hesitate to acknowledge it before the public? I did not say anything to exalt you in any way. I only wrote the truth and I have already received several compliments on my article in the mail. We really talked a lot (in fun) about coming home to surprise you, but knew we couldn't afford it."

Chapter 9

"Comin' Home Soon"

Nelson and Carol were very thrifty, hard working, and did what they could to make monies stretch. If they did not know how to do something, they would read or ask others and find out how. During the winter of 1931 to 1932, they worked side-by-side butchering their first hog. They put up all the meat, including smoked sausage, rendered five gallons of lard, canned the ribs and tenderloin, put hams in salt brine for five weeks—planning on smoking them soon thereafter.

The 1930s were a perilous time for public education, which likely added stress on the young couple whose income depended upon Nelson teaching school. With money so short, parents across the country were finding it difficult to supply their children with the necessary clothes to go to school. A decent teachers wage was forty dollars a month, or two dollars a day.

Even Nelson and Carol's alma mater didn't seem to be immune to educational difficulties; Carol mentioned in a letter to her old room-mate Mary that "there probably won't be any college next year."

Thankfully, it seemed that Nelson's position was secure. Nelson "will apply for [the Halstead School] again," wrote Carol, "and at least five people at Zimmerdale have asked him to apply there. We would like to get back closer to the church and our own people, yet we are willing to stay here another year if that's what God wants. I am simply trusting Him to lead us." As a schoolteacher, Nelson may have been teaching his students to read from the newly published Dick and Jane books, which were introduced in 1931.

With all the numerous things to do, Nelson made time to teach a Sunday School class of boys at church and was asked to be the mission secretary. He appeared to create extra minutes within every half hour. Carol did the same. They were a united team effort in everything they decided to accomplish.

Throughout this time, Carol continually suffered from back pain, a problem she'd been living with for a number of years already. "Oh, I do not know what the doctor will say tomorrow," she wrote to her friend Mary in a cold January 1932. "We have prayed so about it, but it also bothered me ever since it was lanced. I hope the Doctor tells me the truth and is not keeping anything from me." In a later letter, she mentioned that the doctor suggested radiation treatments to help with her back pain.

Still she and Nelson remained active in the church, their hearts set on faithfully serving where ever the Lord needed. "We worked with Vera Kauffman from South Africa, with the Mexicans who lived along the railroad track near Hesston," wrote Carol years later. "We learned some Spanish together, and we thought that perhaps we would be sent to South America some day. We both were willing to go anywhere the church wanted to send us. We even made the statement that we would be willing to wade through fire if needed, to follow the leading of the Lord, because God never closes one door unless he opens a window."

In an undated letter to her parents, Carol mentioned that she traded the typewriter for a fifty-pound refrigerator and gave ten dollars toward a washing machine purchased at Montgomery Ward. Nelson washed all the clothes by hand every week, plus all the diapers every day when their hired girl left.

By March 1932, Carol was in bed because of her back. She decided to go to the hospital for an operation since the pain didn't subside.

She was not getting any better, and the doctor said that he would care for her without any charge. Carol wished that they lived closer to her family so that her sister Esther could help care for her after the surgery.

It would be a more serious operation this time. The doctor would have to scrape or remove part of the bone, depending on what the X-ray showed. The hospital said that Ma Donna could stay there for a dollar a day, clothing and food included. Nelson was very good to Carol and dealt with the situation very patiently.

In addition, Nelson applied for teaching positions at several different schools. If they could make more money somewhere else, they would be willing to move. If they decided to stay in Halstead, Nelson planned to screen off the front porch so they could put the baby outside to play and the flies wouldn't eat her up.

As she had for several years, Carol was still writing her monthly article for the *Youth's Christian Companion*. Carol never used a typewriter. She always wrote all of her stories in longhand, with a pencil (just as is shown in scanned archival images over the following pages). Nellie would type the stories and send them back to her.

One such story was found in the Goshen archives among the many letters and correspondence relating to Carol's life. It was in an envelope addressed to her parents and dated March 17, 1932. The envelope contained several sheets of folded paper upon which was a handwritten story that Carol must have intended Nellie to type, but for some unknown reason never found its way to Nellie. Subsequently, this wonderful gem never saw the light of day, never was typed, and never sent to *Youth's Christian Companion*. How fitting that now, nearly eighty years later, Carol comes to us as fresh and pure as if she wrote only yesterday.

The story is especially poignant when you consider that the heart of the message derives from a letter that also failed to reach its intended recipient, yet the effects of that letter are deeply felt by all those who read it. It is as if God allowed Carol this one last turn at the loom, a moment to weave, in her skillful and simple way, a story that in the course of a few short sentences reaches deep inside even the most calloused heart and there tugs at the strings with a skill and compassion born in the fire of affliction and yet touched by the Master's grace. At the end of this particularly moving story, Carol writes a brief note to Nellie as if dashing off a story like this were an afterthought that she could have, should have, attended to earlier:

Dear Nellie   I think every time I finish one story, I won't wait so long to begin the next one, and every time I seem to let it go till the last minute. The poem, I copied from a book I have. It is not original.

Ma Donna Lee has been cross today. I didn't get her to sleep till one o-clock. I am baking bread and beans now. I wish I could send some over. This has been such a gloomy, rainy day, and such mud, but I am much happier in my heart than I have ever been. One tract you sent helped me most, the story of the sea captain. I say that verse over every day.

Comin' Home Soon

The quartet took their seats. A strange hush like a solemn benediction fell over the church. Even the red and white carnations in the baskets beside the pulpit seemed to drop their heads an instant. The ushers tiptoed to the door to bring in the latecomers. A young man with sandy hair and well-worn shoes and tattered suit, took a seat just inside the door.

The minister rose. "I think it would be fitting after the song to just bow our heads a moment in silent prayer, thanking God for our Christian mothers." The sandy head twitched, then went down with the others.

"We have come here today," said the minister opening his Bible, "to pay tribute to the best friend, the dearest and truest friend you or I have ever known. No human name is so enshrined in humanity's affection like the name of mother. For most of us everything that is beautiful, sweet, lovely and noble, clusters around that name. Think of mother and you think of home. Think of home and you think of the Bible. Think of the Bible and you think of God. And more to the man whose heart does not respond to the music of the two words, mother and home."

For twenty minutes the minister held his audience. Hardly a child made a whimper. Many a heart beat faster than the ordinary Sundays, but no one saw or knew why one spotted heart jumped madly toward his throat. Often throughout the audience a patch of white went to the eyes.

"And now," concluded the minister, "after another song, Marjory Smith will give a closing number, after which we will rise for the benediction."

A slender girl of about seventeen took her place on the platform. Her voice was clear but shyly sweet.

"There's a feeling comes across me,
Comes across me often now,
And it's the deepest, seems when trouble,
Says its finger on my brow.
Oh, it is a deep, deep feeling,

Comin' Home ~~Soon~~

The quartette took their seats. A strange hush like a solemn benediction fell over the church. Even the red and white carnations in the baskets beside the pulpit seemed to drop their heads an instant. The ushers tiptoed to the door to bring in a few late comers. A young man with sandy hair and well worn shoes and tattered suit took a seat just inside the door.

The minister rose. I think it would be fitting after this song to just — bow our heads a moment in silent prayer, thanking God for our Christian mothers. The sandy head twitched then went down with the others.

"We have come here today," said the minister opening his Bible, "to pay tribute to the best friend, the dearest and truest friend you or I have ever known. No human name is so enshrined in humanity's affection like the name of mother. For most of us everything that is beautiful, sweet, lovely and noble clusters around that name. Think of mother and you

Neither happiness nor pain.
But a strange and soulful longing
To see mother's face again.
You don't know how much you love her,
That old mother—till you roam way off,
When her voice can't reach you,

And with strangers make your home.
Then you know how big your heart is.
Seems you never loved before,
When you get this soulful longing
Just to see her face once more.
Mother, tender loving soul!
Heaven bless her dear old face.
I'd give half my years remaining
Just to have her one embrace,
Just to shower love, warm kisses
On her lips and cheeks and brow,
And appease this awful longing
That comes so often now.

The audience rose with one accord. The benediction was pro-
nounced, and the young man on the back seat slipped from the room
unnoticed.

It was dusk when a call was sent into the city hospital that a young
man with an attack of acute appendicitis was found in the north end
park, and was being brought in immediately.

An operation was performed at once. Shortly after midnight the
young man turned and for the first time spoke to the nurse beside
him.

"I'm better, ain't I Miss?"

"Yes, but you are still quite sick." She felt his pulse.

"I, I thought I was goin', once." He choked on the words and
stared wildly from feverish eyes.

"We thought so, more than once." She moistened her lips. "But,
you must not talk yet."

"But I must, I must. You see I ain't wrote or heard from my parents
for 'leven years. Won't you write a note for me?"

He tried to raise a hand, but it remained limp beside him, rough,
brown and helpless on the white sheet.

"You'd better wait a few hours. You must not talk now."

"Now, now," he whispered huskily, "please now!"

Without knowing why, the nurse obeyed him. It was her custom to have patients obey her--but something in the man's voice, something in his pleading eyes sent her quickly after paper. She drew up her chair.

"My old cast-off mother," he began.

The girl looked up sharply. "What? You don't mean?"

"Yes, write it, for that is what she is. I cast her off and left her 'leven years ago. Please write. It's 'leven years, now since I run off and left ye, but I took one look at yer face. You, I left and it's followed me all these years, that dear face like when ye told yer little boy to say his prayers." He stopped for breath.

"It always comes before me, in all the bad places I've ever been, an kep' me from goin' clear down. I'm rough now mother an' I've seen lots of trouble an' knocks, but yer face always smiles at me. Sometimes it has tears on the cheeks, an'—"

"Wait a minute sir." Something blinded her that she could not write. Her hand shook. The man did not notice, for his eyes were half-shut.

"I'm in the hospital now, but I'm comin' home, soon as I get well, an' take care of ye. Ye shan't know a care or worry, only be near me with your dear face. This is Mother's Day and I happened into a church. I was so tired. God forgive me and God bless ye, till I come. I'll come home soon, yer wanderin' boy Jack".

The nurse folded the partly blurred sheet and reached for an envelope.

"Why, Jack! Mr. Jack!" She bent over the man. "What's the matter Jack?" She shook him. "Just a minute Jack. Where shall I send it?" " Your mother—your mother!" "Jack, where is she? Jack!"

"Oh," she whispered, "may her face be among those that welcome you."

She leaned over the man and something from her lips fell on the sandy hair and calm face. And just then [in] the moon pictured on the wall above him, what seemed a face, a mother's face smiling down on her sleeping boy.

A nine-month-old Ma Donna was keeping Carol quite busy during August 1932. The baby walked around things and stood on her tippy-toes and reached for things on the table. One Monday morning just before breakfast, Ma Donna got to the syrup pitcher and poured it all over the kitchen floor, laughing about it. The next day, she got into the icebox, pulled out the Mazola Oil, and again poured it all over the floor. This time she trampled through the mess and made little greasy footprints all over the house. She even pulled dishes out of the cupboards. "Oh my," commented Carol, "so it goes!"

From a very early age, Ma Donna learned through her parents' example the importance of prayer and seeking Lord's protection. On September 11, Carol was cooking when their stove became a raging blaze.

"Nelson, Nelson, come quick, come quick," Carol screamed. "We are on fire! What do I do? What do we do? Oh my! Oh dear me! Help!"

Hurriedly Nelson ran to the rescue.

"Don't worry dear heart, I know what to do. I'll take over. You scurry out of the kitchen with the baby. If anyone is going to get injured, I want it to be me and not you two!"

Carol was positive that their house would be engulfed by the raging flames within and around the oil stove, but Nelson remained calm and was able to keep the house from burning to the ground. It was a day they would never forget.

The three knelt in prayer as soon as the fire was gone and thanked the Lord for his protective care and for the ability to remain focused, calm, and to keep safe. Nelson purchased a new oil stove for Carol; a very early Christmas present.

There had been a lot of robberies in the neighborhood. Their neighbors had six blankets stolen, as well as linens and eatables. Another neighbor had twenty-five gallons of gas stolen. A third neighbor had all their chickens and their supply of lard stolen. Carol was justifiably concerned. "Nelson, daddy, what will I ever do if they steal my long stockings?! We need to pray right this moment and ask for Father's watchful care over all of us!"

Right then and there, Nelson, Carol, and Ma Donna knelt on their front porch, with the clothesline in view and the chicken house in the background. It was their only hope. They knew God's power and grace; it was always sufficient.

They were keeping rabbits for Milo Kaufman, Nelson's cousin, in order to get several litters. The rabbits were worth two dollars and fifty cents apiece for the huge white ones. Their meat was worth twenty-five cents a pound and was very delicious. They planned to raise the rabbits to eat. They hoped and prayed that no thief would take any of their possessions.

Nelson also purchased two pigs weighing thirty pounds apiece, hoping to fatten them up enough to butcher in three months. They had a dog named Tippy. Ma Donna was able to imitate the dog sounds so well that Carol could hardly tell if it was the baby or the dog. "Nelson gets up every morning very early to study the Bible before he goes out to tend the animals," wrote Carol. "I can often hear him praying when I wake up. Of all the men I ever met, I think I have the best, and truest and kindest and most sincere.

Crist Snyder from Portland, Oregon, was at Hesston for a two-week conference. He was on the Pacific Mission Board and was very anxious to have Nelson and Carol come there in the spring. It was an interesting offer for Carol and Nelson as they were looking for opportunities to go into full-time church service. There were three candidates for the place, and they were asked to let the board know by the first of April if they planned to accept that invitation.

The invitation was also a source of worry for Carol. If we went out to Oregon, what would we do with our things?" she wrote in a letter to her parents. "Have a sale or take them along or store them or what? We would have three rooms of our own and share the rest of the house with the other workers. It would sure be a strenuous life, I believe. I told him I could not work in the kitchen much and he said I wouldn't need to. I said I have a baby and if I do visitation work, help hold street meetings and go around with Nelson, it was all I could do, and he said I could be my own boss and manage what the other girls do."

Nelson and Carol were much loved by everyone and enjoyed socializing with their friends as often as they could. They usually had three dinner invitations every Sunday to someone else's house. They attended church in Hesston, a seventy-mile round trip, which cost them fifty-five cents each time they drove it. If they happened to go home for some reason after church, they didn't drive back to Hesston a second time on the same Sunday because of the expense.

One October evening in 1932, the Buckwalter family came for supper, bringing their six children. The children made comments that completely embarrassed their mother:

"This pudding is lots better than what Mama makes." Their mother looked bewildered.

"We never have much for supper at home." Their mother looked red.

"Your baby is lots sweeter than ours." Their mother looked astonished.

"I wish I was your girl." Their mother looked hurt.

Nelson and Carol hosted the 1932 Halloween church social at their home on an exceptionally windless Kansas night—the smoke went straight up, and the candles did not go out. They decorated the backyard with ten jack-o'-lanterns on the fence posts and an arch gate of cornhusks and a dandy fire with logs around it to sit on. Carol baked eighty-two buns, which were almost all eaten up along with three quarts of pickles and a water pail of coffee. Nelson said it was the best social he ever went to.

There was a pie race, to see who could eat the most, a shoe-hunting contest, clothes pin race, stick whirl race, egg race, and a left-handed potato-peeling race. The cracker-eating contest was to see who could whistle first. The "Going to London" race was a relay where each person took a turn dressing up in clothes from a suitcase, running a distance, coming back to the start, putting the clothes back in the suitcase, and giving the closed suitcase to the next contestant.

While they were eating, two boys came out of the darkness dressed up as ghosts to scare everyone. Both the adults and children had a grand time. What laughter and fun for all. They ended the church social with an impromptu program inside the house.

Carol was involved in teaching a monthly "Homemakers' Club" for the women and teenage girls. It surprised her how many skills she had to continually teach:

It is astonishing how I have to explain and re-explain these simple things to women, so they can learn to do them. I hope Ma Donna Lee will be able to figure out some of the things for herself. She (Ma Donna Lee) would rather play all day with a spool of thread and a little pair of child size scissors than anything else. Sometimes I get out a clean washrag and make it damp, and she'll wipe down the window and the icebox and floor and chairs. I give her some lids and a rag and she wipes them over and over pretending to be washing the dishes. Yesterday she spilled a cup of cocoa on her head and then sat in the puddle. What a mess! Today she climbed up to the cupboard and stuck her fingers all over the pumpkin pie. And so it goes.

The doctor examined my back Saturday and said I should count my blessings. It does hurt sometimes, but he said it is a sensory nerve reaction and probably always would be so. It seems too good to be true. I haven't had to dress it now for eight months.

In December, Nelson, Carol, and Ma Donna were so pleased to be able to spend Christmas in Indiana with Carol's parents. They took the train to Chicago from Newton, then another commuter train to Elkhart. They returned home to find nine new baby bunnies, which brought a big smile on Ma Donna's face and delighted Carol—since rabbit was their new favorite food.

Chapter 10

Four Precious Years

Carol was sick in bed for five weeks after the long train ride home from their holiday in Indiana. Again, her back brought horrible pain, and she feared she would need to go to the hospital. The pain crept down into her hip, so she could barely stand it. Since it was very painful to walk, she stayed in bed as long as Ma Donna would let her and returned to bed as soon as Nelson came home from teaching school. Carol wrote of the experience to her parents:

I didn't tell hardly a person, but just took it to the Lord in prayer. Fortunately, at the end of five weeks the pain left me and it has not hurt me since. The bone from my hip to my knee hurt and I could hardly step on my left foot. It was swollen all around my incision. Now, what it was, I do not know, but this I DO KNOW, God heard our prayers and we thank Him for it every day.

Nelson helped me get all the rest I could, and he also helped me with all the work. The doctor said it couldn't be TB of the bone nor cancer, so maybe the pain was to draw us closer to God. Oh, I tell you, was I SCARED!! To think of leaving my baby again was more than I could bear to think of; and the expense. It seems like a miracle to me, and if you prayed for me, I wish to thank you.

February 1933 brought a cold spell to Kansas. "We lived only in the kitchen for two weeks," wrote Carol. She wore her slippers all the time and even a woolen shirt for two days. They even had to take our shoes off every half hour to warm their feet. Their milk froze solid, as did their potatoes and fern. Nelson's school was cancelled for one day. Somehow, through it all, none of the family members caught a cold and none of the rabbits died. "Then a few days later it was so warm we didn't need to wear a coat," Carol said.

Ma Donna continued to be a lively baby who ran all day and woke up laughing, thoroughly wearing out her mother. At fifteen months, she could say: *mama, daddy, bye bye, more, crackers, meat, drink, door, cold, hot, Bible, baby doll, shoe, tick-tock, oh no, bird, ball, give, comb, bottle, pocket, wake, butter,* and *I want to go out.* Carol wished she could spend more time helping Ma Donna to talk in sentences. At such a young age she seemed already to take after her mother. "She sings every day out of a cookbook or almanac or Bible," reported Carol to her parents. "She holds any kind of book that is near and pretends it is a songbook. And she loves to color. When I sprinkle the clothes, she uses a saltshaker and sprinkles the hankies. She sure loves dollies and loves pretending to be a mommy."

As spring approached, it was time for Nelson to once again apply for a teaching position. As they had not heard from Oregon by late February 1933, Nelson planned to reapply for the school where he currently taught. "Anyone who can get a job can do well to just stick with it," remarked Carol.

In March, Nelson received word that he could retain the school in Halstead, but there would be a cut in his wages to seventy-five dollars a month. They were grateful the cut wasn't more. Many teachers were receiving only thirty-five to fifty dollars a month.

Mr. Showalter, who let them live in one of his houses rent free, told the couple they could stay as long as he didn't need the house for a hired man. Carl wrote to her parents, including mentions of some unexpected opportunities:

There will be a bunch of new babies in church again. I am glad we are not expecting any in these uncertain times.

Nelson has been asked to apply up at Hesston. Some of the parents sure want him for their children. Well, if it is my husband, I must say he is a real teacher, but I wouldn't say this to anyone else because it is wrong to be proud or brag, and that goes before destruction.

I think it would be really foolish to move, since we have it so nice here; big garden, no rent to pay, light and milk bill, etc. I'd rather go eighteen miles to church. . . .

We had a letter last week from S. J. Miller, President of the Mission Board, asking if we would soon be able to come to Hannibal, Missouri. We hardly know what to say. Nelson should teach another year and get his father paid off.

In these hard times, I'd rather dread going into a strange city with no money laid up. Everything is tight here. I don't know if Nelson can get his next check cashed or not. By the end of next month, we expect to have the doctor and hospital paid off. Then we owe no one, but Nelson's folks. There is no certain time we have to pay that. Nelson said maybe we could take it out of his inheritance. He is to get one.

We did not hear from Oregon. We were recommended for the Chicago mission again. That would be a HARD place for beginners. If we were at Hannibal, we would be only a day's drive from home.

With the school year coming to a close, Nelson was busy with exams and reviews. He had five eighth-graders and one seventh-grader who would be taking the diploma exam.

Truly the struggles they saw friends enduring must have made bittersweet the relative prosperity Nelson and Carol were experiencing. Carol wrote:

On Monday, Maurice Yoder was severely burned when his torch-light exploded and threw burning gasoline over him. He was working in his shop where he makes toy engines for a toy company. He quickly ran and put out the fire with the garden hose, then fell exhausted and was rushed to the hospital. His face, legs, hips and one arm are badly burned and the paper says his condition is very serious.

My heart goes out for him and his wife. They have a baby a month old and one about twenty months. They named the baby Doreen Mateal. The other one is Marjorie Ann. They have both been so blue after he lost his job teaching. He bought a meat market and failed at that and didn't have work for a long time. Then he started his toyshop. Now this experience! The paper says his burns are third degree. I hope and pray he gets well. Nelson's father is related to him. We are going to prayer meeting tonight and will try to find out how he is.

Carol and Nelson continued to work and provide for themselves. Already they had eight rabbits, and they were looking to buy setting hens and a fifty-egg incubator and try raising chickens. "So, if we have good luck," Carol wrote to her parents, "we will have plenty of chickens and rabbits for summer meat." Eggs, Carol said, were up to six cents a dozen; cream at ten cents.

They planted potatoes, onions, lettuce, peas, and radishes. Soon they had 160 eggs in the incubator and eight hens nesting, so they were hoping to get a good number of chickens. The worms were so bad that year that they considered not planting another garden, and an infestation of flying ants added to their dilemma.

But in March, Kansas was already dry and dusty. "Today we had another one of those days for which Kansas is noted, a windy, dusty one," wrote Nelson. "The air was so full of dust at noon that one could not see more than several miles. Toward evening it let up some, and now is calm. Kansas farmers are not very hopeful for a wheat crop. The cutworms are destroying thousands of acres. Many farmers are feeding them poison. I don't know how effective it is."

In addition to teaching and gardening, Nelson was also busy serving on the Information Committee for the upcoming General Conference. In preparation for the conference, the local congregations were asked to plant potatoes, can beans, bake cookies, furnish breakfast food, and even butcher young beef to help feed the people who attended. Two congregations offered to can eight hundred quarts of beans. The Yoder church planned to grow tomatoes, Harper was to grow cucumbers, and Crystal Springs offered to make noodles. The Missouri churches were asked to dry corn. Other congregations were to raise the potatoes and others to fatten beef. They all determined to have plenty of food to feed the anticipated crowd of two thousand.

Carol hoped it would not be too hot, dusty, or rainy for the conference and worried that with the hard economic times the conference might be called off.

Nelson's folks planned to come out unless they had a crop failure. Carol's parents wanted to attend the conference too. Nelson and Carol were asked to give beds to six people. That meant they needed to make some straw ticks for mattresses so their guests could sleep on the floor. However, Nelson and Carol were hoping to get a room in a home at Hesston. If they had a little tent of their own, they would be willing to use it for the conference stay. Driving back and forth to Hesston from Halstead would not only take a lot of time, but also be costly to pay for the gas. If they did decide to stay in Hesston then they would not take in six guests.

On May 1, 1933, Nelson had only worked two and a half days since school let out for the summer. To bring in some extra money, Carol decided to do sewing for seventy-five cents a day, letting Nelson do all the work around the home and farm, which Carol usually did.

They planned to purchase sixty pounds of beef at just six and a half cents per pound to can, as they had only six quarts of pork left from their last butchering. Their garden continued to provide spinach, lettuce, and peas. Indeed it was so big that Nelson used a horse to cultivate it. Only fifty of their three hundred eggs hatched, the same poor results other neighbors were having. They had expected 175 to hatch. They ate two of their six-week-old rabbits; a tasty feast since the rabbits were fed milk, oats, and sweet clover.

They spent their meager money wisely and got the hospital bill, washing machine, and car all paid for. They had only eight dollars left to pay on their stove and just a few dollars to pay to the doctor. By the end of the month, Nelson had steady work, making one dollar a day; it was a tremendous help during the depression. They had so much to be grateful for.

The flies and mosquitoes were unusually terrible in June, and, with the temperatures higher than one hundred degrees, the potato plants all died. Everyone longed and prayed for rain. The local newspaper reported the fifteenth month of dry weather, with no rain in sight for the Kansas farmers. The rivers were lower than then they had ever been, and everyone was fearful that the wells would go dry.

Two of Nelson and Carol's big laying hens died because of the heat. With the temperature so high, Carol would wash clothes and hang them out on Friday evenings. She would iron on Saturday for Sunday, and then bake on Mondays. Ma Donna and Carol usually went barefooted in the summertime to keep cool.

Ma Donna talked more each day. One Monday morning, she came running onto the porch and told Carol that a birdie ran under the dresser, the bed, and then into the closet. Carol was sure it was a mouse.

Ma Donna couldn't stand to have dirty hands or feet and asked a dozen times a day to wash her hands. They are "dorty," She'd say. Carol thought it was funny how she put an "e" on the end of words such as *milkie, ridie, sleepie,* and *blankie,* to match her favorite word, *mommy.* She was a blessed delight.

Carol taught Sunday School and would take Ma Donna into the class with her. In the class, Ma Donna would sing, point to the picture of Jesus, fold her hands to pray and whisper something before she ate, pretend to read out of the Bible and sing, then kneel down and whisper.

Nelson and Carol started calling their little girl Donnie, because that is what she called herself. One Sunday in church, Carol had to keep her quiet so gave her part of a stick of gum to keep her happy. Ma Donna began begging for *piece gum.* She started calling her bottle a *milkie.* "We have great hopes for her and pray for Donnie every day," wrote Carol.

By June 12 it was 122 degrees in the shade. Nelson and Carol celebrated their fourth anniversary by going to town for ice cream, a favorite treat. She made him a homemade card with an original poem:

Four precious years, you've been my husband
Four precious years, I've been your wife
Four precious years, you've been my darling
Four precious years, best of my life
Four precious years, you've been my lover
Four precious years, no wounds, no strife
Four precious years, you've been my sweetheart
Oh, I thank God I am your wife.

In the same letter in which Carol shared this poem with Selena, Carol wrote:

This is an old house and I am constantly fighting ants, crickets, spiders, mice, moths, wasps, flies, mosquitos, silverfish, and other bugs too numerous to mention. I hope by another summer that we will be living in another place as far as insects and weather is concerned. As far as our neighbors, they couldn't be beat.

Donnie has been sick with a fever of 101. Her glands are still swollen so I won't take her to church tomorrow. The doctor said that we need to keep her condition under control so it doesn't affect her heart.

Carol wrote to her parents in July:

I just think I can't tell you we aren't coming, but we just can't make it. We've been planning on it all spring, but it seems we can't raise the money that we thought we could. I have to buy so many cans and one hundred pounds of sugar and we still owe the hospital and doctor, so we really can't afford it.

Nelson was talking with the banker yesterday and he said things are beginning to look pretty awful. Everyone was bragging that the Halstead Bank was strong. Now no one is depositing anything. Nelson can't be too sure he'll get his checks cashed this fall if things don't get better. Mr. S has had to borrow money a number of times in order to pay his men.

I will still hope to get home for Christmas now. We are talking to a man from Kansas City on Sunday, and he said it gives one the horrors to walk down the streets there and see all the factories that are closed and windows knocked out. So many people out of work, I guess we can be glad we have what we do.

Nelson still has work, but it takes all he makes to pay for the washing machine and gas. We have to drive so far to church and Newton. We haven't heard again yet from Mr. Snyder at Oregon. . . . If we go we won't go before spring.

I told Nelson, I won't go way out there without coming home. I dreamed yesterday that Nelson had to go to war. We sure don't know what to expect. I guess you read the papers too.

The first week of September, Carol made grape jelly, canned apricots, and made two pints of sandwich spread. She kept busy with sewing classes on Wednesdays when the girls would come over to their house. Nelson was busy, enjoying his new school year teaching fifteen students.

Carol writes of their other endeavors in a September 6 letter:

We were gone all last week. I sewed for Mrs. Amy Hershberger and Mrs. Horst. We stayed at the Horst's nights. Nelson went to the institute. I made three dresses, did some mending and made five bonnets. I was glad to be home again where it is quiet. Amy has nine children, and can you imagine the noise and commotion all day! . . .

We want to butcher for Thanksgiving. Well, I had to do my first grief today of disposing of some of my things. We failed to cover our sweet pickle crock tight and flies got in and we had to throw out two gallons of pickles. They had worms. Oh, I felt terrible! They were delicious and crisp as peanut brittle and the choice of all my pickling. I have seventy-five glasses of jelly now and some plums to make up tomorrow. Our tomatoes are over and our sweet potatoes are about as good as cardboard. So dry. I will have to cream or bake them with syrup.

With the approach of spring 1934, Nelson and Carol had to make some major decisions about their lives. Ever since they decided to get married, they were willing to consider serving in a foreign land, but since the depression following 1929, there were no funds for foreign work. They were approached again about opening a mission church in Hannibal, Missouri.

Nelson decided not to apply again for the Halstead school. Three years in one school was long enough, and he was growing rather tired of the same pupils—possibly the students were tired of the same teacher. He wasn't opposed to teaching, but wanted to teach where he could take his religion. (Nelson never received any criticism on his teaching other than one family of no religious profession who said he was too much of a churchman.)

The most important aspect in all of their decision was their determination to go where God would direct them. They wanted to make no mistakes as to where the Lord wanted them to go. Deciding whether to teach at another school near Hesston, leave Halstead, or go to Hannibal, Missouri, intensified their prayers.

In April 1934, Carol wrote a nine-page letter to her parents, going over the various life pursuits she and Nelson were considering:

I thank you for your sound advice and admonition, and much more for your prayers. We both can truly say we felt ourselves being held before God very definitely. Many around here are also praying about this matter with us. We did go and ask advice of Milo Kauffman. He suggested that Nelson should go ahead and apply for schools and take any delay as the leading of the Lord. Surely for some reason, God is keeping us in limbo, but we are not worried.

Nelson takes everything very calm, and I have also committed it all to God. I got a letter from one other woman saying what all we would do when we go to Hannibal, Missouri.

Mattie is J. M. Kreider's daughter-in-law, and they live on the same yard. She said it was J. M. who planted one hundred pounds of potatoes for us. Donnie would soon be playing with her little girl.

I got a letter from Margaret Horst today and she said if we needed a dining room table, we could get hers up at Hesston and use it for nothing. Also, we could take her cupboard along. Kreider's said they had a day bed we could use. The Kreiders are so kind to us.

It may be, I was not ready to receive the verdict yet, even though, I

Picture taken at Nellie's home in Elkhart, Indiana, ca. 1934. Front row, left to right: Esther, Carol's sister; Harold, Nelson's brother; Nelson; Ma Donna; Carol; Mary Histand, Carol's best friend; David Alderfer, Mary's husband; and David Gideon Kauffman, Nelson's father. Back row, left to right: Nellie, Carol's sister (peeking behind Nelson); Anna Kauffman, Nelson's mother; Helena, Carol's sister, holding her son Philip; Selena Belle Miller, Carol's mother; and Abram Miller, Carol's father.

thought that I was. If I understand my own heart, I am willing to go anywhere, or stay as God sees fit.

Our personal conviction is definite. Times are hard to open a new work. Paul Erb said he doubted if we could be happy working where we don't have a definite personal call. . . .

We surely would never think of going to Hannibal without orders from the Board. That is what is so confusing. We had letters from each member of the Local Board, which were forwarded to the President of the Missouri, Kansas Board, and each said we should come. Yet no word has come from the District Board.

Nelson will apply for schools tonight. We have no intention of going without definite contracts on black and white. It surely did excite me though, when Mattie Kreider asked us to be there the 22nd. We have a burden for souls, but no definite call for Hannibal.

Chapter 11

Their Decision Was Sure

In spring 1934, Nelson sang with a men's quartet that visited all of the small country churches near Hannibal, Missouri. During the trip, he visited with Bishop J. M. Kreider and Ruth Buckwalter from Palmyra, Missouri, to further discuss preparations for opening up a mission outreach in Hannibal.

After school was out, Nelson attended a General Mission Board Meeting in Elkhart, Indiana, and received an official call to go to Hannibal. Lena Kreider, Bishop J. M. Kreider's daughter, had been doling out clothing and needed supplies to the poor people living in Hannibal, and the Board felt that Nelson and Carol should give their full and undivided attention to opening a mission there. The call was official. The call was definite. Their decision was sure.

The Mission Board felt a great need for a Mennonite witness there. They wanted a dedicated couple able to work together to make a definite difference in the lives of those seeking the Lord. The board knew, from the evidence of their united dedicated service in Kansas and North Dakota, that Nelson and Carol Kauffman could and would unitedly fill that need.

Hannibal is an old historical town on the shores of the Mississippi River in northeastern Missouri. It is centered on the famous character and author Mark Twain. Although there were already about fifty churches in the town, they were outnumbered by taverns.

Nelson, Carol, and two-and-a-half-year-old Ma Donna loaded up their Model A car and trailer with all their earthly possessions and ventured to Missouri. Their first stop was in Palmyra, to the Kreider homestead where Bishop J. M. Kreider lived with his son's family. Harold Kreider, Bishop Kreider's grandson, recalled that the Kauffman's arrived in the evening. "I was ten years old then, and I ran out our lane to meet them. People who came to Grandpa's house to visit and stay overnight always interested me. Grandpa's visitors were always great people that I wanted to learn to know."

On June 3, 1934, under the supervision of the South Central Conference, Nelson and Carol Kauffman opened a Gospel Mission in what was once a barbershop, located on the wedge of Market Street and Lindell Avenue. The wedge-shaped building, known as the "flat iron," was the perfect spot in town for the church. They held church services on the main floor and lived in five upstairs rooms.

The local newspaper printed the following:

MISSION WILL OPEN SUNDAY

A gospel mission will be opened by the Mennonite Church at 1213 Market Street on Sunday morning, with services at 10 o'clock.

Services will be held each Sunday under the direction of the Rev. Nelson E. Kauffman, who was graduated from Hesston College, Hesston, Kansas. At 10 o'clock, Sunday school will begin, followed by preaching services at 11:15. The evening worship, consisting of Bible study and preaching, will begin at 7:30. There will be two services during the week. On Tuesday evening Bible class will be held, and on Friday evening there will be a prayer meeting. Both of these services will be at 7:30.

The Rev. Kauffman stated that the Mennonite Church takes its name from one of its early leaders, Menno Simons, and had its beginning in the Anabaptist movement, of the early sixteenth century. The church, he stated, has always held to the doctrine of non-resistance as the real peace teachings of Christ.

Carol's following write up appeared in the *Gospel Herald*:

The first services were held at the Mennonite Gospel Mission located at 2313 Market Street, June 3, in charge of Nelson Kauffman. There were twenty-one present in Sunday School, and one woman responded in the evening meeting and asked for help to get right with God.

Hannibal has a population of twenty-two thousand and offers a real opportunity for the preaching of the gospel. The mission is located in a busy part of the city. We expect to begin our Bible School on June 11.

Their [the church's] three weeks of vacation Bible School closed with a public program Friday, June 29, with 67 children enrolled and we had an average attendance of forty. Fourteen were rewarded for perfect attendance. Sadie Bissey and Martha Detweiler of Cherry Box assisted in the work.

Nelson and Carol had visited at least a hundred homes, and they found many people in need of spiritual as well as material help.

The Mission Board sent Nelson and Carol twenty-five dollars a month for rent and living expenses. The room downstairs was heated by a little old coal stove. To power the kitchen's propane-fueled stove, Carol had to deposit twenty-five cents at a time in the meter. With Nelson's ingenuity and Carol's artistic taste and ability to make something attractive out of scraps, they soon had a pleasantly cozy place to live. But they really had to live by faith. They received much love and assistance from the local Palmyra, Cherry Box, and Pea Ridge congregations.

The following are a few selected paragraphs from the *Gospel Herald*, written by Bishop J. M. Kreider:

Bro Kauffman and his little wife are earnest workers for God, and very sound in the faith for which they are contending. Bro Kauffman was raised on the farm while Sister Kauffman was raised in the city, which seems to be a great advantage to her in handling the people.

The building on Market Street has been used for a church by the Church of God and a barbershop. The Kauffman's live upstairs and have a cozy little home. The man that owns the building has been very good to us in getting it ready for his new renters, by papering each room and painting them, and Sister Kauffman lets no opportunity pass by without keeping everything exceedingly clean and tidy. Bro Kauffman as well as Sister Kauffman put much time in visiting among the members as well as among those who are not members.

Any one passing through Hannibal will do well to visit the Mission, where you will always find a hearty welcome. Any one in Hannibal can direct you to Market Street. So don't be afraid to come. May God bless all the members of our dear church, as well as all others. Pray for the work in Hannibal.

At the height of the Great Depression, moving to a new town held frightening possibilities. However, Nelson and Carol continually received support from other congregations and remarkable answers to their prayers. Sewing circles from a number of states, especially Iowa congregations, showed interest in the work at Hannibal by sending supplies of clothing, bedding, and household furnishings.

On one occasion, Carol's sister Nellie had a church visitor stay the night at her and Cleo's home. To Nellie's surprise, she discovered that the man had left two dollars on the dresser when he left. Dumbfounded, as no one had ever left money before, she felt bad this visitor thought it was his duty to pay for their hospitality. She didn't want to keep it for herself, so that day she sent it to Nelson and Carol, little realizing how desperately they needed it. Carol baked bread to save expenses, but their flour supply was exhausted. They had no money to replenish their flour supply or to buy a loaf of day-old bread at the bakery down the street.

In simple faith one morning, Nelson and Carol had laid their needs before the Lord, praying earnestly for help from above. Would the Lord be pleased to inspire someone to send them money enough to purchase some flour? The Mennonite congregations in Iowa were generous in supplying them with money for food. When members of these congregations visited Hannibal, they brought boxes of nonperishable food for Nelson, Carol, and the new members.

But that morning there was no letter from Iowa. Nelson was dejected. He sat with his head in his hands and his elbows on his knees. No mail from Iowa!

"Our prayers were sincere, our hearts are clean and the Lord knows our desperate need," said Carol. "I know somehow, some way the Lord will provide either flour to make bread or bread already baked for us. We can't give up so easily. We must keep or faith strong! I know He cares for us!"

The mail had brought only a letter from Nellie, which Nelson tossed over to Carol. She opened it, saw the two-dollar bills, and jumped up, waving the bills in the air and shouting, "Praise the Lord, Praise the Lord. Here's the money for the flour!"

"And this is the confidence that we have in Him, that, if we ask any thing according to His will, He heareth us: And if we know that He hears us, whatsoever we ask, we know that we have the petitions that we desired of Him" (I John 5:14–15).

Truly, Nellie was inspired to send those two dollars days before Nelson and Carol's flour supply was gone. The Lord knows our needs and supplies them for us long before we even ask. He does this for us by inspiring others to provide for our need. Those who give often do not know themselves what specific needs are urgent, but the timing of the Lord is exact.

Many persons traveled through Hannibal on their way to Hesston College in Kansas and often stayed for the night at the mission home. Of course, Carol and Nelson provided meals even when it was the very last food that they had to give; often leaving little, or nothing, for their next meal. Not all the food donated by congregations wanting to support the mission outreach remained in Nelson and Carol's cupboards. It was generously given to others in the congregation.

On one occasion, a couple was traveling through and stopped for a meal and night's stay. This, too, was a common occurrence for the young pastor and his wife. Carol was very concerned when they arrived because she had used up fuel for the propane stove at lunchtime and did not have a quarter to turn it back on.

"Oh dear, dear Heavenly Father, what am I going to do?" Carol silently pleaded. "These dear people are so hungry. Me too, and I don't have any propane to cook them an evening meal. I don't even have a quarter to put in the meter. It's getting late. I need your help dear Lord. You know my need. You know everybody's desperate need. My need may be simple and little, but it is really huge to me right now! Help me Dear Lord. I'm really counting on you right now this very minute!"

It was getting late. She was too embarrassed to tell the visitors that she couldn't start cooking supper because of her plight.

"Carol, I am in desperate need of a new covering," the welcomed visitor inquired. "Mine is getting rather worn. I heard that you sew them for the women in your congregation. Do you happen to have an extra one for me to buy?"

The price was exactly right—twenty-five cents to be exact. Precisely what she needed. Carol thankfully reached for the box of coverings for the lady. Then, quietly with a prayer of thanksgiving in her heart, went to the kitchen and started preparing their simple, nourishing meal. The lady never knew how her request was an answer to prayer. A miracle happened. Carol's prayer was instantly answered.

In another touching experience, occurring in July 1934, Nelson was deeply concerned and tenderly spoke to his little wife, "Carol darling, what are we to do? Donnie needs milk and we don't have enough nickels and dimes or even pennies to buy her any. We don't even have enough to purchase skimmed milk. We pray every morning, noon and night together for the Lord's tender mercies to rest upon us here. I know he knows our desperate need."

Within the hour they unexpectedly received a five-dollar check in the mail from their congregation in Kansas. It was sent with a note saying that it was specifically for buying milk for little Ma Donna. "The Lord always comes through for us when we do what is right," Nelson declared with strong conviction.

When the envelope came with the check, Carol could hardly talk; she was so overwhelmed with gratitude. Nelson and Carol were almost positive that Ma Donna had German measles. It was going around in town; others in the congregation had children suffering with the dreaded illness. Ma Donna had not eaten anything for over a week. She would only sip a little milk at a time. Milk for her was essential at this particular time since she wouldn't eat anything else.

July 1934 was unbearably hot; three people in town had died from the extreme heat. Their upstairs apartment sometimes got a slight crosswind in the evenings with all the windows opened. When there wasn't much of a breeze, and the upstairs was so insufferably hot, the three of them would take their blankets to a nearby park and try to rest as best they could. They covered up completely with sheets to ward off the mosquitoes.

There was an ice cream factory directly across the street from the mission home. Every night Carol could watch out the window and see clerks serving the seemingly constant line of customers. They were the most delicious looking ice cream cones she had ever seen. How she wished to be in that line! She craved some ice cream.

Could she spare a nickel for such a special treat? No, there was no change to spare for such things. She seemed to have no appetite for anything other than some strawberry ice cream. One night she decided that if ever in her life she craved a cone, it was on that exact night! Disappointed, she fell asleep.

The very next day she received a one-dollar bill from her mother, telling her to spend it on something special just for her, Nelson, and Ma Donna. Little had Carol dreamed that she actually could have and ice cream cone so soon! All three were able to walk across the street that night, stand in that special line, and order their favorite flavors. Not only does the Lord know our specific needs, He also knows the desires of our hearts.

"Trust in the Lord and do good; so shalt thou dwell in the land, and verily thou shalt be fed. Delight thyself also in the Lord, and he shall give thee the desires of they heart. Commit thy way unto the Lord; trust also in Him; and he shall bring it to pass" (Psalms 37:3–5).

In late September, Nelson, Carol, and other church members went door-to-door passing out cards with a special invitation to attend Hannibal's Mennonite Mission's first Revival Meetings. The cards they passed out listed five blessings they hoped to pass on to those who attended:

1. Hope to the hopeless.
2. Pardon to the penitent.
3. Peace and joy to the believing.
4. Victory to the defeated.
5. Eternal salvation to the lost.

J. D Mininger, pastor of the Gospel Mission, Kansas City, Kansas, was the visiting preacher at their very first Revival Meetings. A men's quartet from Hesston College came. They had large crowds who expressed special interest. Forty confessions were made, which included thirteen mothers, two fathers, and seventeen Sunday School-age children.

Congregations also sent books of all kinds to start a library of good reading for the members. Harry Buckwalter provided wood for the potbelly stove, to help heat the building that fall and winter. John and Mattie Kreider of Palmyra, Missouri, continually provided time, offered spiritual support, and gave the most wonderful produce from their gardens: green vegetables, cabbage, beets, radishes, lettuce, beans, cauliflower, turnips, carrots, Chinese cabbage, sweet potatoes, and more. They also provided eggs, milk, and chickens. What a tremendous blessing for both those giving and those receiving.

Nelson, with Carol's assistance, visited the local Old Peoples Homes on a weekly basis and held services in the local jail. Both Nelson and Carol spent countless hours doing all they could to provide both spiritual and material help to all they came in contact with. Visitations were continual. Carol spent many hours a week going to poverty-stricken homes to help scrub floors and do any cleaning where ever she could assist.

When widowed, Carol found herself at the six-week Bible term at Hesston College in winter 1928, where she'd determined to prepare herself for Christian service. "Where He could use me now, it did not matter," Carol had said back in 1928. "I told Him I'd go back to the sticks, the mountains, the jungles of Africa, yes India, or even an old peoples home close by. If nothing more, I told Him, I'd get down on my knees and scrub spit or urine for His glory."

Now six short years later, Carol was proving her dedication to the Lord. She was actually scrubbing up spit and urine!

So many Bible verses and hymns describe the kind of wonderful Christian service Carol was so willingly rendering. "I'll do thy will with a heart sincere," wrote Mary Brown. "I'll go where you want me to Go, I'll say what you want me to say, I'll be what you want me to be." Carol likely thought and sang the words to this and other hymns: "Where He may lead me, I will go"; "My life to give, my vows to pay"; "More consecration for work He bids me do"; "Serving God thro' all our days, Toiling not for purse or praise"; "All my days, and all my hours"; "I will go with Thee all the way."

Similarly, Christ himself spoke of such selfless service:

"For I was an hungered, and ye gave me meat: I was thirsty, and ye gave me drink: I was a stranger, and ye took me in:

"Naked, and ye clothed me: I was sick, and ye visited me: I was in prison, and ye came unto me.

"Then shall the righteous answer him, saying, Lord, when saw we thee an hungered, and fed thee? or thirsty, and gave thee drink?

"When saw we thee a stranger and took thee in? or naked, and clothed thee?

"Or when saw we thee sick, or in prison, and came unto thee? And the King shall answer and say unto them, Verily I say unto you, Inasmuch as ye have done it unto one of the least of these my brethren, ye have done it unto me" (Matt. 25:35–40).

Harold Kreider, grandson of Bishop Kreider, shared this story:

The effects of the deep economic depression created much hardship for many people. One day a man stopped by the church and asked Nelson if he could have some money to buy something to eat. Nelson said, "Wait a while, and my wife will fix you something to eat." So Nelson asked Carol to make the man some lunch. Upon giving it to the man, he walked up the street. Nelson watched to see where he would sit down and eat the food. To his amazement, the man threw the lunch away without eating any of it. Nelson ran up the street and gathered up the sack lunch and caught up with the man, and confronted him. Nelson exclaimed, "I am going to stay here with you until you have eaten this lunch. We don't waste any of our food and since this is now yours, you will not waste it either!" The man had no choice, so he ate it then and there!

Martha Detweiler, from Cherry Box, Missouri, was the mission's first full time "worker." The Mission Board paid her two dollars a month for her help. She helped with caring for Ma Donna, with house-work, and with anything and everything related to the missionary outreach. This wonderful lady made it possible for Carol to work hand in hand with Nelson, assisting and visiting new members and contacting all who would listen to their message of hope.

The district Mission Board of the Kansas–Missouri Conference began to look around for a brother and a sister that were willing to consecrate their time to assist at Hannibal. Sister Naomi Detweiler, of Cherry Box, Missouri, Allan White and Oliver Miller of Newton, Kansas, and Junior Lind, a student at Hesston College, assisted in the work at Hannibal. Because of news printed weekly in the *Gospel Herald,* many wonderful people sent financial donations, bedding, and clothing. The work was progressing. Carol wrote in a letter to her parents: "I know that our success is due to the many prayers given in our behalf."

By November 1935, diphtheria was a dreaded illness in Hannibal. Two children had come over to play with Ma Donna, and the next day they were quarantined. Nelson, Carol, and Ma Donna had the special Shick test, which checks whether a person has immunity to diphtheria. Nelson and Ma Donna both were okay, but the doctor said Carol was susceptible. Carol had a hard time deciding whether she should have the three shots of antioxidant because she was afraid of it affecting her heart, so she wrote to her sister Esther for a nurse's opinion.

On November 3, Carol wrote the following letter to members of a Sunday School class in Elkhart, Indiana:

Greetings in the Master's name,

We wish to express our sincere thanks to you for remembering us in the Lord's service at this place. It is not our work, but your work and the Lord's. We have felt His very real presence with us since we came the first of June.

Our Sunday school attendance has grown from 21 to 92. We attribute not one bit of it to ourselves, but all to the Lord, and to the prayers of consecrated ones such as you. May the Lord richly repay you for every effort of yours in behalf of the work here. We can say that we truly enjoy the work. It is a busy and strenuous life, but *"He giveth more grace."*

When the days are long and full of hard work, He giveth more grace. When trials come, He giveth more grace. When funds are low, He giveth more grace. When we can not see one step ahead, He giveth more grace. Praise His name and we know that His promises are true.

We seldom pass a day that we don't visit in some home. We have three evening meetings a week and hold jail services every Sunday and do some visitation work besides. We pass out tracts and "The Way" on the streets every week.

If the weather permits, we will sing at the Old Peoples Home in Palmyra tomorrow. There is much sickness in town. So much diphtheria, causing several deaths. There are so many blind people in Hannibal.

Most of the forty converts seem to want to go on with the Lord. They need your prayers very much. Bro. Kauffman has two instruction classes a week. We expect to have special meetings November 16 through 18 with Norman Hobbs. We have a sewing class every Saturday for the girls and a manual training class for the boys on Wednesday night.

Most of our people are very poor. Many of the children have no idea what a Christian home is like. We frequently have a drunken man stagger into the church. We meet up with all kinds of problems, but He giveth more grace.

May God give you all more grace for every passing day and make His face to shine upon you and give you peace.

In Loving Service,

Nelson and Carol Kauffman

On November 19, 1935, Nelson and Carol were blessed with a second child, a son, Stanlee De Von. Ma Donna's complexion was very fair, and it was a welcome surprise to find Stanlee with very dark brown hair and eyes. He was a very welcomed precious addition to the family. Ma Donna celebrated her fourth birthday just five days before the new baby's birth. Little Stanlee was the best birthday present she could have had!

That fall they had some of their hardest times since they came to Hannibal. Donations were down and the letters slow. Nelson gathered a big load of wood to sell. Carol decided to sell a beautiful comforter and three quilts that were sent in by sewing circles.

"Dear Lord I said I would give anything up to serve you," Carol sobbed as she prayed. "I really did promise that to you long ago. Now my faith is really put to the test, Dear Heavenly Father please don't make this hurt me so much to give up my beautiful blankets that were especially made just for me."

Heavenly Father gave her sweet peace as she wept when she parted with them, but they had no choice but to sell them for much needed money. Carol also decided to sell her high school class pin, so Nelson took it to a jeweler and got enough money to purchase stamps and envelopes to send out letters of appreciation to those who had blessed their lives in support of the Hannibal Mission. Nothing was too much to sacrifice for His work and glory.

On another occasion, they went two weeks without being able to wash their clothing because Carol didn't have a quarter to put in the meter to heat the water. H. R. Buckwalter gave them a bushel of apples that Carol hoped to can, but the apples rotted because there was no money for sugar and rubber rings for her canning jars.

Nelson was invited to preach in Palmyra, but they had no gas for the car.

"What are we to do?" Nelson inquired of Carol. "We need to drive to Palmyra. We have no gas in the car. Can you think of anything we can sell to get even a few pennies to be able to keep our commitment to go preach tonight?"

Carols mind went into a spin. She could always think of something to remedy the problems. She went from closet to closet, from kitchen drawer to cupboard. She went near the washing machine and found the solution.

"Daddy, Nelson," she cried, waving several old rags in the air. "I have it. I have the exact things we can part with. We can sell these old rags to the man at the gas station down the street! I've got it, by George I've got it."

So they gratefully gathered together a gunnysack full of rags and sold them to the owner of the local gas station for six cents. This gave them exactly enough change to buy a half-gallon of gas. They were able to get to Palmyra and back without anyone knowing of their situation. They lived each day by faith.

Carol's sister Esther surprised them with five dollars—enough to pay the electric bill and purchase some sugar. Someone stole Carol's long stockings off the clothesline; fortunately she had just enough money to buy a new pair.

There had never been one time, since moving to Hannibal that they didn't have the money when a bill came due. Yes, food was scarce, but they somehow got along on almost nothing. Carol was inspired to make delicious food in spite of the bare cupboards.

Newlyweds Le Roy and Naomi Zook were the first of many couples who came to Hannibal to help with the congregation and then decided to make Hannibal their home. Le Roy was appointed superintendent of the Sunday School, and Naomi became a Sunday School teacher. They were best friends who met in Iowa and decided to help Nelson and Carol in Hannibal. Naomi became a much-needed "worker," living with Nelson and Carol. Le Roy was at the right place, at the perfect time to fall in love in Iowa, then decide to be married in the Hannibal mission church.

Many individuals met at Hannibal as workers, fell in love, got married in the mission church, and decided to stay and support the mission outreach. Hanging in Carol's master bedroom were about twelve framed wedding pictures of couples who met at the mission. The workers greatly helped in the service of the church. They gave their support in many ways, such as serving as Sunday School teachers, Bible School teachers, song leaders, choir directors, and youth leaders.

With so many new converts and members, mostly women, Carol was very busy making coverings and bonnets. In a postcard she sent her parents on December 16, she said that she made twenty-four bonnets and twenty coverings in five days. She was so tired that she had to take medicine to be able to rest.

With Christmas on its way, the church members in Wayland, Iowa, sent 125 quarts of canned food and forty quarts of canned chicken. Wonderful new and used clothing, quilts, and comforters also came in by mail to provide many with very thankful hearts.

Nelson's brother Herbert passed away from complications of severe diabetes. Nelson was able to go to North Dakota on the train because of the kindness of Bishop J. M. Kreider, who provided the monies to go.

While Nelson was gone, Ma Donna became very sick with tonsillitis to the point of being delirious and unconscious. Carol lost much sleep tending to her needs. The doctor advised that as soon as her tonsils were healed, they should be taken out or they would affect her heart and legs.

"It always pays to say, 'Not my will but thine be done,'" wrote Carol in letter to her parents that told of Herbert's death. "I often think of my past experience, but I can truly say now, I am glad for it all. I am glad that I am where I am, and God sure gave me one wonderful husband. The longer I live with Nelson, the deeper and purer he is. I surely have learned a lot from him."

By January 1936, they were experiencing a most wonderful problem: church attendance was becoming too large to accommodate everyone who came. In a few short years since opening the mission, the downstairs Mission Hall was too small! Besides that, Nelson and Carol's living quarters were not adequate to provide comfortable space for visitors traveling through. Nelson called a special meeting to begin looking for a suitable new location.

There was a Holiness Mission near their present location, and everyone was hoping that it would still be available when funds would be forthcoming. Nelson found out that the Holiness congregation had been hoping to sell their building to the Mennonite Church for some time. The decision of where to relocate became a priority to the local leadership and also with the Local and South Central Conference.

The *Gospel Herald* printed the following statement written by Nelson: "The Hannibal Holiness Band, which they called themselves, reported to us that their board unanimously decided to sell the building to us for $5000.00, which we thought was quite reasonable. They had an audience room 40 by 70 feet, a basement under most of the building with a steam heater in it, and eight nice rooms upstairs, four on each side of the hall. We thought it was just the right place for us."

However, right after the third meeting of the Holiness people, ten of their congregation board members decided not to sell. It was a disappointment since it seemed like the perfect place to relocate. Immediately everyone began looking for another location. They knew the Lord would provide for their needs.

The Hesston College Alumni notes of a 1935 publication printed the following:

Mr. Nelson E. Kauffman, '25, '29, is the Mission Superintendent and pastor. Mrs. Carol (Hostetler) Kauffman, '29, is enthusiastic with this calling and the results of only a year's work reveal the blessings which have attended their work.

The Kauffman's wrote: "We were attracted to the present work because of the opportunity it presented to do definite work in soul saving. It had for years been our conviction that the Lord wanted us in mission work, so naturally our hearts were in this kind of work and any opening that presented opportunities was an attraction.

"The most enjoyable feature of the work is seeing the change that comes about in the lives of individuals and realizing that we have had a part in it. The work with the young people is especially rewarding."

Chapter 12

Home on Broadway

During the Christmas season of 1925 and into January 1936, Sunday School classes and sewing circles from far and wide made the Hannibal Mission outreach part of their daily concerns and prayers. Congregations from Ohio, Pennsylvania, Iowa, Kansas, and Oregon boxed up and sent clothing of all kinds, including bedding and towels. Blankets and quilts were also donated to help bless the lives of the new converts of the mission church.

Carol wrote the following for the *Gospel Herald*:

I only wish that every member of the Church in this country could have heard the testimonies from men and women, boys and girls, miraculously saved from sin the night of our New Year's special midnight prayer meetings. There were 47 present. Before dismissing, a delicious but simple supper was served, furnished by the Kreider families at Palmyra. The members, most of who are on relief, know what it is to go hungry often. They all enjoyed the meal immensely.

Every Sunday School pupil got a nice sack of good homemade candy furnished by the sewing circle from the Sugarcreek congregation in Iowa, and each family got a box of homemade candy made by the sisters of Kalona, Iowa. Bibles were furnished by Rose Buckwalter's Sunday School class at Hesston, Kansas. About 100 pieces of clothing were handed out during the holidays.

248 meals were served to visitors at the Mission last month, besides 40 meals for charity cases. Not a day passes without praises with thanksgiving to the Lord for the gifts of love sent by friends. We have not been able to meet all the expenses of the revival. Milk, light and gas bills for the month were extra large.

Every penny contributed was counted. All offerings donated were much appreciated; an offering of only one dollar was considered very generous considering the low wages and cost of living during the mid-1930s. Those who sacrificed to provide needed funds for the Hannibal Mission were, in turn, greatly blessed. That's how the Lord works. An honest full tithing brings tremendous blessings, both material and spiritual. Added generous offerings bring even more!

By March the local board of the Hannibal Mission had an ongoing effort in soliciting funds to purchase a larger building. They knew that the efficiency of the work was being hindered: The meeting place downstairs was inadequate for the growing congregation, and the upstairs living quarters was too small to take care of the many visitors passing through from east and west. With Bible School coming soon and revival meetings in continual progress, there was not enough room to accommodate everyone who came to serve as singers and teachers.

Carol and Nora King, one of the mission workers who blessed their lives with her kind service, were continually preparing meals, changing bedding, doing extra laundry, and providing a welcome stay for all who visited the mission home. Nelson and Carol gladly entertained both friends and strangers, and many strangers became instant, lifelong friends.

As the local mission board sought to find and raise funds to purchase a new building, the *Gospel Herald* printed the following invitation: "One thousand dollars has been promised [to purchase the Hannibal Mission's new building] to date, by a brother as an annuity. The local board is endeavoring to raise the remainder on the same plan. If anyone should read these lines who wish to provide a treasure in the heavens that faileth not, surely it could be done by investing in this property for the Lord's work in Hannibal. If you are earnestly longing to help souls find the Lord, may God help you to consider this need prayerfully!"

The first week of April 1936, Ma Donna became very sick. On April 18, she had her tonsils removed in the local hospital. She came through the operation in a remarkable way, improving day by day and regaining her appetite and strength. Prayers in her behalf had been answered.

After looking at many properties, and with the help of a real estate man, the board found the perfect location. It was an empty lot on the corner of Lyon and Huston Street, eighty-feet long by forty-feet wide. At one thousand dollars, the price was perfect for building a new church!

A nice seven-room brick house adjoined the empty property. Located at 1417 Broadway and right on U.S. Highway 36, the house was easy for all those traveling through Hannibal to find. The house was rented on Friday, May 22, 1936, for twenty-five dollars a month. Church members from neighboring states immediately donated beds, bedding, and furniture for the newfound dwelling.

In direct answer to prayer, lumber (including shiplap eight-inch boards, No. 2 lumber) was donated to construct a temporary tabernacle on the empty lot. Immediately, they decided to build a shell twenty-six by fifty feet. Brotherhood from different congregations near and far raised the money to help build the new structure and gladly donated many hours of labor. They arrived by the carloads. By June the building held its first meeting. J. M. Kreider of the local board wrote the following, which was printed in the *Gospel Herald* on June 8, 1936:

The brotherhood in different places has been good to us by giving the money whereby we could buy the ground and put up the tabernacle. We raised most of the money by annuity and are paying four and five percent interest. Some of the money was given as a direct gift to the Mission.

Last Monday and Tuesday there were seven brethren working on the building from West Union and Lower Deer Creek churches of

Iowa. Later, four brethren came from Cherry Box, and gave their time. And still later, five came from Pea Ridge, and then the Palmyra brethren gave some time on the building.

So you see, practically all the work on the tabernacle was donated. A few of the Hannibal men who worked, we paid a little, as they are all poor and needed their time for other purposes, but gave it to us, so we thought it was more than right to compensate them a little.

The building is almost finished now. And the first meeting was held in it on last Sunday with an attendance of 84 in Sunday School, with a larger crowd that night. The building is on the corner of Huston and Lyon Streets. The dwelling fronts on Broadway and is located just at the rear of the tabernacle, and the plot on which we expect to build the church sometime in the future.

The home we rent is a brick building with seven rooms and bath. It is situated in a nice cool place, much more than where we had been. Several nice shade trees are about the present dwelling. We pay $25.00 per month rent, just what we paid for the building that we left last week, but you will understand the rent we paid over at the other place was for both the audience hall and the living quarters.

Throughout the building process, Carol kept busy providing clean beds and delicious meals for all those who helped. Nora was a most valued, wonderful helper and friend. The new parsonage was bustling with happy, excited volunteers.

The tabernacle was dedicated just in time for their first revival meeting at their new address. E. M. Yost of Greensburg, Kansas, came as their visiting evangelist.

By June 12, the attendance at their Summer Bible School was more than 50 percent higher than the year before. Now that they had a house with three large bedrooms upstairs, each with two double beds, Nelson and Carol were able to accommodate those who were willing to teach and help with the mission.

The growing faith of the converts and those who taught and served was exactly what Nelson and Carol earnestly prayed for. Their prayers were definitely answered. Many college-age people came from both near and far to help teach Summer Bible School; the parsonage was gloriously full.

There was room made for all who came. Oren and Martha Detweiler, from Cherry Box, stayed in Hannibal for the ten days of Bible School, so they wouldn't need to make the long drive to and from home each day. Carol and Nora provided breakfast, lunch, and supper on a regular schedule, even when the cupboards had little. Carol had a talent of increasing the amount served by adding rice, noodles, and flavorful spices to satisfy anyone who was hungry. Carol always taught a Bible School class too. Everyone pitched in to lighten the load. Everyone was busy from sun up to sun down.

And, of course, Nelson and Carol were also very busy tending to Ma Donna and Stanlee. This meant laundry piled high, including extra bedding and towels. Wringer washers and two tubs for rinse water were used. There were no clothes dryers in the 1930s. Everything was line dried, sometimes in the church basement when it was going to rain. Everything needed to be ironed, including the sheets and pillowcases.

Because of the added guests, friends from Cherry Box, Pea Ridge, and Palmyra brought boxes of wonderful food from their gardens as well as chickens and other meats. Many baked delicious homemade breads and pastries that helped satisfy all visitors. The blessings never ceased for those who came to help and for those who came to learn.

In July 1936, Simon Gingrich of Wayland, Iowa, came to Hannibal as the principal speaker of an all-day home conference. They discussed "dealing with home life and its problems," a topic of unusual interest to all who attended. A brainchild of Nelson's, this was the first conference held of its kind. He wrote the following paragraphs for the *Gospel Herald*:

As the New Jerusalem has twelve foundations, so the Christian home has in its foundation twelve elements; love, peace, kindness, gentleness, forbearance, self-sacrifice, helpfulness, truthfulness, honesty, purity, devotion, and loyalty. God's order in the home is man, the head, woman, the helper of the man, and children obedient to parents. The child should have due consideration in the home.

The occupation and material part of the home should never hinder the highest physical, mental, and spiritual development of the child. It is the duty of every parent to provide and direct wholesome recreation in the home. Attitudes and principles manifested by parents will be adopted by the children and carried into the church, and the rise of many of her problems are found there. Moments spent in spiritual fellowship at the family altar and other times, are happiest and make lasting impressions for good.

When burdens of the home are carried to Jesus at the family altar each day by several members of the family, the scriptural injunctions to bear one another's burdens and cast them all upon Jesus are obeyed and wonderful blessings realized. Home may have many of the blessings of heaven, but in the ideal home of Abraham and all others before and since, sorrow and tears have come; but in heaven there will be none of either, nor any thing enter that defiles, or works abomination, or makes a lie.

Regardless of the blessing of home life here, the life of the heavenly home will far surpass the blessing of the Christian home.

The hot, muggy July weather made it very difficult to carry on all the phases of church and mission work. With fall approaching it was evident that the tabernacle wouldn't provide adequate shelter from the summer's heat or the winter's cold. Actual construction of a new replacement church building needed to be a reality, not just a dream. Blueprints were drawn up. Prayers for donations became an even greater priority and faith continued to increase even more day by day for the advancement of their united, dedicated work for the Lord. Nelson made sure that the friends who read the *Gospel Herald* knew of their detailed efforts in Hannibal. What a wonderful blessing to see the work of the Lord progressing!

In late August 1936, thirty-four brethren from Iowa and Missouri helped tear down the tabernacle and started digging the basement for the new church. In September, forty-six men from Wayland, Iowa, drove 135 miles to build a concrete footing for the foundation of the new church building. These valiant men drove early and worked late, then drove back home the same day. What dedicated service! In the meantime, church services were held in a garage located nearby.

Aline Sommerfeld, one of the mission workers, wrote an article for the *Gospel Herald*:

For 12 days we couldn't have services, because the town was under partial quarantine for infantile paralysis and encephalitis. In one way the quarantine proved a blessing, in that the members and Sunday school pupils seemed to appreciate more than ever the assembling of themselves together.

The work on the new church building is progressing nicely. God has been leading very definitely in this work in the way of sending in working men, provisions, and offerings. We praise God for every part of it. And we extend our appreciation to every one who has helped both materially and in prayers. There have been over 100 different men who have helped on the building.

Carol wrote:

We praise our loving Lord for His unfailing supply of grace that it is our privilege to draw upon continually. He is able to do exceeding abundantly above all we ask or even think. Such has been the way He has blessed the work on the new church building being erected in Hannibal.

Bro and Sister Leroy Zook and son Marlin, were among those who came to assist in the work of building the church. Their presence is appreciated by all of the members. We ask that the brotherhood continue to pray for the Hannibal Mission, that God may bless and have His way in everything. "Now thanks be to God which always causeth us to triumph in Christ [2 Corinthians 2:14]."

Mission worker Nora King wrote:

The thought of being away from home soon vanished, because Brother and Sister Kauffman took me into their home as one of the family and I was not alone because I felt quite at home in my new surroundings. After being here a year, I love the city life and all that it brings.

The people with whom we work are not of the high class, but I have learned to love every one of them. To get into their homes and to see how some of them have to live has made me appreciate my own home more. Then to see under what trying circumstances some of our dear young people live the Christian life has created within my own heart and life, a greater thankfulness to God for my Christian parents.

I remember very distinctly the first time Sister Kauffman sent me out on visitation work. I was into the home of the daughter of one of our members. This family lived in a house with three other families, but separately. Into this home had come a new baby, and I took some clothes, which had been sent by the sewing circles for the little one. The mother was very thankful for them and treated me nicely.

I went on to visit three more homes. One of them, I shall never forget. It was the home of a dear old sister who always had a testimony for her Lord. The house in which she lived was made of wide boards covered with tarpaper and not even sealed on the inside. The floor of her kitchen was the bare ground and the room was very dimly lighted. But here we had prayer together, and God seemed just as near in her humble little shack as in any beautiful church.

As a result of the excellent work and the progression of the Hannibal Mission, Nelson was asked to conduct a series of revival meetings throughout the United States. He was becoming very well known throughout the church because of his articles published in the *Gospel Herald*.

In November 1936, Nelson was in Harper, Kansas. It was expected that the brickwork would be completed on the new building by year's end. One hundred and ten men had helped to build the church. The monies for building the church were raised in many different parts of the United States, as annuity gifts and free will offerings. The electrical wiring, plastering, and front entrance steps were soon to be completed.

Chapter 13

Tests of Faith

In February 1937, the mission home was partially quarantined because of scarlet fever. Mission workers Aline Sommerfield and Nora King both contracted the disease and stayed on the second floor of the parsonage. Both women remained upstairs, so Nelson and Carol could go on with all the business of mission life downstairs. There were about forty cases of scarlet fever reported in Hannibal; most likely many more went unreported because of fear.

Scarlet fever, a very contagious disease, develops with a sore throat and fever as high as 104 degrees. The glands in the neck become severely swollen. The patient has a red rash and, in severe cases, small blood vessels burst under the skin, which leaves the skin peeling away. Large pieces of skin may drop off of the hands and feet in large scales. Because individuals who care for scarlet fever patients are directly exposed to the germs, they need to have already had the disease.

Carol had been stricken with both typhoid fever and inflammatory rheumatism and was close to diphtheria and polio in her childhood. She never had scarlet fever, but she had no choice but to care for Aline and Nora. Eventually the doctors suggested that since Nora was not doing well, she would need an extended rest. She left for a two-month stay with her parents in Iowa.

Nelson traveled even more extensively, holding revival meetings throughout the Untied States. He was usually away for a period of two or more weeks. It was a burden for Carol to have Nelson gone so much, especially when five-year-old Ma Donna started crying both day and night with severe leg pains. She became seriously and critically ill.

"Oh, No! It can't be that!' Carol screamed. "Not rheumatic fever!" But it was. The doctor declared the horrible news.

Carol remembered when Ma Donna was sick with a fever and the doctor was concerned that the condition could develop into something more serious that could affect her heart. She remembered Ma Donna's hospital stay not even a year earlier when she had her tonsils removed. Carol worried about the coming days, wondering what she could do now and what she could have done differently in the months before.

Rheumatic fever is characterized by painful arthritis and heart damage, causing pain in leg muscles. Temperatures rise to 104, the pulse becomes rapid, and there is profuse sweating and swelling since the joints swell with fluid. The disease causes grave heart damage, which can recur after the disease is gone. And children with rheumatic heart disease are especially susceptible to secondary infection.

Carol later remembered the experience:

And this is one thing we often wondered about. When we went to Hannibal, our baby was two and one half years old, and when she was five she got very ill with rheumatic fever. It's a big thing on my horizon. Our little darling, our sweet little dolly got so sick. And she was in bed for eight months. And the doctors said she just couldn't live past nine years old, and she'd have to learn to walk all over again.

But I remembered when my own mother missed six weeks going to the table too. What my mother did while I was young; I remember that!

As I sat by Ma Donna's bed and told her about the angels I saw when I was seven years old, I thought in my heart, "Oh God, if I could be as pure in my heart, in faith believing as I was then, to pray for this little girl." And we prayed. And we prayed!

Oh, did they pray! Many friends both near and far prayed for Ma Donna's recovery. Could Ma Donna have had a very mild, undetected case of scarlet fever? Could this have lowered her resistance, allowing her to get this horrible illness now? Did Ma Donna's sickness a year before make her susceptible to this unbelievable condition?

Carol was under tremendous stress. How could she continue her duties as a pastor's wife and at the same time take care of little Ma Donna's dire needs? How could she give fifteen-month-old Stanlee the time and attention he needed? How could she continue on with all that needed to be done at this trying time while Nelson was gone so much?

The help of the workers was a tremendous asset, especially after they were well enough to help Carol with the entire household and with Ma Donna's grave illness. In Nelson's frequent absences, Carol clung to the support of congregation friends and the mission workers to assist with Ma Donna's needs.

Ma Donna's condition improved, and she began to regain strength. It must have been difficult trying to keep that five-year-old on continual bed rest so she could recover. Carol dreamed up and created all kinds of exciting things to keep her precious little girl occupied. Thank God for workers who loved and cared for the two children and Carol during this most difficult time.

On June 21, 1937, the *Gospel Herald* printed an update to Ma Donna's condition: "Ma Donna, daughter of Brother and Sister Nelson E. Kauffman, has been seriously and critically ill. Her condition at this writing is considerably improved, but she must be confined to her bed indefinitely. The Lord definitely touched her during the regular Thursday night prayer meeting. Pray for the Lord's will to be done in this time of affliction. Our little girl is still quite weak, but is happy to feel God's healing hand over her. Please pray for her."

By the end of the summer, Ma Donna was feeling well enough to travel. Nelson, Carol, Ma Donna, and Stanlee spent a wonderful vacation with Carol's family in Elkhart, Indiana. To make it even more special, Nelson's parents and brother were able to join them in Elkhart.

In September they were back in Hannibal, again searching for ways to improve their mission. On September 8, a note from Carol appealing for a mission car appeared in the *Gospel Herald:* "The 1929 Nash we have been driving is beyond repair and we are in desperate need [of] another car very much because we haul around twenty-five persons each time we have church services. These members live at a distance and need our help. Who will help provide a better car?"

Donations from kind friends and congregations made it possible for Nelson and Carol to purchase a 1936 Chevrolet four-door sedan. It was a tremendous blessing. J. M. Kreider described the blessings of this new car in the *Gospel Herald:*

The work in Hannibal, all told, is very encouraging; but not without some things that we would see different. The devil is busy here, as he is at other places. Not long ago he was allowed to be used by some young men in bad conduct during the services. The word got to the police office and they sent an officer up there, but as it happened the boys had gotten out of the building. The officer saw them on the street, and told them that, "We want you to go to church, but you must behave yourselves while there, or I will take every one of you to the county jail." We think the boys were somewhat frightened, as they have not showed up since.

When Brother and Sister Kauffman came to the Mission, they had a Model T Ford that they were driving, but knew that is was pretty well worn. So through the kindness of the Elkhart brethren, money was raised to purchase a Nash, not a new car, but one that gave better service than the Ford.

During the General Conference at Turner, Oregon, Brother Kauffman received a letter from Sister Kauffman that the Nash had given out and that the garage man says it will not pay to get it fixed up. So she said, "I just don't see how we can get along without a car." "Well", I said, "I will see what I can do in the way of getting another car."

So I began to tell it to a few brethren as I met them, and without exception all said, "Yes, we will help." After we got home, we began to look around for another car, and finally bought a real good car that had been only run in the city by a city man.

Then, money began to come until enough came to pay the car and the 1938 license. We did not use any of the money to pay [for the] license, however without first taking it up with the donors, who said, "Use the money that you don't need, to pay for its upkeep." Dear Herald readers, you don't know how much we appreciate this wonderful gift.

After eight months of serious illness, Ma Donna's health was completely restored. It was a definite answer to prayer. The church debt was wiped out and the new mission car was providing excellent transportation.

Exactly two years later, to the month, Ma Donna was suddenly ill again—with rheumatic fever. Two years earlier, the doctor warned that recurrence was a grave possibility. How could this be happening all over again for this precious little dolly girl? Carol shared this devastating news in the *Gospel Herald* on February 17, 1939:

Since our last letter to the Herald, we have had some very happy experiences, and a few sad ones. Visitors in our midst usually bring with them cheer and new courage to the mission family and congregation.

The one sad experience we have had recently was caused by the sudden illness of our little daughter, Ma Donna, who was so very sick in 1937. From that sickness she was completely restored to perfect health and God will always have the glory for it. Praise His Name! For well over a year, she was in the best of health and was able to go to school. She became sick again on February 6. We are looking to the Lord in submissive faith to heal her again if it will be His will. Will you please pray for her? That is such a comfort in this hour of trial.

Nelson wrote Carol the following letter of comfort while he was away at a two-week revival meeting:

My Dear Sweetheart

I am here in this hotel where I have a table to write on and must wait until 5:00 to get the bus. I had a nice trip, but oh, how my heart went out to God for you! I just prayed that such sweet peace and calmness might come down upon you that you might be rewarded for your tears and sacrifices.

I told your father at the depot that it seems harder to leave each time and it is especially at this time. He said he thought I should go in perfect faith and confidence, and so I am going. I said, "Lord, let me die if I cannot be a rich blessing to others."

The conductor sat down beside me to give me some tips for the trip; how to enjoy it more. It seems I don't care about that. All I want is to be used of God. Oh, how I long to pray mightily. I read that Moses fell on his face before God for his people. I so want to lay my form before God, for my child, my wife and my people and church. I said, "God, take me back home if I can't be a power for blessing and revival.

Oh, dear mother, trust in the Lord. This seems the most heart-searching experience we have ever had, again to have our little Donnie so sick! I do so much appreciate the attitude of your folks. It makes me feel surer that I am doing the Lord's will. I want you to tell Martha that I said I would like to have her make it easy as possible for you at night. Let her get up.

My mind is rather hazy yet. I am as in a dream. But I feel the real presence of God. He is so sweet and dear to me. I just thought how the heart of Jesus must be moved because of the need of those for whom he died and whom he loves. I love Donnie so, and how my Lord must love me. Even if I didn't shed tears, my heart is almost broken for her and you. I wish I could bear all your burdens. I thought, how different all would be if you were with our children and me as well. Sometime we will see the reason why, I believe.

I wish I had a room where I could pray alone. I surely hope I can have one alone at the Institute. I am going to spend hours with God, and I know he will hear. I want the prayer passion that Knox and others had. I surely praise God for the experiences in fasting and prayer, which we have had in the past few weeks. I just want to be all God wants me to be. I don't know what lies before us, but I know I am going to give all to God, as I never did before.

I love to think how we searched our hearts and asked for forgiveness and plead before God. Oh, darling, how I love you! I'll be true to you. There's no other like you. Oh, the times of sweet fellowship we have had. I will never forget you for the most beautiful scenery or in the greatest crowd of people, or at any time at all. You will be in my thoughts always.

When I preach, I will do it because I have confidence in God and love you. When I sing, I will be thinking of you and that deep peace of conscience because of sins forgiven and being in God's will. I want his will to be mine.

Oh, God bless you, bear your burden and give you peace and comfort! God bless Donnie and heal her. God have his way with me. Amen.

Your loving burdened husband, Nelson

PS: for Donnie,

I must tell you again, I love you and praise God for you and pray for you always. Oh, God bless and strengthen you. Just look into His face at night and see him smile back at you. I will ask him to smile and shine on you. Daddy

"I can't believe this is happening to our precious little dolly again!" Carol sobbed uncontrollably. "Oh Lord. I wish it was me instead of her! I can't bear seeing her suffer. Let me do it for her. Oh please let it be me! O Please, God, save me from the anguish of this horrible trial!!"

The second time around for rheumatic fever! What were Nelson and Carol supposed to learn from this anguish again? The Lord knew what was to be. Patience was an attribute he wanted Nelson and Carol to experience. It is an attribute we can learn only through experiences that require it.

"That the trial of your faith, being more precious than of gold that perisheth, though it be tried with fire might be found unto praise and honor and glory at the appearing of Jesus Christ:

"Whom having not seen, ye love; in whom, though now ye see him not, yet believing, ye rejoice with joy unspeakable and full of glory:

"Receiving the end of your faith, even the salvation of your souls" (I Peter 1:7–9).

We cannot really come to appreciate our loving Father in Heaven without Him creating opportunities in our every day lives that demand that our faith be stretched to the limit. Sometimes we forget that a test of faith must really be a test of faith: a trial. We forget too that when our sore trials come to us, they are carefully shaped to wring us and to wrench our souls, otherwise they would not purify us, like a refiner's fire, like the purifying of gold. It is a measure of both the love of a living God and His perfect awareness of our needs.

When our hearts are pure and in tune with the Lord, we know this. Even so, sometimes in our human frailty, we resent it. Sometimes challenges trouble or puzzle us. We can't figure them out. Could it be that the Lord knows exactly what we need to endure to help us prove our faith?

It is often so difficult for us to be patient in tribulations, especially when they involve our beloved children, so innocent, so pure. Jesus said that we would have tribulation in the world, but in Him we could have peace in the midst of tribulation. We should be of "good cheer" because He has come to overcome the world.

When sore trials come, if we put our trust in God, the support that He gives us in times of disappointment and discouragement can be turned into blessings that are greater understanding of Him. Such understanding leads to greater assurance of the Lord's power to strengthen us, so our hearts are in tune with His divine will in our lives and in the lives of our children.

"Therefore being justified by faith, we have peace with God through our Lord Jesus Christ:

"By whom we have access by faith unto his grace wherein we stand, and rejoice in hope of the glory of God.

"And not only so, but we glory in tribulations also: knowing that tribulation worketh patience;

"And patience, experience; and experience, hope;

"And hope maketh not ashamed; because the love of God is shed abroad in our hearts by the Holy Ghost, which is given unto us" (Romans 5:1–5).

Nelson and Carol searched their hearts; their broken hearts created contrite (humble) spirits, which helped them grow closer to the Lord. Their faith was strengthened. They learned the reason why. They knew from their personal experiences His love, His will, and His depth of understanding their hearts. They learned acceptance to his divine will.

Nelson and Carol opened a "Good Samaritan Hall" for men as a Rescue Mission. Nelson shared the reasoning behind this Rescue Mission with the *Gospel Herald:*

There is in our land, a great multitude of men, young and old, who have no homes, no work, and some, no relatives that care for them. These men are often in this condition, not by their own choice, but because of circumstances over which they have no control. Some are men of ability and education that have seen better times. They spend their time traveling back and forth over the country, eating what they can beg, sleeping where they can find a place to lie down, and wearing what is given them. Misfortune has come their way and their stories are heart-rending. They live at the mercy of a cold and heartless world. These are among those of us for whom our Lord Jesus left the glorious courts of heaven to be homeless and unwanted that we might be saved.

It is because of a love for these men and a desire of Carol and mine, to bring them the good news of God's love in Christ for all men, that last year the "Good Samaritan Hall for Men" was opened on South Main Street in Hannibal. It was our privilege to hold 37 services there, preach to a total audience of 781 persons, 63 of whom were transients, and serve as many meals. Among this group were also men of the town that seldom go to church. To all that attended we gave Scripture portions and Gospel tracts. Every one was spoken to personally concerning his soul and pointed to the Lord Jesus Christ, the Friend of the friendless.

The expense of this work was not as great as might be expected. Bakeries usually furnished bread, rolls and doughnuts. Grocers gave soup bones and sisters of the sewing circle gave other soup constituents.

At the last meeting of the local board, it was decided that the work of the "Good Samaritan Hall" should continue again this winter. Would you that have homes, loved ones, and an abundant measure of blessings, like to share in the work of bringing Jesus to these men? If you could sit in the service some evening, watch their faces as the message is given, and afterwards see them enjoy the simple meal, I am sure that you would feel that you would like to have a part in ministering to them. We are asking the Lord to make it possible, if it please Him, to open this work before Christmas. As you pray, will you not remember this work with Carol and me, for our Father? We then will be working together with God.

Carol reported further on the progress of the mission for the *Gospel Herald*:

Although the work is not a large one, it gives us one more opportunity to preach the Gospel Story to men who otherwise would not hear it. Transients, some young, pitiful looking boys, some old shaky men have been in nearly every service.

One more thing that makes us sad in a way is the giving up of our beloved worker, Martha Detweiler; but we know God can use her to His glory when she goes to her home in Canton, Kansas, and has a home of her own. We are sad to see her leave, but glad she is marrying in the Lord. Sister Cleo Miller of Hutchison, Kansas, has come to take her place, and she is doing this very well too.

Our average attendance in Sunday School for the past year was 80. That means that all but the mission family is from the city and non-Mennonite homes. Our problems are many. Your prayers are appreciated much.

Christmas 1939 didn't look like Christmas; the weather was so warm. No snow on the ground, but everywhere there was Christmas in the windows and, best of all, in their hearts. The blessed Christ Child had found a place in the hearts of some who a year ago didn't know of the Hannibal Mission and the wonderful friends there to offer love and support like they had never known before.

A week before Christmas, boxes and packages arrived from the ladies Mennonite Sewing Circles and young people's groups in Iowa and Kansas. That year Nelson and Carol gave each boy and girl in the congregation a sack of candy and an apple—one hundred in total. Every mother received a pretty apron, a tea towel, a bookmark, and material for a new dress.

The Young People's Literary society from Elkhart, Indiana, sent a box of thirty toys. Toys also came from Iowa congregations. Each child knew they were loved and remembered. Many needy children received clothing, and every baby on the cradle roll was given a gingham animal that was made by generous young people from an Iowa church. Truly, for the children, it was a Christmas to remember. In addition, every family in the church got a dressed chicken.

The church pews were filled for the Christmas program. Parents who had never been to the church were present to see and hear their children participate in the annual Christmas program.

Finally, by the following May, Ma Donna started rapidly regaining her health. It had been a long hard road to travel, but the prayers offered in behalf of not only Ma Donna, but for all of them, strengthened Nelson and Carol daily.

Meetings in the Good Samaritan Hall were discontinued for the summer. Thirty-seven services had been held, sixty-three transients came to the services, and 781 meals had been served during the winter. Carol was often in the hall's kitchen preparing and serving meals to the men. Some of the men who attended services in the Samaritan Hall began to attend regular church services. All were grateful for their interest in the Lord.

Edna King came to work in the Mission home in the fall of 1940. "It was a very warm afternoon in September, when I arrived in Hannibal," she remembered. "I received a very hearty welcome and was made to feel at home. Having worked in worldly homes for ten years, the change was great. The Christian love and spirit that prevailed thrilled my soul. The privilege of joining Nelson and Carol and other Christians in family worship in the morning and in prayer at the after noon meal has blessed my soul."

Nelson and Carol's commitment and dedication to blessing the lives of others continued to bless each and everyone who came to Hannibal to help in the work of the Lord. Their lives of genuine service made a lasting impression in the lives of those who came.

The Savior taught about losing one's life in the service of others: "For whosoever will save his life shall lose it; but whosoever shall lose his life for my sake and the gospel's, the same shall save it" (Mark 8:35).

Carol was living a promise that she made to the Lord back in September 1928 when she told Paul Bender she was ready to go into full-time missionary service anywhere the Lord would call her. Her cup of joy was overflowing because she was living that dedication in both word and deed.

J. M. Kreider requested an assistant bishop in the Hannibal area. The Missouri-Kansas Conference granted this request with Nelson. In September 1940, Nelson was ordained to the office of a bishop by three senior bishops: J. M. Kreider, of Palmyra, Missouri, Abner G. Yoder, of Parnell, Iowa, and Milo Kauffman, from Hesston, Kansas. The service was well attended by members of all the district churches, as well as some city visitors. Nelson would begin assisting J. M. Kreider in overseeing five churches in the conference district. This meant even more time away from home for Nelson.

On December 7, 1940, just before Carol's birthday, Nelson and Carol were blessed with a precious baby boy, weighing more than eight pounds. James Milton was a very welcome addition to the family. This baby had been five years coming, and the home was filled with joy and excitement. What a blessing to have Ma Donna happy and healthy again after such a lingering illness. She was now nine years old and loved playing "mommy." Five-year-old Stanlee was overjoyed to have a brother!

Christmas preparations were well under way again. Each Christmas seemed to be more wonderful than the previous year's, as the friends of the Hannibal Mission generously donated valued items to be given to the needy. Each person was blessed with things they needed, and hearts swelled with deep gratitude for those who cared enough to send items in support of the Hannibal Mission.

Chapter 14

He Giveth More Grace

The very first convert of the Hannibal Mission Church was Bessie, a dear lady who had been a devoted and faithful member for seven years. Carol kept getting impressions to ask her if she would be willing to let her life story be written and shared with many thousands of people, if it was ever published into a book.

When Carol came in contact with this humble woman, Carol was impressed with Bessie's deep sense of devotion to Jesus Christ. Ever since she found the Lord and Savior in her life, this precious woman centered her entire existence around emulating His life and following His teachings. She sought especially "to do unto others as you would have them do unto you." She never complained about her poverty but accepted her life as a definite avenue for "Leaning on His Everlasting Arms," her favorite hymn.

Carol found out about Bessie's life situations as she visited regularly in her humble home. Some wouldn't even call it a home, but it was for Bessie. "I went on to visit three more homes," mission worker Nora King once wrote. "One of them, I shall never forget. It was the home of a dear, old sister who always had a testimony for her Lord. The house in which she lived was made of wide boards covered with tarpaper, and not even sealed inside. The floor of her kitchen was the bare ground and the room was very dimly lighted. But here we had prayer together and God seemed just as near in her humble little shack as in any beautiful church."

Bessie never took anything for granted and always expressed great appreciation for everything she had, which was very little. She respected life as a challenge to experience and made strides to improve upon what she found wanting.

Carol prayed feverently over the idea of sharing Bessie's tender but tragic story, knowing that it could and would touch the lives of each reader and show how to value the Lord's tender mercies in their lives. Knowing of Bessie's many trials and concerns might motivate readers to improve upon their own life's conditions. Carol desired no glory to be hers, and Bessie desired the same. They both shared a testimony that Heavenly Father watches over and cares for everyone, no matter how weak or how insignificant they may feel or appear to others.

Bessie's response was: "If just one young or older person would profit by all the mistakes I've made, I am willing to share it. Never would I tell it to bring glory or attention to myself. I want none of that."

Carol spent as much time as she could with Bessie, recording all the details and events of her life, with the desire to someday begin what she always dreamed of doing—writing a full-length story that could possibly change its readers' lives. In the story, Bessie was renamed Lucy Winchester.

Carol hoped to develop in her readers a greater testimony of the blessing of having the Savior in their lives, creating a deeper gratitude for home and family, and the guidance of the Lord in everyday life.

Nelson had the privilege of speaking at the regular assembly for the Eugene Field Junior High School in Hannibal. This was the first time for this kind of opportunity. He spoke to an assembly hall filled with parents of students from the school district. His subject was "Three Aims of a Successful Person." He named three aims: be able to say "no" to those you believe to be wrong; aim to do the hard things, not to say it can't be done; and be dependable. He used for illustration the biblical character Daniel, who fulfilled all these aims and was a successful man.

It was a great opportunity for him to share biblical principals that would hopefully touch the hearts of those in the audience that might not step a foot in a church but would come to a school assembly.

On January 20, 1941, Carol shared the following with the readers of the *Gospel Herald:* "Today, Brother Kauffman is with Ma Donna who is a patient in the Kirksville Hospital. She had a severe fall ten weeks ago, and two weeks ago her condition became serious. We have committed her to the Lord. We thank you for your prayers. God's will be done."

A month later, when Ma Donna was ten, the unspeakable happened again: the crippling effects of rheumatic fever returned once again. The third time! It was almost too hard to believe. Only this time was even worse. Oh, Dear God, what more do you want us to learn? This time she suffered from St. Vita's dance, which often accompanies rheumatic fever. Her feeble body jerked uncontrollably.

Carol knew exactly what needed to be done; she had been through this ordeal twice before. Ma Donna knew what she was in for too: months of pain and months of extreme weakness. This time the doctors declared that her heart was even more severely damaged. Carol was now a pro at caring for her dolly. Stanlee was just six and in the first grade. James was barely a year old.

Praise God for the workers. Praise God for the faithful prayers of friends across the country. Thank God for the previous miracles preformed in Ma Donna's behalf! The days were dim. The nights were long, and the cries of an innocent, tender little girl were heard in heaven. Again faith was stretched. God's almighty will was all they had to rely upon. Nelson and Carol were like clay in the Master's hands, formed for His will, being prepared for His glory.

"He giveth power to the faint; and to him that hath no might he increaseth strength.

"But they that wait upon the Lord shall renew their strength; they shall mount up with wings as eagles; they shall run, and not be weary; and they shall walk, and not be faint" (Isaiah 40:29 and 31).

Jesus Christ is our perfect example in suffering. He understands what we experience. He knows our pain more than anyone else. He knows our hearts and can help renew our spirits if we ask Him to come in and cleanse our souls.

Faith in Him and faith in His promises, as well as our attitude about our suffering, help make us whole inside because it renews our spirit. This process helps us to accept His divine will, whatever it may be. Whether we gain a wholeness of body isn't as important as developing a wholeness of Spirit. Both spiritual pain and physical pain help us to understand and accept His great atoning sacrifice that was freely given in our behalf. It is both for sin and for pain of any kind. It is for each and every individual; for Carol, for Ma Donna, for every other person.

As we approach our Heavenly Father by seeking to endure any kind of suffering successfully, we will experience a spiritual change and become "born of the Spirit."

Experiencing any kind of suffering is never easy. It is especially difficult when we see our children suffer. Often because of parental love, we wish it were us instead of them.

Even Jesus Christ had difficulty approaching and passing through His suffering in Gethsemane. He suffered alone while the apostles slept. He asked that the bitter cup might pass from Him. Regardless of the pain, He was obedient to the will of the Father. So how do we attempt to become more like Him?

There is something about our own suffering that perfects our individual spirit, if and when we draw closer to Our Lord and Savior Jesus Christ. The whole experience can teach us patience and hope when we call upon Him to bear our grief and pain. With Jesus Christ by our side, no trial is wasted. No pain is wasted because the Savior becomes our closest eternal friend. We learn patience, hope, and trust in the Lord no other way, but through experiences that require these Christ-like attributes. Our prayers in our trails are hour-by-hour, minute-by-minute. Our pleadings draw us closer to his side, bringing us sweet peace and solace, as expressed in the hymn "What a Friend We Have in Jesus:

"O what peace we often forfeit, O what needless pain we bear, All because we do not carry – Everything to God in prayer. Are we weak and heavy laden, Cumbered with a load of care? Precious Savior, still our refuge; Take it to the Lord in prayer. In His arms He'll take and shield thee, Thou wilt find a solace there."

Nelson and Carol clung to Christ's promise: "Peace I leave with you, my peace I give unto you: not as the world giveth, give I unto you. Let not your heart be troubled, neither let it be afraid" (John 14:27).

Their hearts were not afraid. Their hearts were not troubled. They wanted to be taught by the Lord through their experiences. They had hope in tomorrow. The act of suffering with the illness of little Ma Donna helped identify the tranquil, the peaceful, the calm, and the serene that comes within and through Jesus Christ.

"If ye love me, keep my commandments.

"And I will pray the Father, and he shall give you another Comforter, that he may abide with you forever;

"Even the Spirit of truth; whom the world cannot receive, because it seeth him not, neither knoweth him; but ye know him: for he dwelleth with you, and shall be in you.

"But the Comforter, which is the Holy Ghost, whom the Father will send in my name, he shall teach you all things, and bring all things to your remembrance, whatsoever I have said unto you (John 14:15–17, 26).

Jesus Christ understands our pain, and with His spirit by our side we will receive the answers we desperately long for: Why is this happening? What are we to learn because of personal trials? Through the comforter, the Holy Ghost, we will be guided as we seek understanding as to why this suffering is necessary.

When we seek Heavenly Fathers will, we are not alone. With His divine help we learn patience and humility and love Him even more because of the suffering He personally went though for each of us.

His atoning sacrifice becomes personal for each and every one of us. His love begins to overshadow our personal grief and pain. His love envelopes our souls and brings healing within.

"Blessed be God, even the Father of our Lord Jesus Christ, the Father of mercies, and the God of comfort;

"Whom comforteth us in all our tribulation, that we may be able to comfort them which are in any trouble, by the comfort wherewith we ourselves are comforted of God.

"For the sufferings of Christ abound in us, so our consolation also aboundeth by Christ.

"And whether we be afflicted, it is for your consolation and salvation, which is effectual in the enduring of the same sufferings which we also suffer: or whether we be comforted, it is for your consolation and salvation.

"And our hope of you is steadfast, knowing, that as ye are partakers of the sufferings, so shall ye also of consolation" (2 Corinthians 1:3–7).

As Nelson and Carol received the comfort of the Holy Ghost, they in turn were able to give comfort to others who needed succor. Because of this most cherished refining and spiritual experience, they knew the blessings of these promised truths as they served others, living a most righteous life. As we serve others our own burdens are lightened. Being partakers of consolation means that we therefore receive hope, strength, comfort, and solace in and through our trials because of the Savior.

Through their trials they were living examples of their beliefs. "When days are long and full of hard work, He giveth more grace," Carol previously wrote to the Elkhart, Indiana, Sunday School class. "When trials come, He giveth more grace. When funds are low, He giveth more grace. When we cannot see one step ahead, He giveth more grace. Praise His name, and we know that his promises are true."

There was absolutely no doubt in Nelson and Carol's hearts the love they felt from the Lord. Likewise, there was absolutely no doubt in the Lord's heart, the love that Nelson and Carol had for Him.

On September 2, 1942, Nelson and Carol's fourth child was born. Marcia Marie was a full-term baby but weighed only four pounds, thirteen ounces. As a result of her tiny size and weight, she was kept in the hospital's incubator for a month until she weighed at least five pounds. For some reason, Carol could not push out the baby, and forceps were used to deliver little Marcia.

Interestingly, Carol's recovery time in the hospital inspired her to finally begin writing her full-length book:

Some people say, have you been writing ever since you were a little girl? No, I was twenty-six years old. I was a student at Hesston College when I wrote my first short story, as a class assignment, and Paul Erb sent it to the publishing house. I had no idea he was sending it. I had no idea it would ever be published. But that is how it got started. And Brother Yake wrote and told me that I had ability to write.

I didn't believe it. I couldn't believe it, but I wrote to my mother and she promised to pray for me. He (Paul Erb) asked me if I would write a short story a month for the Youth's Christian Companion, and I promised I would try. And I think it is because my mother prayed that God would help me.

Every time I sent one in I thought, "Oh, this one won't be accepted, it isn't good enough." But when I made my consecration, I had no idea that God wanted me in this field. Brother Yake wrote me a letter one day. I will never throw it away. And he said, "If you are speaking to a group of people you can only speak to about so many. But, if you will dedicate your ability to write stories, just think how many thousands can read them."

And it was, when our last baby was born. God blessed us with four children; two sons and two daughters. And our youngest, when she was born, I asked the doctor if I couldn't have a table across my bed in the hospital. I said, "I'd like to write." And he said I could. He said, "Maybe it is a good thing to take your mind off that baby over there under oxygen, because, I don't know whether she is going to make it or not."

And he said, "You have a nervous heart and if you write, that will keep your mind off the baby and yourself." And I said, "Oh Doctor

Bernie, do you think that life begins at forty?" He said, "Why?" I said, "Cause, if Ma Donna doesn't get rheumatic fever any more, and the baby lives, and I can write a book, and I'm forty years old, then life for me will begin at forty." And he said, "Well, I tell you right now, you are the writinst [writingest?] patient I have ever seen. But, if you write a story that makes a book, I'll buy the first copy." So I wrote the first thirteen chapters of "Lucy Winchester" in the hospital with my baby Marcia.

I had to leave my baby there three weeks after I went home. So, during those three weeks, I spent most of my time in the basement of the church trying to finish "Lucy Winchester", because she was one of our first converts and she had such a marvelous healing, that I think that's the reason why I asked her if I could write the story of her life.

Carol with youngest baby Marcia Marie, Ca. December 1942.

She asked to be anointed one night in church and so did another lady. And, Lucy had five running sores on her one leg and had been to many doctors in town and they said there was no cure. And she asked to be anointed. And in simple childlike faith she asked to be healed. And this I saw with my very own eyes. She was healed over night. And her leg didn't bother her any more till her dying day.

And from that day on she was Ma of the church. And whenever any body was in trouble or sick, we called on her to pray. And I said, would you be willing to tell the story of your life so I could write it and she said like this: "If anybody could profit from the mistakes I have made, I am willing to share it."

I started gathering information about Bessie two years before Marcia was born. So when Marcia was born I was ready to create that information into a story. When Bessie was baptized, I knew of her circumstances. Her testimony of Jesus Christ and His love, especially for her and her children brought her to her knees in gratitude for what she found. When you write about someone, you put yourself in their shoes, so to speak.

Life at the mission home was very busy. I lost myself in service to others. That's what makes one the happiest; serving others, so when it became evident that I would write a full length story to hopefully be published, I had to devote many hours above taking the time necessary to make the story not only true but interesting to read.

Nelson was a great support and so were the workers, in granting me the time alone to create the story from the facts that I knew to be true.

Carol said that the reason she wrote in the church basement was that the walls were bare. Any pictures on the wall or looking out a window to see people walking by would have distracted her mind. Carol always wrote with a pencil, and she always wrote her manuscripts standing up, because she said that she could think better on her feet. She would stand up to an ironing board because she could adjust it to a perfect height for her small frame. She would place a cutting board on top of the ironing board to give her a firm surface to write on. So with a box full of sharpened lead pencils, a stack of new (or used) paper, and a tall glass of water, she would begin each day, writing from morning to night.

Carol did not type, but there was always someone close by that she could hire to type the story from her hand-written pages. Her penmanship was larger than most, so she wrote twice as many pages.

In 1943, again in the second month, Ma Donna started showing signs of a rheumatic fever reoccurrence. Nelson and Carol were bewildered. The doctor had told Nelson and Carol that Ma Donna couldn't live past the age of nine. She was twelve. The doctor was bewildered also. All the same procedures were followed. This was the fourth time she had contracted the disease. Nelson and Carol spent time fasting and praying for Ma Donna's complete relief from any more effects of this horrifying illness.

She became critically weak after having the same taxing burdens on her heart again. Nelson and Carol thought for sure they were going to lose her this time around. The thought of losing her ripped their hearts.

Everything seemed to be on hold, story writing and all. For some months, the doctor came every day to the house. Ma Donna almost seemed like his very own child, he had become so attached to her over the years. He sensed a deep religious commitment in this home that he had never experienced before, a spiritual strength he privately longed for. What made them able to endure such physical hardships?

For weeks on end, Carol did not eat meals at the kitchen table with others in the home. Often she did not undress at night. She seldom left the house. This was the absolute worst case the doctor had ever witnessed without certain death. Thank God the workers were in the home around the clock to help care for Stanlee, James, and Marcia.

In desperation, after eight months of what seemed to be no change in Ma Donna's condition, Nelson spent an entire day in the cold, damp woods pleading with Father in Heaven to take his life in place of Ma Donna's. "He laid on the ground face down, sobbing and crying out to Almighty God for deliverance from this repeated attack on Donnie's frail body," remembered Carol. "He searched his soul. He confessed any sins that he could have unknowingly had in his heart. He pleaded for the Lord's mercy."

Finally, after many hours in prayer, he found inner peace. It came after he told the Lord that he and Carol were willing to give Ma Donna up and let the Lord take her home. He found freedom in being sincerely and completely willing to let Father in Heaven take her lifeless like body to His bosom. Carol continued:

I remember the day that Nelson left and went seven miles out into the country, behind a big hedge fence where nobody could see him. And he laid most of the day with his face in the dust and prayed for our little girl to get well.

We were finally willing to give her up. And we prayed, "Take her, or, if it be thy will, raise her up that she might bring glory to you and that we might get glory through this experience."

And that day, when he came back, our Sweet Little Dolly hadn't stood on her feet for months. She got up and walked across the room when he came in. And she said, "I know I am going to get well."

Now, why other people haven't had that blessed experience, I don't know. And again, I feel like we weren't worthy. But today when she gets up in church and remembers all this and gives her testimony, I just thank God that he took us through it, although it was awful hard at the time.

Chapter 15

The First Book Published

Carol was a distinguished, one of a kind, Mennonite author. Her stories became a part of many everyday household conversations. Thousands found her books inspiring. Many readers desired a closer, more fulfilling relationship with Jesus Christ as a result of reading her books. This was her primary goal.

The correspondence between Carol and publishers paint vivid, interesting pictures of how Carol found the main characters of her stories. Carol remained in close contact with her main characters as well as her lifetime friends at the publishing house.

It is easy to recognize the determination of both author and publisher to have the Lord's influence in all the decisions that were made for the benefit of the readers.

The archive folders have very little personal memorabilia about Carol between 1945 and 1969. Nelson and Carol did not keep journals. Thankfully they saved and kept wonderful detailed files related to her writing.

Carol finally completed *Lucy Winchester* even though she was in severe pain caused by an unknown source. In spite of her extreme discomfort, she kept on going. *Lucy Winchester* first appeared as a

The Kauffman family, ca. 1943. Back row *(left to right)*: Nelson, Carol, and Ma
Donna. Front row *(left to right)*: Stanlee, Marcia, and James.

serial in the *Youth's Christian Companion*, in which all her short stories were published.

Carol's mother, Selena Belle, passed away on June 25, 1943, just
twenty days after turning seventy-seven. Nelson and Carol traveled
to Elkhart for the funeral. She and Nelson were the only ones who
had to travel some distance; Carol's sisters Nellie, Helena, and Esther all lived in Elkhart. It was a very sad time with many tears,
along with tears of gratitude for precious years they shared, all the
happy memories, but most of all the assurance that someday they
would see her again.

In July, Brother Yake wrote a letter to Carol with this opening
paragraph: "The YCC readers have received 'Lucy Winchester' with
great interest. Everywhere I have gone, I have been battered with
numerous inquiries, and letters coming to my desk frequently refer
to it. Others bring reports of inquiries and comments. The story has
'gone over the top' as no other contribution of recent date. This tells
me of the reading public's interest and taste, and makes an editor sit
up and take notice."

On December 16, 1943, Carol received another letter from Brother Yake regarding the many stories contributed to the *Youth's Christian Companion*:

Your contributions have been much appreciated, and the services that they have rendered to our readers are very commendable. This is merely an extra blessing from the Lord for the good turns which you are doing for the young people.

We are certain that your worthy hubby will share this pleasure with you. May God richly bless and make you a continued blessing in every sphere of your work together. Kindest regards also from our family.

Carol's name became increasingly known throughout the country, and she was asked to speak at churches in neighboring states. On February 28, 1944, she gave a talk in Wellman, Iowa, at the biannual sewing circle meeting. She chose a timely subject: The Challenge of a Chaotic World.

June 3, 1944, marked the Hannibal Mission's tenth anniversary. The following are some selected paragraphs that Carol wrote in "Echoes from the Hannibal Mission":

When the time came to instruct the new converts, we found that the seed had fallen on more than one kind of soil. Some took four or five lessons and gave up. Some took four or five lessons and said, "The way is too hard." Others took instruction lessons up to the last one, and were found to be living in adultery. This caused some unspeakable heartbreak and anguish of soul. Half of those who confessed, however, were willing to accept the full doctrine of the church. Those twenty-eight became the charter members of the church.

At that time Brother J. D. Minniger said to us, "I have not been in Mission work for over thirty years without learning a few things." His words of encouragement and his fatherly advice during those ten days that he was with us have been priceless.

The war brought about many changes in the city of twenty-two thousand. Many families moved away to find suitable employment. As a result, we have lost eighteen members, and quite a few Sunday-school pupils. Most of the members, however, are still faithful where they are located, and we have been able to keep in touch with them. The membership at the present is forty-four.

Approximately seven percent of the city of Hannibal is colored, and if it were not for the strong race prejudice here, we might be able to do more for them. We have been permitted however, to sing and witness to the inmates of the old people's home for colored people and on several occasions, Brother Kauffman has spoken in their churches. Every house in the city has been contacted by Brother Wm. Myers one of the older converts who volunteered to distribute "The Way" and other tracts.

Just recently we received a letter from Brother Harold Kreider, who has been helping whenever possible. One paragraph in the letter reads: "It is impossible for me to tell what this Christian work has meant to me. My life has been richly blessed. This activity has given me a greater zeal for the lost. Never can I thank my Lord enough for cheering my own life, and I helped bring cheer to converts and fellowshipped with the workers. This is a work I love so much."

A close neighbor passed away and her body was taken to St. Louis to be cremated. The husband had three huge baskets of flowers brought to the Mission; so that day we started what we call "The Flower Mission." From these sprays, we made fourteen lovely bouquets, which we took to the hospital and gave to patients who had no flowers, the poor, the neglected, and the friendless ones. How their faces glowed! With every bouquet, of course, a portion of scripture and several tracts were given. One undertaker in town has promised to send us floral pieces for this "Flower Mission" whenever a body is sent out of town.

Two classes of older girls have organized a sewing class. They are making baby clothes for the needy.

The most pathetic work we have undertaken is that in the city jail, in broken homes, and in the juvenile court. It would take books to relate the heart-breaking stories we hear and the pitiful things we see. We were called in to one home to pray for a very sick lad. His bed was a table board, which rested on two broken chairs. Then a colored boy, about eighteen years of age, confessed Christ in jail one Sunday afternoon. His tears looked sincere; his gestures seemed sincere; so Brother Kaufman called at a tumbled-down shack to tell the boy's mother the glad news. "You say my boy says he's sorry? You think I'll believe it? Ha! He's told me that too often. But God bless you any-way, and may He shine on you," the mother commented.

Since gas has been rationed, we have discontinued our young people's literary society, which met once a month. Our young people miss this social get-together.

Sewing circles have given splendid support to our work.

As we look back over the last ten years it is with deepest gratitude to God for the way He has supplied our every need; it is with praises and supreme joy because of those who have been lifted from the depths of sin and darkness and are now walking in the light; it is with sincere appreciation for the co-operation of brethren of God; it is with a "groping for words" as we recall how the workers gave unsparingly of their energy without wages; it is with humiliation that more has not been accomplished.

It is not God's fault. Nothing has been accomplished without the aid of the blessed Spirit. We ask an interest in your prayers. We crave them as nothing else. Prayer started this work, and it must go on by prayer.

Throughout its decade of existence, the mission survived by rely-ing on the Lord. "One of the things that impressed me most is that we lived by faith," wrote Hilda Brenneman King, a Hannibal Mission worker, on May 12, 1944. "I will relate one experience. The flour bin was empty and the bread was all gone. As we knelt for prayer in our morning worship we unitedly asked the Lord to remember us when the mailman came, but he came to the door with nothing special for us. There was only a dime in the house and out-of-town guests were to arrive in the evening. Brother Kaufman was gone. The Lord heard our prayer by supplying our needs abundantly, but not in the way we had requested." (She did not mention how the prayer was answered.)

On June 1, 1944, Hannibal saw the worst flood in years. The downtown area of Hannibal is right on the shores of the Mississippi. Flash floods came as the creeks running throughout the town quickly rose, overflowing their banks. The mud brought in by the high waters caused insurmountable damage to homes and places of business. Boats were used in a number of streets, and railroad traffic was suspended for seven days. Many members of the congregation helped those who were hit hard by the devastation of the flood.

On June 23, Brother Yake sent the following words of praise about *Lucy Winchester,* which was still being published in the *Youth's Christian Companion* as a serial:

It seems that each chapter of "Lucy Winchester" is the concrete evidence of increased accomplishment in the fine art of good story telling. Certainly I have received much inspiration in editing the last four chapters in particular. They are splendidly developed, they have very good movement, and the thread of interest is strong. And, too, the chapter endings are rightly placed. Surely we believe that the Holy Spirit is directing the writer in this task for the young people of the church.

In the meanwhile, keep up the good work. And "Say It With Flowers" or any other way you desire. The young people thoroughly enjoy your contributions, and the missionary work which is being accomplished, can never be measured. May God richly bless and make you a continued great blessing to His name.

"I certainly appreciate your work and contribution, which you have been to the YCC," wrote Brother Yake a month later. "Our big concern is, what next? May the YCC continue to expect something equally as interesting from you in the days ahead? And may we have this expectation without imposing on you and your ministry? Somehow or other it will become the task of the editor to secure stories of equal merit to fill the place of "Lucy Winchester" when the last chapter has been printed. I pray the Lord's blessings to you in your future tasks, and in your consideration continually of young people."

For the moment, at least, Carol was busy with her children. The last week of July, all four were very ill with the whooping cough. Nelson was away. Carol always missed his tender care, not only for her, but his concern and help with the children.

In August, Brother Yake sent yet another letter to Carol: "We do want again to express our deep appreciation for the ministry of which you have rendered to the church at large through this story, and for the splendid way in which you have rendered this ministry. The Lord alone knows and eternity alone will reveal the amount of good which has been done. You will hear from us again about this whole matter [of Carol writing another story]. And don't forget to keep thinking and planning for additional contributions for our readers in the days to come."

He asked Carol to estimate the number of hours she spent writing *Lucy Winchester.* Her reply was:

It is rather difficult for me to estimate the time I spent in writing this story, for I was often interrupted. I have written a chapter in four hours, but some chapters took me as much as nine hours to complete. I suppose all together, I spent around five hundred hours on the story. I spent some time reading it over and making some corrections after it was in typewritten form.

I would like to know what your personal reaction is after reading the last chapter. Is there anything you would have me change or add? I am glad to tell you that the evangelist in the story who helped Lucy find peace was Brother J. D. Minninger.

Lucy told me this morning after church to remember her younger daughter in prayer, for she is reading the story and with interest and seems to be under conviction.

On September 4, 1944, Carol received a letter from Paul Erb, who worked in the editorial office of the *Gospel Herald,* telling her that the Publication Board decided to publish *Lucy Winchester.* The very next day she received a letter from A. J. Metzler stating that the Mennonite Publishing House in Scottsdale, Pennsylvania, would publish *Lucy Winchester* and requested an immediate reply. The *Youth's Christian Companion* printed the story in two different sections. On September 16, she sent the following reply. Three paragraphs read:

It is correct that part one and part two go together and in the book there would be no such division, for it is one continuous story. The reason for the lapse between the two parts is that I wrote part one while in the hospital with my baby and never intended to continue it.

But, after receiving upwards of one hundred letters from people throughout the church requesting me to continue the story, I took up the matter with Brother Yake, and talked it over with Lucy, then decided to go ahead.

I have in my desk a statement signed by Lucy, granting me permission to write this story of her life. She told it to me humbly with a desire that others would profit by her mistakes. I tried to stay by the facts as she related them. I have asked her several times since she is reading it if she is satisfied, and she replied she was.

In September, Carol also received a welcomed letter from Zondervan Publishing House in Grand Rapids, Michigan. Nelson told the publishing house's founder about Carol's short stories. The founder expressed great interest in taking on more manuscripts of Christian fiction.

They requested that Carol send *Little Pete*, a short story that she had written, and asked for her to send copies of a group of short stories that were published in the *Youth's Christian Companion*. In October, Carol sent twenty-five of her short stories to them. Nelson met with A. J. Metzler, general manager of the Mennonite Publishing House, about publishing *Lucy Winchester* as a book-length story. Brother Metzler also considered the possibility of a joint publication with Zondervan Publishing House, hoping that it would be a good plan for both organizations. Zondervan wrote back that they always enjoyed working with the Mennonites.

To Carol's disappointment, Zondervan sent back all the short stories because they were not satisfied with them. They felt that a compilation of short stories did not interest people like a full-length novel, and they wanted to work together on a complete book. The editor did not feel that with the present paper shortage they could issue anything other than a full-length book.

Carol's writing was in full swing again. Her mind was busy as ever finding new things to write about. By October 1945 she had sent in a story to *Youth's Christian Companion* titled, *Up Shumack Lane*. Brother Yake inquired as to whether the Mennonite Publishing House could have the pleasure of listing Christmas Carol Kauffman among "Who's Who" for 1946.

Even before the first book was copyrighted and came off the press, Brothers Yake and Metzler were requesting that Carol begin a second story as soon as possible. In October, Brother Yake corresponded with Carol again:

I am happy for your willingness to stay by the work of the Youth's Christian Companion, in its service to the church. Thank you for this dedication to the Lord's work, which He has made possible through endowing you with talent for such service.

I can sum up my needs in less than two points: a continued story again, if and when it is ready for publication; and in the meantime, a number of short stories from you from time to time to keep your name before the readers and to keep up the interest, while the continued story is in preparation. I would vote for a Christian romance as the type of continued story at this time. However, I am willing to fit into the writer's pattern, if such would not be practical for her.

The Lord's blessings to Lucy. May she be faithful unto the end, and may her life history prove a real inspiration to others to live true to the Master.

"We need you, of course, and our readers keenly appreciate you," wrote Brother Yake in a letter dated October 9, 1945. "Furthermore, as mentioned before, we want to do everything possible to make your service possible to the young people. If when replying, will you kindly state what materials you have possibly in mind for the coming year, it will help us in making some announcement which will have an especial appeal to the readers."

Nelson and Carol held their breath as February 1945 approached. Could Ma Donna possibly get rheumatic fever again for the fifth time? Months passed with no relapse. By June the doctor felt that she was finally completely free of any other episodes of the illness because of her becoming a young lady. But the devastation of this repeated illness left her heart with major damage. She had a private teacher for almost all of her eight grades of school. The whole family, along with the entire congregation, celebrated triumph in the Lord's healing in Ma Donna's life.

By March Paul Erb wrote to Carol and told her that the typesetting for *Lucy Winchester* was beginning immediately. On March 10, Carol wrote a letter to Paul Erb thanking him for his editorial corrections and expressed appreciation:

I deeply appreciate your story and your permission to leave the death scene as it was. This in particular was still vivid in Lucy's mind and I made quite a few trips to Lucy's house to ask for details.

While some may feel that the story is too emotional, the fact that several hundred letters that have come in, most were written by parents and active church workers makes me feel that a good many appreciate the feelings that the story contains.

Two letters of appreciation from Sunday school classes bearing the signatures of sixteen to eighteen parents have come to me from the east. If this story has been an encouragement to our praying mothers or fathers, God must get all the glory. I spent many hours fasting and praying to this end while writing.

Lucy Winchester was first published on December 15, 1945. Carol dedicated the book "To my husband Nelson E. Kauffman by whose side it has been a joy to work these sixteen years, this book is dedicated with love." Carol submitted the following synopsis:

This is a story of a girl who was born and reared in a modest country home along the central Mississippi River. When she was a small child, she read these words engraved on a silver dollar: "In God We Trust." From that day on, she had an intense longing to know God and how to trust Him. This tragic story of her life reveals some of the physical and spiritual struggles that she endured. In these pages are portrayed the hardships of rural life decades ago. The heroine experienced the adolescent longing for God, trials of many kinds, with tears, heartaches, and misunderstandings. There is romance, disappointments, bereavements, poverty, homelessness, sickness, despair, and domestic trouble, with burdens almost unbearable, but in the end she found hope eternal and heaven's peace through the promises of God.

The introduction reads:

Christmas Carol Kauffman here shares her deep understanding and appreciation of the Missouri life of which she writes in *Lucy Winchester*. She has lived, worked, and prayed with the people who vividly live before us in this true story.

Through all the trials and defeats of life in a home with ungodly influences, through many personal difficulties of her own from her teens until at last she finds the God that satisfies her soul—Lucy will capture your sympathetic interest to the end.

This popular story has the right emphasis and has already been read and enjoyed by thousands. It will live in your memory as a living testimony to the grace of God and His faithfulness in revealing Himself to the earnest seeker after Him.

The paper jacket written by Carol states:

It seemed but yesterday when that soul-bewildered face and those truth hungry eyes cried out to me in silent desperation before she invited me in out of the rain. Out of the rain! I shifted from place to place, for the roof was leaking in more places than there were pans or cans to catch the droppings.

The bedspread was gunnysacks pinned together with nails. The walls were covered with sheets of the local newspaper, and the kitchen floor was the naked rusty-brown, hard-beatened earth.

No one but God told me then and there to take a special interest in the struggling yet uncomplaining woman. Under the face of the long lived-in troubles, I detected a fascinating and unusual beauty; and with God's help, we together tried to lift her burden.

For some reason the archive folder on this story has two different prefaces. Carol wrote both of them. The first states:

This story of the life of Lucy Winchester begins when she was twelve years old and closes when she was fifty. It was written by her permission with the prayer that some who read it might begin counting their blessings, some tempted souls might be able to resist, and that some ministers of the gospel might take fresh courage, remembering that after many days the Bread of Life cast upon the waters shall return.

Many additional incidents of interest in Lucy's childhood could have been related, but the book would have become too large. In conversation with some of Lucy's near relatives, it has been verified that only part of the trials she actually experienced have been related. The entire story is founded on fact. Only two of the characters retain their real names. Norvena Seller and Gussee Jenkins.

Special gratitude is extended to Paul Erb, Professor of English at Goshen College for his editorial work on the manuscript.

Should this simple composition depicting the tragedies and triumphs of the life of Lucy be the means of helping just one heart to understand better the tricks of the enemy of souls and cause that heart to get a fresh hold on God, the prayer with which this story was started and ended will have been answered.

When she first held the book in her hands her eyes glistened with tears. Her lips quivered as she said, "Now the greatest wish is, that God will let me live to learn of one soul influenced to accept Jesus Christ because I told my story. Then I'll know I didn't go through all this in vain.

The second reads:

This is a true story about real people. It is surprising to learn there are those who think when a story is labeled "true" it means every word of conversation, every detail of each incident must be as it actually happened. For a writer to reach this level of accuracy would be humanly impossible. Lucy concluded that this story is ninety percent fact.

While *Lucy Winchester* was appearing in a serial in the *Youth's Christian Companion,* a weekly magazine, a woman came to me and said, "If you wanted a real thriller of a story, why didn't you come and ask me? Mine would have put this *Lucy Winchester* all in the shade."

It was after knowing and closely observing Lucy for several years, that I approached her. "Lucy," I began with a good deal of hesitancy, "would you consider telling me your life story, and allow me to write it for a youth magazine?" She neither smiled nor frowned. Instead, she looked at me full in the face, a prolonged thoughtful minute. "If," she answered quietly, "just one young or older person would profit by all the mistakes I've made; I am willing to share it. Never would I tell it to bring glory or attention to myself. I want none of that."

It was well over a year before I could find the time to start working on it. The first thirteen chapters were written in the hospital bed after the birth of our fourth child. Because the doctor detected a heart murmur, he kept me in bed for two weeks. The moment I was given permission to sit up, I asked for a bed table.

As soon as Lucy learned her story was accepted for publication in book form, she insisted on giving me a notarized statement certifying the entire story is founded on fact, it's true, correct, told to me by herself, written by her permission, that she gave me the right to add or deduct what I deemed wise, and that she gave me consent to the book publication. It was signed May 12, 1945.

To be sure Lucy never told me she was a beautiful young woman. Her brother showed me photographs, which unquestionably proved it. Never did she intimate she had a sweet, loving personality. Those who knew her best told me that, and much more.

It was Lucy's wish that all names be fictitious except for two, Gussee Jenkins and Norvena Seller, both deceased before the story was written. Too, all names of towns and places she preferred fictitious. I complied.

When she first held the book in her hands her eyes glistened with tears. Her lips quivered as she said, "Now my greatest wish is, that God will let me live to learn of one soul influenced to accept Jesus Christ because of my story. Then I'll know I didn't go through all this in vain."

Chapter 16

One in Sixty-Two Thousand

In December 1945, Carol began gathering information for a second full-length story. She pulled her characters from real life, preferring stories of individuals who made definite, quiet, humble impressions on other people; someone who was willing to share their story, only if it would help the readers find greater faith in the Lord and motivate them to develop a deeper sense of commitment to change their lives for the better. She was never interested in someone begging her to write his or her story.

Carol found Joseph's story when a common acquaintance told her about his tragic childhood with a hypocritical, abusive father and a suffering mother. The minute Carol heard about this boy's heart-rending story, she knew it should be told. The triumph of a faithful mother and a forgiving son would bless the hearts and lives of those she wanted to share this story with.

"My eyes filled with flowing tears as I tried to imagine the tender broken heart of both Joseph and Annie," said Carol. "I have come to appreciate even more through this experience in writing this story, the blessings of a gentle, obedient father in my life and a gentle, faithful husband. My heart goes out in prayer and concern for those who are not as fortunate as I am."

Carol traveled to Joseph's home and wrote down all the details necessary to begin writing. The words flowed, and the story took shape. With the help of the dedicated mission home workers she found the hours to write. It was the manuscript that would become *Light from Heaven.*

Carol sent a letter to A. J. Metzler, which included the following:

At the present, I have twenty-three chapters completed on another story of true life. It is of a boy born in a Mennonite home. I am also writing this by permission. To my mind it is equally as pathos and human interest as "Lucy." The purpose of the story is to show the influence of a godly mother on her son.

I have been preparing this for the YCC. The longer I work at it, the more I wonder if it might make a book. Since Nelson came home and is reading it, he feels that Brother Paul Erb might evaluate it, if you think you would want to consider it. I can tell now that it will have forty or more chapters. If I have been presumptuous in even thinking of such a thing, just say so.

"I could hardly lay it down," wrote Paul Erb to Carol, after reading the *Light from Heaven* manuscript. "I will talk to Brother Yake, and will talk it over with him with the matter of getting it into type as a book so that it would be ready to come out immediately when it is finished as a serial."

Mrs. Clyde (Iona Miller) Stutzman introduced *Gospel Herald* readers to *Light from Heaven:*

It has been my privilege to read the carbon copy of Sister Kauffman's new story "Light From Heaven," which will soon appear as a serial in the Youth's Christian Companion. You will certainly not want to miss one chapter of this touching true story of a boy. It is even better and more full of human interest and pathos than "Lucy Winchester." It is entirely different from "Lucy Winchester," but even better and more fascinating and stronger in many ways. Every line from start to finish is filled with breath-taking interest.

The author is a Spirit-filled woman, enabled by God to write; her gift from God is definitely felt in this book. Sometimes you'll laugh and again you'll cry, and in the end you will have that happy-sad, yet satisfied feeling that comes at the end of a good book; happy because of triumph at last, and sad because the book is done. "Light From Heaven" is based on an actual life story and truly it is light from heaven to the reader.

The *Youth's Christian Companion* started publishing *Light from Heaven* as a serial in October, and Carol was pleased to share her second full-length story.

Amid her writing, Carol remained active in her role as pastor's wife and mother. "The Lord leading, the congregation will have an assistant pastor in the near future," she reported in the April 1946 *Gospel Herald*. "We are prayerfully waiting for His will to be made clear."

By June their Summer Bible School enrollment was 145 with an average attendance of 107. The most blessed thing of all was that they had their largest representation of parents attending their annual public Bible School program in eleven years. Forty-eight children received their own special New Testament with Psalms for perfect attendance.

The *Gospel Herald* printed the following, written by Carol, in June 1946: "Our 13th summer Bible School is over. In several respects we feel it was the best school we ever had. In spite of the fact that several other denominations in our community were having Bible school at the same time, our enrollment was one-hundred-fifty-nine. At this time we have three workers, Alice Detweiler, Florence Snyder and Arland Miller. It was our happy privilege to realize another definite answer to prayer when a used school bus was purchased just before our Bible school opened. This proved a great help to us in the past two weeks."

During February 1947, several new families with children started coming to church. The mothers brought their babies, and they were added to the cradle roll. On such occasions, the mothers would bring their children to the front of the church for a prayer of consecration.

The superintendent of the city hospital where three of the church members were employed asked to have the Mennonite Church secure a service unit of two young men and two young women to work as nurse's aids. They hoped that the voluntary service would be around four months. At the conclusion of the voluntary service, if both the young people and the hospital agreed, they would be employed as regular staff. "We would like to get in touch with those interested in such service," stated a note in the *Gospel Herald* informing of the hospital's interest. "The hospital renders much free service to the poor of the city and we consider this a worthy project."

The young people of the Hannibal, Palmyra, Pea Ridge, and Cherry Box congregations started getting together once a month for a literary program. They would take turns meeting in different peoples' homes, including in the mission home. Those literary meetings were among Harold Kreider's fondest memories of Norman and Carol. "Literary meetings were always a special time for me," Harold said, also recalling the fun Norman and Carol always created as well as Carol's laugh. "My deepest impression of Carol was her passion for the mission congregation. She expressed deep sadness whenever a member left the faith, called backsliding then."

On March 31, 1947, Christmas Carol Kauffman became an honorary member of the Eugene Field Society. It is the National Association of Authors and Journalists. The certificate reads: "Known to all men, that Christmas Carol Kauffman, having by her writings made an outstanding contribution to contemporary literature; and the Board of Governors of the EUGENE FIELD SOCIETY being desirous of granting recognition of Authors who distinguish themselves in the field of letters."

On June 1, 1947, Bear Creek overflowed causing floodwaters like were never witnessed before. Downtown Hannibal became a swirling river, several feet deep. Many downtown-area homes and businesses near the Mississippi River area had water close to the ceiling in the ground-floor rooms. Floodwaters rose to touch the bottom of the C. B. and Q. Railroad Bridge. Several hundred homes were evacuated as rainfall reached 3.26 inches.

City "refugees" were evacuated from their homes and taken to the Admiral Coontz Armory, where the Red Cross established headquarters. An emergency shelter was also set up at the Central School.

The following Sunday, only forty-five people came to Sunday School. Four-hundred families had to evacuate, and the young men of the congregation gave many hours of voluntary service in helping those in need. Thank God the parsonage and church were on higher ground.

Carol continually looked for stories that taught valuable life lessons. When she heard of the life of Daniel "Dannie" Martin of Waynesboro, Virginia, she felt impressed to seek out his story. She made a trip to his home, finding him to be an elderly man. He, his wife, and his children shared most of his life story as Carol took many notes.

Upon returning home she felt even more impressed that this man's story should be shared to show the commitment he had to help prepare a way for future generations. He helped many, especially those of the Mennonite faith, to find opportunity to receive further education and training for life.

In the midst of Carol's mission and home, she was able, with the help of the workers in the home, to find the time needed to spend the many hours that it took to write Dannie's story, which became *Dannie of Cedar Cliffs*. Even so, she somehow was still able to fulfill her assignment as a true friend and helper to those souls that needed a listening ear. This pastor's wife filled that need, especially for the women of the congregation.

As we look back upon our lives we often ask ourselves, Was I able to make a difference in someone's life, to create within them a desire to become a better more dedicated, more righteous person? Was I humble enough to allow the Holy Spirit to teach me, through its whisperings, so I could in turn teach others—either by my words or actions—the truths that would motivate individuals to desire a closer relationship with our Lord and Savior Jesus Christ? Did I allow myself to be used for His service? Was I true to what I know in my heart is right and pure?

As Carol wrote, she knew in her heart that she was fulfilling a promise she made to the Lord years earlier. She wanted to use whatever talents the Lord gave her to strengthen that previous promise.

Dannie was a man dedicated to blessing others, so in turn Carol knew she could use his story to do the same. It becomes a chain reaction—a chain that leaves a legacy to be remembered. Carol is being remembered for her obedience to the Spirit, not only as a writer, but also as a pastor's wife who deeply cared for others, and the best part is that everyone knew it.

On December 19, 1947, Carol received signed certification that she could write and publish the life story of Daniel Roth Martin. "D. R. Martin, Dannie," "Savlia F. Martin, wife," "Marie E. Weaver, daughter," and "John D. Martin, son" each signed the certification.

As Carol began work on *Dannie of Cedar Cliffs*, her second full-length book, *Light from Heaven*, was getting closer to publication. On February 24, 1948, she received a letter from J. C. Wenger, secretary of the Mennonite Publication Board's publishing committee:

Permit me to state that I read "Light From Heaven" on Saturday, February 14, and enjoyed it tremendously. I submitted to Paul Erb a few small criticisms that he will undoubtedly hand on to you.

In response to your letter, I would like to urge that you write one more chapter, giving the reader reassurance and joy in the successful ministry of Joseph. The way the story now ends, the reader is somewhat distressed and uncertain about Joseph's stability. Such a chapter should strengthen the faith of the reader in the power of Christ to enable effective service and spiritual victory.

Allow me also to call your attention to the great need of an accurate, true, challenging, historical novel dealing with Conrad Grebel and the founding of our brotherhood in Zurich in 1525. I will be glad to bring to your attention such historical tools as may be necessary to give you proper background. Such a work is urgently needed. And it would do more to increase love and loyalty for our faith than all the writings of the historians and theologians put together. Truth stated as history or doctrine is insignificant compared with the presentation of this truth in a living story, tinged with emotion.

May the Lord bless your writing to His glory.

J. C. Wenger

Two days later, on February 26, Carol heard from A. J. Metzler—the publishing house approved *Light from Heaven* for publication. Carol wrote back to Brother Metzler and agreed to write a concluding chapter. An accomplished artist, Miriam Kreider (Bishop J. M. Kreider's granddaughter) from Palmyra, was working on the illustration jacket cover for *Light from Heaven*.

"I am glad you are getting so many testimonials concerning your story," wrote Paul Erb on March 2. "There is certainly a widespread interest, and the book should sell well. I am glad too, that you are getting other materials together for stories. What do you think of Brother Wenger's suggestion concerning the Conrad Grebel story as a possibility for you?"

Carol started thinking very seriously about the huge endeavor of writing a historical novel about Conrad Grebel and the beginnings of the Anabaptist movement. She wondered how this could possibly be done without visiting the actual places in Switzerland that would help this story come alive.

Carol wrote the following to Paul Erb, refusing to reveal the identity of Bennet (the abusive father in *Light from Heaven*), indicating her interest in the Conrad Grebel story, and asking for an opinion on the book she was already writing—*Dannie of Cedar Cliffs*:

Some folks still beg to know who Bennet is. I got stamped envelopes for answers. An unsigned letter states that they know exactly where Bennet lives and he attends their church. Bennet died years ago. I absolutely will tell no one except for Nelson who Bennet really is.

About the Conrad Grebel story, I am interested. It might be fall before I could get at it. I would want to make it a romance.

Nelson thought on this trip you might perhaps have a chance to read ten chapters of another story I'm working on. It is not a tragedy. It is not sad except when two of Dannie's children die. After J. W. Hess, Elias Culp, and J. R. Mumaw urged me to go to Virginia to get Dan Martin's story, I went. I spent all of four days in taking notes. I had a long talk with the two oldest children and with a near neighbor who has known him for forty years.

This story is to show early Mennonite family life, the beginning of Sunday School and other church organizations, and how good layman made a contribution to the church. I'm told Dannie did more than any other one man to help E. M. C. [Eastern Mennonite College] get started.

But before I go any further on this story, I want your opinion. Does it appeal to you at all? Would there be any chance of it being published? I did not mean it for a serial in the YCC. Dannie said if the Publishing House wouldn't publish it, he would. He impressed me as being a worthwhile and unusual character.

On May 1, 1948, Brother C. F. Yake sent the following words of appreciation and admiration to Carol:

I appreciate very much the spirit of your last letter and the willingness, which you express for the writing service. One thing that "your superiors" should always bear in mind is the fact that there is possibly only one in ten thousand who can do what Mrs. Nelson Kauffman can do. And, may I as well increase that to one in sixty-two thousand, for there is not another writer in the Mennonite Church that can produce material of the type and the way, which you produce it. It is distinctively your product, and some other person, who may write very well, simply cannot write just as you do. That makes your service, therefore, distinctive in ministering in the Lord's kingdom.

In the light of that, your "superiors" should be happy to grant you the time necessary to do the creative writing, which you like to do, and which serves so many thousands of readers. The amount of good and the extent of the influence accomplished through your pen can in no way be measured, and much less can it be compared to other types of service.

Here is one place where the might of a pen is indeed much mightier than the sword and all that goes with it. It is a great work which you are doing, and you know as well as I how far we together have come along in this growth of service and compare notes today. We claim you as a product of God for a ministry of distinction. Even though we have not seen one thing of "Dannie," if that is the correct title, we are anticipating another good product for the extension of God's kingdom.

Carol spent fifteen days in the Kirksville, Missouri, hospital, undergoing major surgery in February 1948. A doctor there finally was able to pinpoint the reason behind the last six years of continual chronic pain: during the birth of her third baby, James Milton, she tore the primary muscle that holds all her internal organs together, especially those pertaining to carrying a full-term baby. James weighed more than eight pounds. Carol was a very tiny woman. The doctor assured her that she would have a complete recovery and have no more chronic pain, a tremendous blessing.

"Christ for Today" tent meetings were underway for the second summer. In connection with the tent meetings, the local radio station KHMO aired a weekly Sunday morning broadcast with Nelson giving a spiritual message. The evangelists who came also had an opportunity to share in this broadcast effort.

Nelson's father, David Gideon, was able to spend four days in Hannibal with the family.

On June 10, 1948, Carol received her first copy of *Light from Heaven*, the book was published in fall 1948. "To every boy and to every young man who has, or has had a praying mother," Carol wrote in her dedication. "This book is dedicated with Christian Love." She spent a minimum of 460 hours writing the story. One wonders how Carol was able to continue writing amidst all her extreme suffering, during this time she had five hospital visits, which included three operations. The Mennonite Publishing House advertised the book as, "A Book With a Telling Story Purposeful Discerning Pointed. Those who have read it are talking about it. Those who have not read it wish they had."

Carol's preface reads:

A number of years ago, when my husband held a Sunday afternoon jail service, his group sang for the inmates, "If I Could Only Hear My Mother Pray Again." One young man stepped close to the bars, and said indignantly, "Don't ever sing that song in here again! I never heard my mother pray. Maybe you did, but I didn't. All I've heard from her was cursing. If she had prayed for me, I might not be here."

About that same time, the evangelist who preached on the night Joseph Armstrong, the hero of Light From Heaven, gave his heart to God, became one of my close friends. After learning about the tragic story of this boy and the tremendous influence his praying mother had on his life, it gripped my soul. Having two boys of my own, I was deeply touched. I immediately asked God to make it possible for this story to be published so that other young men and boys who have, or have memory of, a mother's prayers, will appreciate what a blessing is theirs. No other force on earth is equal to their power.

I was quite taken back when someone asked if the motive for writing this story was to reveal hypocrites. That would be my last motive. To depict adequately the misery and the soul struggles this boy went through, it was impossible to do other than reveal, in part, the character of his father Bennet, who would have ruined his life, had not his mother, so characteristic of true Christian motherhood, held him continually before the Lord.

It is surprising the number of letters of confidence which have come to my desk since this story started as a serial in The Youth's Christian Companion, telling of other Bennet Armstrongs still living. To every Joseph, to every Annie, to every Lowell and Virginia, my heart goes out in true concern and sympathy. May this sad but true story somehow give you a little comfort and courage.

It seems fitting that I should here express, in part, my gratitude for the many letters of appreciation for this serial. Two are most priceless.

One came from an eleven-year-old boy, the other from a bishop past eighty, but who is still young at heart.

A young mother of five boys who was not a little disappointed when her sixth child was a son, looked wistfully at another young mother holding a small baby girl in her arms.

"So you have another boy?" The second mother asked. There was a hurtful little tinge of unmeant pity in her voice because the infant was not a girl.

"Yes," answered the first mother, softly, looking lovingly at her own baby, caressing him, and smiling bravely, "But little boys can be sweet too."

It is my sincere prayer that the sweetness of the life of this boy Joseph will inspire every other boy and young man, who has a praying mother, to cherish those prayers and to live and respect her as Joseph Armstrong respected his mother; that he will choose for himself the kind of wife who will make a praying mother for his children; that he will not quench the voice of the Spirit when He calls; and that he will learn how to live a victorious, winsome, fruitful, beautiful life in spite of any or great difficulties—this alone was my motive for writing "Light From Heaven."

The introduction was written by C. F. Yake:

It is a privilege to introduce "Light from Heaven," by Christmas Carol Kauffman, the author of "Lucy Winchester," which has been so widely read. Indeed, an introduction to this volume is hardly necessary because of the extensive publicizing of this splendid work through the pages of "The Youth's Christian Companion," and its thousands of readers. The fact that many of them have inquired about securing this story in book form is an evidence of the great amount of interest created by the writer.

That truth is stranger than fiction is once again proved by this remarkable story, depicting the events in the lives of characters who actually lived and made their contribution to their homes, their church, and to society in the communities in which they lived. These characters portrayed spiritual living on the one hand and extremely selfish and self-righteous living on the other. The author brings to the reader in most conspicuous contrast these two types of lives.

There is an extant today in literature of all kinds and types, but little is found of the true-story kind, which teaches forcibly great and noble lessons from life. So-called true stories are either written in popular romance style to gratify passion of readers, or in the form of biography or narrative. It is very exceptional to find a true story of the noble type, such as is "Light From Heaven," written in romance style! Christmas Carol Kauffman is found to be at her best in this story.

The reader will find the thread of interest running through every chapter that will motivate their reading the book uninterruptedly until finished. The lessons in life to be learned will prove valuable helps in Christian living; and when they have finished reading, they will be satisfied that his time was well spent. I count it a privilege to recommend to the public, this book for wholesome Christian reading, which is entertaining, as well as profitable.

Carol had a passion to write. She barely had completed *Dannie of Cedar Cliffs*, which was being considered for the *Youth's Christian Companion* for publication, and she was already beginning another, titled *Unspoken Love*.

The *Youth's Christian Companion* offered to pay for a writer's scholarship, put out by the Christian Writers Guild. Carol was very interested in the scholarship, hoping she could find the needed time to both study and write her assignments. She could hardly keep up with the demand of the publishers. They welcomed all new short or book-length stories created from her pencils!

When Carol decided to write any new story, she would literally lock herself in the room she chose to use and have meals brought to her. Sometimes she skipped meals to avoid even that distraction. There were to be no phone calls or interruptions, unless dire emergencies. She often wrote from very early morning till late at night, especially when the words flowed from her heart and mind.

In September 1948, Carol received a letter from A. J. Metzler saying: "While there has been no formal decision concerning the publishing of your book "Dannie of Cedar Cliffs," I do feel that it is quite certain that we shall do so."

Chapter 17

A Great Honor

On March 21, 1949, Carol introduced Paul Erb to her fourth full-length story, *Unspoken Love:*

Before you start reading "Unspoken Love," I'd like to tell you that about a year ago Marlin Brooks in the story started corresponding with me about the experiences of his brother-in-law. He asked if he might come to Hannibal to tell it to me. I told him I would prefer if he would come some time when Nelson would be at home so we might hear it together. We set several dates, but because he is busy in church work, every time at the last minute, he or Nelson would have some other arrangement.

Finally after several unsuccessful efforts to have a meeting, Marlin Brooks decided to send his wife. She stayed here three days, and with great emotion related this story to me. She brought with her over 60 letters, also the contents of the box.

I thought it would be only courtesy to send the carbon copy to Marlin to read it first. He has passed his approval of the story. Two other members of the family have also read the entire story and have passed approval.

This was Myra's personal expression. "If the publishing of this story of my boy will help just one other boy like mine to decide for the right, I am willing to have it done."

It will be much appreciated if you will read this story and criticize it before it goes to Brother C. F. Yake. I want him to get it as soon as possible if it passes your approval.

I would like to have you discuss any point of criticism with Nelson when he comes to Scottsdale, Pa. in the near future if you could find the time to read "Unspoken Love" before he comes. Nelson has read the story.

Robert Baker, another Mennonite author who attended the Belmont Mennonite Church along with Nelson, Carol, and their children in Elkhart, Indiana, was one of the persons that evaluated *Unspoken Love* and sent a lengthy letter to Carol. His last comment was: "There is one thing about the story that amazes me. The author can have no actual knowledge of war (except vicariously), yet her story is an authentic story in many details and pictures it, as it actually is, a nasty, ugly business. I believe it speaks well of the author."

Unspoken Love was not published in book form during Carol's life. She wrote to Brother Yake concerning the story after it was decided that it would not be published: "Never before in my Christian experience has my faith been so strengthened in my story writing. Once more I am convinced it pays to go to Him for every task assigned and with prayer and fasting, seeking His divine help. Otherwise I am sure my work on this manuscript would have been a failure. In deep humility I received your words of appreciation only with the same desire that in the future, God can use me in a greater capacity for the honoring of His Word and its interpretations in the lives of our youth."

Unspoken Love was published in 1971 after Carol's death, under the title *One Boy's Battle*. It was Carol's only story not published while she was alive.

By December 1949, Carol was anxious to see *Dannie of Cedar Cliffs* published as soon as possible. She wrote a letter to Brother A. J. Metzler:

My greatest concern is that I serve the church I love and serve her well. I want to take this opportunity to thank you again for all you have done for me so far in the way of remuneration. While the money is not my main propose for writing, it does give Nelson and me some satisfaction to put away a little for the education of our children.

Just now I'm especially anxious that "Dannie of Cedar Cliffs" is completed in book form because Dannie has a serious heart condition. Many nights he cannot lie down. His wife keeps me informed and it seems that all he is living for is to see his book. If he passes away before he gets to see it, I wonder if his family can forgive me. I have 57 orders for this book. I am ready to serve in whatever capacity the church sees fit to use me.

She requested that Brother J. L. Stauffer consider writing the introduction for *Dannie of Cedar Cliffs*. She wrote: "I would like to add that the commendable things in the story about Dannie were related to me by his sister-in-law, his wife, his children, and by a neighbor who has known him for over forty years, and not by himself."

Carol later said: "'Dannie Of Cedar Cliffs' is an entirely different type of story, but one I knew needed to be shared to help the Mennonite people recognize the blessings of this faithful man."

Dannie of Cedar Cliffs was published in 1950. "To the children, grandchildren and great grandchildren, and many friends, young and old of Daniel Roth Martin," Carol wrote in the dedication.

Carol's Preface reads:

Edgar A. Guest, in his poem entitled "A Friend," wrote, "He comes by chance, but stays by choice." Another unknown poet wrote,

"Thy friend will come to thee unsought;
With nothing can his love be brought,
His soul thine own will know at sight,
With him thy heart can speak tonight."

When recently, a new friend came across my path, I found in him a character that has inspired and enriched my own life and stimulated my thinking as a wife and mother. The story of Dannie was given voluntarily from his own lips, with the sole desire that his friends and his posterity profit by his mistakes and successes.

It was told to me with keen wit, drollery, and pleasantly, and again with seriousness, even genuine solemnity. It gripped me with the conviction that others too might enjoy the same. His children, his neighbors, and some of his closest friends sanctioned the publication of this story. Few of the names are fictitious.

My motive for writing this biographical narrative is threefold: to portray early Mennonite life, to show what part a layman can have in the progress and up building of the church, and to preserve for my own children and others of this generation the story of the heroic struggles of the fathers of the past generations in providing for us today the institutions which at present are so much a part of the life of the church. It is quite unlike either "Lucy Winchester" or "Light From Heaven."

Dannie at the age of eighty-five, stately, sincere, and kind in heart, has but one desire—to do the will of God in his last days on the earth. His wife, who has shared with him every joy and disappointment, every sorrow and hardship for over fifty years, is a most charming picture of sainted, silver-haired loveliness. Even today though footsteps falter and shoulders bend with the lowering of life's dim shadows, love's sweet song comes from this godly husband and wife as fresh and melodious as ever.

Dannie and his companion join me in prayer that in this simple and imperfect narrative, the reader will grasp the soul satisfaction, which comes with the union of these great powers, which lifts soul's heavenward-love, pity and assistance—and the regrets that come from ignoring them. Chaff and grain have been emptied out together with confidence that a faithful and all-wise Hand will reach down and sift them and help each reader to keep what is worth keeping and with the breath of charity blow the rest away.

May God bless every faithful father and mother who have been good stewards of the manifold grace of God, and may the present generation honor their memory, treasure their memory, and hand on to the next generation the same creed, the same courage, the same devotion that holds to the faith.

John L. Stauffer of Harrisonburg wrote the following introduction to *Dannie of Cedar Cliffs* on April 3, 1950. Seven days before this introduction was written, the "real" Dannie passed away on April 10, 1950, at the age of eighty-five years, nine months, and twenty-seven days:

Reading the manuscript, "Danny of Cedar Cliffs," containing the life story of one whom I have known for the past thirty years has been illuminating and pleasurable. His life story involves communities in the states of Maryland, Pennsylvania, and Virginia. While I am acquainted with the communities in which he spent his early life, yet I knew nothing of his early life. Dannie's interesting personality, as I have known him, becomes more meaningful after learning of his boyhood and early manhood experiences.

Dannie still lives in the beautiful Shenandoah Valley, having passed fourscore years.

Yesterday I was in his community and it was my privilege to spend a brief period of time with Dannie and his companion. While the years are definitely telling, yet his interest in Christian work has not abated. His children and grandchildren are real persons living among us and bear witness to his early training which he has in turn passed on to his succeeding generations.

Dannie began life in the midst of Civil War times. Rural life then involved many more hardships than at present. But the virtues of industry, thrift, honesty, economy, and consecrated Christian living triumph over adverse circumstances and develop sterling character and a pleasing personality. Rural life in the days of his youth utilized the services of all members of the family, and thus the family was kept more intact than seems possible in these days of what might be called urbanized rural life.

Today with the modernization of the country and the strong influences of industry over the population, the modern conveniences of transportation and information have helped to make us better off than in the days when Dannie was developing into manhood, but they have not made us better.

This life story deserves a place on our reading table and should be an encouragement to parents in these days of uncertainty when the very foundations of society seem to tremble and social and moral values are seemingly on the bargain counter. Real investments in the rising generation will still pay off well as similar investments have done in the past. The character qualities and the Christian virtues depicted in this life story are as interesting as fiction, as but more refreshing than fiction because the story is true. It is not idealistic, but realistic.

On December 5, 1950, the local Hannibal newspaper, the *Courier-Post* printed an article about *Dannie of Cedar Cliffs* and included a picture of Carol. Below are a few paragraphs from that article:

Mrs. Kauffman states her motive in writing this biographic narrative, was to portray early Mennonite life and to show what part a layman can have in the progress and up building of the church, to preserve for the present generation the story of the heroic struggles of the fathers of the past.

John L. Stauffer, recently retired president of Eastern Mennonite College and one of the starters of the college with Mr. Martin, wrote the introduction of the book, having been personally acquainted with him for about thirty years. The book has 12 illustrations and 15 actual pictures.

By the end of December, 5,260 copies of *Lucy Winchester* and 5,253 copies of *Light from Heaven* had been sold.

Mrs. Clyde (Iona) Stutzman wrote the following book review for *Lucy Winchester:*

It was my happy privilege three years ago to type "Lucy Winchester" for Christmas Carol Kauffman, which gained its first great popularity in the "Youth's Christian Companion." It was read by thousands then, and since, has been published in book form and read by thousands more.

Those who are personally acquainted with the author know she does everything, especially her writing, with prayer and deep sincerity. Her many friends, her church people, her family, and those who know her best are drawn to her and her stories because of these and other sterling qualities of character.

By some rare gift of God she has been enabled to transmit life as it really is on to paper and into the minds of her readers to help them upward. She makes every detail of the story live.

The real Lucy Winchester has for twelve years now given a ready testimony for the Lord who saved her soul. Hers is a story of a girl who was born and reared in a humble home. All her life she longed to know God, and hunted and searched for Him. Several times in her life she had a taste of what she wanted, but there was no one to help her quench her thirst. She went through terrible hardships, disappointments, misunderstandings, and deep sorrow, almost to despair. But, through them all and to the very last she longed for God.

Finally, after 48 years of wondering and after burying two husbands, and eight children, she did find the God that satisfied her soul.

The tragedies of the deaths in her family, her want of the necessities of life, her kind friends, Mrs. Watson, good Brother Buselton, and Gussie Jenkins, the colored lady who befriended her in a time of sickness, are some of the book's incidents and characters that portray in their own way the realities of life. They live on in the memory as a help to a more understanding and sympathetic heart and inspire one Godward. This story has been a means of helping many souls to take fresh courage and has also led souls, who never knew God, to find Him.

Have you read the story from the book? It gains new strength and is more vivid when read from a book. If you have read it once in the "Youth's Christian Companion," it will thrill your soul to read it again, and you'll be happy to have it in your library, too.

Do you know about the special deluxe edition that has a beautiful white leather binding, a picture of Lucy herself, a picture of the author and her family, and the author's autograph? Only the author sells this edition. Order from Christmas Carol Kauffman, 1417 Broadway, Hannibal, Missouri. The price is five dollars. It would make a lovely keepsake or a valued gift for any special occasion.

Within the Hannibal Mission, by April 1950, a special committee was set up for the purposed Old People's Home. An older man of the congregation, who was much interested in the home, arranged that his small property become the possession of the church, later to be used for the welfare of the aged.

The regular services that were given at the county jail brought a tremendous blessing to the faithful members who assisted Nelson, Harold Kreider, and Le Roy Zook. A man by the name of Johnnie Allison was converted and baptized in July 1951. He was later sent to the state prison in Jefferson City, Missouri. As a result of his conversion and the influence he had on inmates at the state prison, several men joined Johnnie's newfound faith, and a Mennonite Church was organized in the prison.

The largest clothing drive in the history of the mission was underway. Surrounding communities donated clothing that was to be distributed by the Mennonite Central Committee, which had offices in Tokyo, Hong Kong, and other countries where there was a tremendous need for their poor. The greatest need was in Japan, Korea, Hong Kong, Formosa, the Middle East, and for refugees in Europe. Persons irrespective of race, color, or creed would receive clothing of all kinds, including shoes. As soon as the military opened Korea for relief work, the donations would move in from Tokyo. The four congregations in the northern Missouri district were involved in the collection.

All the huge piles of clothing were sorted, repaired, and processed by all the youth groups and women's sewing circles from each congregation. Clothing not good enough for shipment was used to make comforters or rag rugs. The mission gathered several hundred pounds of processed clothing, which was picked up by a Mennonite Central Committee truck that made several stops throughout the United States, providing a total of twelve tons of clothing that was sent to Korea. Hundreds of tons of new and used clothing were being sent by the Mennonite Central Committee to various war stricken areas of the world. The first shipment from Hannibal was ready to be shipped by November 15.

About that same time Brother Yake notified Carol that her name was going to be published in "Who's Who for 1953." This was a great honor.

In September the mission home was in the process of being remodeled. The Reschley brothers of Wayland, Iowa, who were the same Mennonite contractors who helped with the building of the church, made the blueprints for the remodeling. They sent a group of experienced carpenters, eight of their own, who came down to Hannibal twice to work on the house. A service unit of three young men stayed at the parsonage and worked for six weeks. Carol's father, Abraham Miller, came from Indiana to install a new gas furnace. By December, forty-five men from other communities came to donate labor. The Wayland, Iowa, congregation had the highest representation of laborers. It was already three degrees below zero outside, but the inside work was continuing as help was provided. It was hard to believe that sixteen years had already gone by since Nelson and Carol drove across country in their Model A car.

The 1933 bus that was used for the mission was replaced in 1953 with a 1946 bus that held thirty-two passengers. It was very generously donated as a gift from the Anna Smucker family of Bird-In-Hand, Pennsylvania. The bus was purchased in Manheim, Pennsylvania, and driven to Hannibal by brothers Paul and John Smucker. It was presented as a free-will offering to the church after the Smucker family had visited the mission and saw the great need for a better bus. The members of the church sent a letter of appreciation to the Smucker family with eighty-five signatures. This new bus became an essential part of the mission outreach. Many of the converts who attended church meetings had no cars. Two routes were driven for every meeting, one on the south side and one on the west.

Chapter 18

No Dull or Idle Moment

In all their years of marriage, through poor times, even while rearing four children, Nelson and Carol always shared a powerful, deep-seated love for each other. On March 25, 1951, a few months shy of their twenty-second anniversary, Carol wrote the following letter of love to her Nelson:

To My Beloved Husband,

On this Easter morning, I want to express to you intense love and complete satisfaction for you and all you are to me. Truly darling, I have discovered in you, all my dreams for lasting happiness. You have not been a disappointment in any way. Trivial things that do not touch character are too small to mention. The you of you is divinely beautiful, sparkling with sacred love and devotion first to God, who brought us together, and for our children and me.

We rightly should be most happy. We are. Truly I am thankful to God for you and bless the day your mother brought you into this life. All of life's duties and cares and drudgeries are easier because of you dear Daddy Nelson.

These four months have been very strenuous to me, but in my heart I am just as young and vigorous with deep-seated love as ever. You are so precious to me. You inspire me always. I wanted to be a truer Christian and church worker, because of you. You have a refreshing effect on me. I want to be true as truth to you, dear.

Together we want to raise our family for God and all that's prayerful and right in God's sight. How I long to see our little Kauffmans all happy as we have been. What he's done for us I pray he will do for Donnie, Stanlee, James and Marcia. My very bowels yearn for them. Sweetheart, pray for them.

God bless your testimony today, over the air. God use you, keep you, and bless you, darling. I am one hundred percent for you in everything from ground to sky. Honestly, true eyes, no one but you could ever satisfy my need for spiritual and emotional support. You know me so well. I love, love, and you are it. Carol

Carol and Nelson on the front steps of the newly built brick Mission Church in Hannibal, Missouri, ca. 1950.

In October 1951, Brother C. F. Yake had notified Carol that her name was presented to the Christian Writers Guild for a scholarship-writing course from Mrs. Osteyee. "We are always in need of the best, and we are willing to co-operate to secure the same," Brother Yake commented. "May the Lord richly bless your ministry through your pen, which indeed has a far-reaching influence."

Carol began the course with Edith Osteyee. Carol wrote:

Through the courtesy of the YCC, I took Mrs. Osteyee's course "Writing for Christian Publications." I cannot begin to express my appreciation for what this course has taught me. It will never correct the mistakes I have made in the past; no matter how crimson I turn or how low I hang my head, but by God's help it should reveal some improvements over former writings. I only wish I had known such a course was offered by a Christian tutor years ago.

Even though I enjoy writing when the inspiration comes, it is harder work than any other work I've ever done, yes, even housecleaning. For real relaxation, I enjoy making dresses for needy and neglected young and old in our Sunday School, or providing an evening of fun for the young people of the church. I hope I never get too old to laugh and play with the children or too busy to drop everything and pray for the sick and sorrowing. This is my slogan.

What good is a song that is never sung?

What good is a meal that is never eaten?

What good is a game that is never played?

What good is a faith that is never demonstrated?

What good is a faith that is never demonstrated? How do we continue to demonstrate our faith; our testimony? As we seek for greater truths to fill our individual longings for a closer walk with our Lord and Savior Jesus Christ, the adversary does all in his power to discourage and defile that which is right and just before the Lord.

In the case of the early martyrs of the Anabaptist movement, the statement they made to the entire world, and the statement they still are making to us today in the twenty-first century was and is one of eternal substance, but with grave mortal consequences.

When one searches his own heart and allows a testimony to grow within because of the light of the eternal gospel of Jesus Christ our Redeemer, one is willing and able to go through any fiery darts because of the confidence derived from the Holy Ghost. Jesus Christ said: "He that loveth father or mother more than me is not worthy of me: and he that loveth son or daughter more than me is not worthy of me.

"And he that taketh not his cross, and followeth after me, is not worthy of me.

"He that findeth his life shall lose it: and he that loseth his life for my sake shall find it" (Matthew 10:37–39).

The early Anabaptist leaders and their faithful followers were willing to be victims of torture and give their lives for the defense of what they knew, without a shadow of a doubt. They could not, and would not, deny the truth they found.

How many of us today are able to stand firm to our testimony of His eternal gospel? How many of us today know without a shadow of a doubt that Jesus truly is the Christ and that our Heavenly Father gave his Only Begotten Son (John 3:16). Truly, without hesitation, are we willing to go though any kind of trial, no matter how small or enormous, because of that sure and concrete testimony locked in our hearts?

Jesus Christ lives. His promises are eternally true. Conrad Grebel, Felix Manz, and George Blaurock, along with countless others knew. We must thank our Heavenly Father daily, even hourly, for their incomprehensible courage to search for greater truths the scriptures contain about our Lord and Savior, our Redeemer and Friend.

"On the completion of my course through Mrs. Osteyee," Carol said, "she suggested having me write a long story as post-graduate work. I would welcome her criticism and do my level best to improve the story. My only desire is to do better work for God and the church."

Carol wrote Mrs. Osteyee the following letter in May 1952:

I have always appreciated your letters to me from time to time, the help I received from taking the Writer's Course, and the last long letter I received upon completing the course first.

I have always appreciated your criticisms and have tried my best to follow your suggestions. Mrs. Metzler told my husband recently that I have improved in my writing. Nevertheless, where I have failed, I am at fault and must be told again. I do want to make good.

In your letter to me upon completing my course, you called me a ten-talent woman. If this is only half true or less, I dedicate once more all that I have to God and to the church I love to serve. Your other letters have always spurred me on. I realize that there is no hope of my succeeding at anything I undertake unless I first admit my need for improvement. This I do.

I ask you to pray for me. Surely they can find some capable Christian who can give me helpful counsel and advice. I want to be teachable and will endeavor to cooperate. If I can't do that capable of this task, Romans 8:28 remains my promise. "And we know that all things work together for good to them that love God, to them who are called according to his purpose."

May I express to you once more my sincere thanks for all the things I have learned from you. Meeting you last summer has remained a pleasant memory. I enjoyed the writer's course immensely. You may use the part of my letter you care to in the "Compass" [a bulletin of the Christian Authors' Guild].

The principal, or rather the superintendent of the Hannibal Public Schools asked me for the third successive year to act as one of the judges in a minor prose contest conducted each year among the sixth and seventh graders of Hannibal schools. Some over thirty stories entered the finals.

Six days later she received a reply from Edith Osteyee:

Thank you for your nice letter. I appreciate your wonderful spirit, and know that you do try to follow advice and correct your typescripts according to my suggestions given. I maintain that you are a ten-talent woman, and the Mennonites are fortunate to have such a consecrated writer in their midst. Many other Mennonites (even one of their scholarship students) want to write for other denominations!

Affectionately, Edith Osteyee

In July 1952, Howard Hammer came to conduct Revival Tent Meetings, and, soon after, the young people helped the congregation conduct another church-wide clothing drive. They gathered and processed more than seven hundred pounds of clothing. The basement of the parsonage was used as the center for sorting and repair.

In August 1952, Nelson and Carol had the wonderful privilege of traveling to Europe! Just before their departure, Carol and Nelson's pictures were in the *Hannibal Courier Post* newspaper with the following article:

Rev. Nelson E. Kauffman, 1417 Broadway, pastor of the Mennonite Mission Church, and minister of the "Christ For Today" radio program and Mrs. Kauffman plan to leave Hannibal Thursday morning to attend the Mennonite World Conference in Basel, Switzerland, August 10-15. . . . Rev. Kauffman, president of the Mennonite Board of Education, is being sent by his board, as a delegate. Approximately 350 delegates are representing the Mennonite church of America.

Mrs. Kauffman . . . is planning to become acquainted with the Swiss Mennonites and with the places of historical interest, where the Anabaptists lived, witnessed, and suffered martyrdom four-hundred years ago, in order to write a story depicting early Mennonite life. She will visit various parts of Switzerland, August 17-September 5.

A second newspaper article described what they did and saw on their European adventure:

While in London they witnessed the changing of the guards at the palace, visited Shakespeare's home and Ann Hathaway's cottage. While in France they saw bones gathered from Word War I and were told that a wagonload every hour, for ten years had been stored in a building designated for that purpose.

World War II ruins were most prevalent in Germany and they contrasted that with the peaceful farm scenes and beautiful mountains of Switzerland. From the ruins created by a devastating war, they continued their travels to Rome and the ruins created not by man, but time.

Rev. and Mrs. Kauffman showed some wonderful pictures of Old Jerusalem and New Jerusalem, one being the tomb where Christ arose from the dead. They were not allowed to take close-ups of refugee camps, but did have a few of the scene in general.

In September the Kauffman family took a nine-day, much-longed-for vacation in Mountain Home, Arkansas.

Nelson and Carol *never* lived in the parsonage just as an individual family. From the time they moved to the house on Broadway, two girl workers and two boy workers (usually in their early twenties) joined the household. Most stayed for one or two years.

The boy workers loved playing tricks on the girl workers. One day while the girls were gone, the boys snuck into their room, short sheeted their bed, put Rice Krispies between their sheets, hid their shampoo and bar soap, covered the toilet seat with Vaseline, and hid their toilet paper, shampoo, and perfume. The girls decided to not even acknowledge their prank, leaving the boys in sheer disbelief.

The girls, together with Carol's suggestions, decided upon a perfect plan to get them back: Many days later, Carol helped the girls prepare breakfast. They first filled the sugar bowl with salt for the boys to sprinkle over their breakfast cereal. They spread Vaseline on the toast, and, instead of cinnamon sugar, they mixed chili powder with baking soda. The two forlorn boys ate the surprise breakfast and dared not even show any evidence of the surprise attack. Since the girls had refused to respond to the boy's attack, both young men had to swallow their pride along with the horrible tasting breakfast.

Esther Stoltzfus joined the Hannibal Mission staff in 1950 when she was eighteen. She met Nelson and Carol at a Winter Bible School where Nelson was the visiting teacher. They were looking for a secretary for Nelson to assist in his duties as President of the Mennonite Board of Education. Esther remembered:

They asked me if I would come to Hannibal for several years as a volunteer to be secretary and help with the work of the church. I put my nursing career on hold, and decided to go. I had a very strong sense that this is what I was meant to do.

The staff consisted of two young women and one young man, and the personnel changed several times. We lived in with the family, helped run the house, do visiting in the community, help with the services, drive people to and from meetings, and everything that needed to be done. Christmas Carol was in charge, and she was a very pleasant person to work with. We all had a very harmonious relationship.

One of the things that must have made it difficult for the children was the constant stream of visitors stopping in. Many times during the summer, as we would be getting dinner ready, someone would come to the door and announce that they would like to visit, which meant meals and overnight lodging. Many people were "Mennoniting it," which meant that in their travels they checked the Mennonite Year-book for mission churches for an overnight stay. Most times people left a donation. But out of this came support for the mission both fi-nancially and personal interest . . . sometimes very significant support.

I really don't know how Christmas Carol and Nelson managed to have such a good family unit with all the outside disruptions in their lives. But they did, and the children were close to each other. It was great living and working with them. . . .

One of my warmest memories of Christmas Carol was one day when she and I were alone in the kitchen, she told me her life story . . . how her first husband had died, how she met Nelson, many things that made me realize what a warm, loving person she was. She could be a sentimentalist but at the same time a critical realist, and she often didn't hesitate to say what she thought.

[Carol] was often teased about being a matchmaker, which she never denied, because she thought the most important thing in a woman or a man's life was to find a mate; this was the foundation of happiness.

Mel Lapp joined the Hannibal Mission in October 1952, when he was twenty-two years old. During his eight-month stay, he drove the mission bus, visited the state prison once a month to encourage prisoners, and was in charge of repairs and maintenance at the mis-sion home in Brother Kauffman's absence.

About the time Mel joined the mission, Carol was beginning to write *Not Regina*. In Mel's regular letters to his future wife, Pearl Stoltzfus, he mentioned Carol's work on the book. His correspon-dence also paints a precious portrait of Carol's personality and influ-ence over daily life at the mission home:

June 25, 1952—"We all went for ice cream. We were carrying on tonight, and Sister Kauffman was just as [silly] as any of us. When she gets started shes just as [silly] as any of us. What a fun person she is to be around."

October 11, 1952—"Every Day after breakfast we have family worship. The folks here are really nice. They really make us feel like one family. Another thing I appreciate is the good meals Sister Kauff-man makes for all of us."

October 24, 1952—"There's company here again for the night. Just since we came upstairs to go to bed, someone drove in. You can expect just about anything here in this home."

November 3, 1952—"Sister Kauffman is writing a new story. She read the first 5 chapters to us. It is really interesting, but we're not supposed to tell anyone about it, as it's still probably at least a year before it gets in the YCC. She's spending most of her time writing. She says it really takes a long time to iron out all the wrinkles and make it all come out alright."

November 9, 1952—"Sister Kauffman was going to read more of her story to us this evening but she didn't say anything about it after supper, so I suppose she either forgot or changed her mind."

December 22, 1952—"Sister Kauffman really tickled me this morning at the breakfast table. She said that Nelson is so lonesome for her. He's been in Goshen, a week and is coming home tonight. He wants her to come to Keokuk, Iowa which is 65 miles away and meet him and then ride home with him on his train. She said she's going to do it. Brother Kauffman is gone a lot. Sometimes he comes home just long enough to get a suitcase of clean clothes and he is off again for another 2 weeks."

Ruth King started her two-year volunteer work in the Hannibal Mission in May 1953:

1417 [Broadway, the address of the mission home,] was a passage to the west and a stopover for many Mennonite families going that way, if we knew them or not. There were no reservations. They would stop by for church and dinner or just ring the doorbell. Everyone was welcome.

What a challenge it was to raise a family with all the obligations of the church along with usually four young adults on hand! There was never any mention of a shortage of funds, but I know that there were times when there just wasn't much to go around. There was a pantry with canned goods and gifts, some of which created a few chuckles.

I always enjoyed Carol's slow smile. There was always popcorn on Sunday evening donated by the "Popcorn King."

Carol did spend a lot of time behind her closed bedroom door. She had the wisdom to make that her sanctuary. She was always available to her children and for any need that arose. I appreciated that she wrote about real people. Inspiration must have come to her quickly because her writing was a large scrawl that filled a page quickly. Deciphering it for typing wasn't as easy, especially when it was ethnic conversation. I did, however, manage to type part of a book.

When someone needed prayer or it was time for Nelson's Sunday morning radio broadcast, she would round up everyone who was available to participate. She supported Nelson in everything he did, even when he was gone so much. . . .

Then there was the time . . . I stripped and refinished the wood flooring in the dining room. [Carol] took two steps out of the living room and went flat on her back. I was so sorry. When I was about to leave [the Hannibal Mission], she lamented, "Who is going to iron Nelson's shirts?" I appreciated that.

There were times when the workers would play pranks on each other and sometimes it would be quite visible. Carol would slowly go into her sanctuary with that slow smile. She would always let us work it out. . . . She dared to be a mother to her family and a dear friend to all the workers.

Stanlee and James, Carol's sons, got great satisfaction from teasing their mother. Many nights they would run around the table holding the serving dishes way above their heads because they could get Carol to scream frightfully. They both knew Carol could not keep herself from reacting to their mischievous ways. Carol knew where the yardstick was stored and would soon be running in circles around the table trying to whack them on the arm to get them to stop, but the two boys were way to fast for her short legs to catch up with them. There was no way she could win the race. Any threatening screams would only make the game more exciting for the boys. Eventually she would literally give up in dismay and threaten to tell Daddy when he came home!

Marcia, Nelson and Carol's youngest, was eleven years old when Carol wrote *Not Regina*. She vividly remembers her mother standing at a drawer in the downstairs bathroom. It was the perfect height for her to write. She laid a large cutting board across the opened cupboard drawer, and wrote while facing the bare wall so as to free her mind of distractions. She spent hours each day writing; seldom even coming to the kitchen to eat. Leaving her "creative hiding place" too soon would ruin her concentration.

Esther Stoltzfus, in addition to being Nelson's secretary, had the opportunity to type much of *Not Regina* for Carol. She vividly recalls the once-in-a-lifetime experience:

A writer recently said, "A writer can't not write." If ever a writer had good excuses for not writing, it was Christmas Carol Kauffman. Here was a person who had a church community that involved endless time-consuming tasks, a family to care for, and many visitors to make welcome.

In addition, she had no private place to do her writing except her bedroom. Even though she sometimes closed the door, she could be constantly interrupted. I can see her sitting on her bed or at her desk with a tablet of paper, writing her stories. But she never had the privacy the most writers take for granted. Her writing experience was more like that of the early women writers of England who had to do their writing in the middle of family activities. Her powers of concentration were amazing.

I had the privilege of living with the Kauffman family during the time she wrote "Not Regina." She and her husband, Nelson, had been on the Mennonite World Tour and had visited the countries where the early Anabaptists originated. She used the information she gathered as the basis for a story about a young woman who joined the Anabaptists and experienced the consequences of this act.

Christmas Carol would write a chapter, then give it to me to type. She would then revise and revise it before she was satisfied with it. Imagine how interesting it was for me to be there at the time of the development of this novel.

I loved living with the Kauffman family. I adored Christmas Carol and Nelson. They were so talented, generous and fun-loving. Here were two people who could have chosen any area of life to excel, but they chose to give their lives to build the church in Hannibal, to endlessly care for its people, and to help them find salvation. They did excel in what they did. I thank God I had the opportunity to be with them for several years.

By April 25, 1953, Carol wrote her first letter to Edgar Metzler of Goshen, Indiana, concerning the manuscript *Not Regina*, a historical novel about the early Anabaptist movement in Switzerland. She also sent a copy to Brother J. C. Wenger hoping that the two men would offer their combined suggestions. She also was planning on giving it to Melvin Gingerich.

By June she was carefully going over the manuscript, using the men's combined suggestions and encouragement to prod her. J. C. Wenger sent a handwritten letter telling her that he was very glad to review it out of his love for the cause and the good it will do for future readers. "I have read it with pleasure," wrote Brother Yake, "and feel that it will be a good contribution to our Mennonite literature." Esther Stoltzfus and Ruth King, both workers at the Hannibal Mission, typed the manuscript for Carol.

Carol received a postcard from Bro. Yake that stated: "I just now finished reading chapter eleven, and you left me in so much suspense that I had to write this card to tell you how effective your psychological skill has worked. There is a long letter coming."

In August, tent meetings with J. R. Mumaw from Harrisonburg, Virginia, were held on the Eugene Field School ball fields, just a few blocks from the church. More than two hundred people attended the first meetings.

Persons from every denomination and race were invited to join in the revival. Part of the two-week campaign included holding nightly street meetings on North Main Street, an attempt to reach those unable to attend the tent meetings at Eugene Field School. This was done with the cooperation of the city officials.

Carol wrote the following for the *Gospel Herald*:

Do these tent meetings pay? Those of you who contributed financially toward this program or sent up prayers must know that it has been infinitely worthwhile. Space will not permit to tell of other miracles of mercy.

Special gratitude has been given to our Heavenly Father for the ideal weather he sent us during the entire campaign. Also for splendid cooperation of the city officials of Hannibal, the local school board, the Courier Post and KHMO radio station and many of the merchants.

This has been no doubt, the most effective "Christ For Today" tent campaign launched in this particular area. On the closing night, scores of non-Mennonites expressed their appreciation for the evangelist's well-chosen messages and a real reluctance to see the meetings close.

Webster's dictionary defines "revival" as "a bringing or coming back to life, an awakening or increase of interest in religion, to restore to a new life." When we make a commitment to Jesus Christ and promise to follow His ways, our individual lives are changed anew, and we make every attempt to become like Him and to obey His teachings and His divine ways.

True repentance and acceptance of Jesus Christ create a change of heart and a change of lifestyle. Revival or a recommitment to Him and His grace and salvation renews within each of us a commitment to again live according to His teachings because we love Him with all our heart, mind, and soul.

Jesus said, "If ye love me, keep my commandments" (John 14:15). Following His ways and living as He would have us live shows to others that we have been truly born again.

1 John 3:23 and 24 states: "And this is his commandment, that we should believe on the name of the Son Jesus Christ, and love one another, as he gave us commandment.

"And he that keepeth his commandments dwelleth in him, and he in him. And hereby we know that he abideth in us, by the Spirit which he hath given us."

Nelson and Carol were living the truths of these scriptures.

They continued to make weekly visits to the local city jail, monthly to the county jail, and twice monthly to the Missouri State Prison in Jefferson City, Missouri. Carol accompanied Nelson, the mission workers, and church members who could go along.

The two-hundred-mile trip to Jefferson City was made by at least six individuals. Carol and Nelson drove with the group each time they went to visit prisoners who were influenced for good by Johnny Allison's friendship inside the prison walls. With a carload going, each prisoner was able to receive an individual visit. Occasionally, a group from Cherry Box or Versailles congregations would join the Hannibal group. It was a challenging work and a huge task that was done faithfully.

Since the Palmyra congregation was so few in number, they began worshiping with the Hannibal congregation twice a month on Sunday mornings and evenings. They also attended prayer meetings on Thursday evenings, and the women came to support the all-day Sewing Circle in the church basement. The women of the congregation met on a monthly basis.

They once more sponsored the annual clothing drive to collect good used clothing, shoes, bedding, towels, yard goods, and non-perishable food for needy people in their own area, as well as in Korea, Palestine, and other areas suffering from the ravages of war.

The women of the Hannibal Mission would process the clothes, making sure they were in repair. Carol and other congregation women repaired clothing. Carol also taught the sisters how to mend, when needed.

The Mennonite Central Committee's large truck picked up the packed boxes of clothing, which were to be distributed to anyone in great need, regardless of religion or nationality. This huge distribution was rendered without political implications and at minimum cost.

As Christmas approached, the Hannibal Mission again collected clothing—this time to aid local individuals. Piles and piles of clothing literally filled two rooms of the mission home's basement. Boxes were lined up all around the kitchen counters, with a family name from the congregation written on each box waiting to be filled. Each and every member of the congregation, whether they were faithful in attending or not, received a Christmas box for their family, including enough food to have a wonderful Christmas dinner.

Each person who served in the Hannibal Mission has fond memories of wrapping the Christmas gifts handed out to every child and adult at the annual Christmas program. This tradition occurred each year without fail since the mission's first Christmas. Huge boxes (previously picked up at the local furniture store) were filled to the brim and placed in front of the chapel where the gifts would be distributed after the Christmas program.

Katherine Rickert, a nurse who worked at Levering Hospital just across the way from the church, purchased a crate of oranges every Christmas, enough to give one orange to each person in the congregation. What a wonderful treat for everyone.

On February 10, 1954, Carol received a surprise letter from Ralph Buckwalter who was serving as a missionary in Kushiro, Japan:

We have been greatly interested in your continued story, "Not Regina" which is now appearing in the "Youth's Christian Companion." This type of an approach to church history appeals especially to young people and is certainly an effective teaching device. We are glad that you have poured your soul into this most fascinating story.

. . . One project, which we decided to carry out, was the production of a small book, which would present the essentials of Mennonite doctrine and history, not only for the benefit of our own people in Japan, but the wider Christian circles. . . .

This is the idea that we would like to explore with you a bit further. If we could use your story "Not Regina" as the main part of our book, we think it would have a popular appeal and would whet the appetite of many to read the appendices which would be included—a brief-as-possible outline of the Mennonite Origins (perhaps using H. S. Bender's booklet as a basis), a summary of Mennonite beliefs, and perhaps a few pages of footnote explanations to your story. . . .

These are our dreams. . . . Maybe we are "jumping the gun" but our first impression, which is also shared by our Japanese co-workers, is that your story, "Not Regina" could be used very effectively in this way.

Carol ca. 1954 in Hannibal, Missouri.

Carol responded in a March 1954 letter to Levi Hartzler: "It has always been my endeavor to have my writing serve the Lord and the church, and I would be very happy if this story could be used to give help to our Japanese friends. I will appreciate the privilege of cooperating with you and with all concerned in any way to make this story serve the church here and in Japan in the most effective way."

In March 1954, concerned that *Not Regina* would not be published in book format, Nelson wrote the following to John C. Wenger in Goshen, Indiana:

In my recent travels in various parts of the church many, both old and young, have talked to me and told me how they enjoy and appreciate my wife's current serial "Not Regina," in the "Youth's Christian Companion." Many ask me if it will be coming out in a book. Last week a bishop asked me this same question and I told him we did not know yet. He said he felt this is a very good type of story our young people need, and wondered what our Publishing House is for, if it is not serving the church.

I, as well as my wife, appreciate what you and Paul Peachy did to check the story for historical accuracy. I am going to be very disappointed if the Publishing House will not publish this in book form and I will investigate having it published some other way.

I know that there are other books waiting for publication, but this is the type of story you had earlier suggested that my wife might write to help our young people to appreciate our history. If you would feel led to give a word of encouragement for its publication, I would appreciate it. Brother Yake told me some time ago that if this is to be published in book form, I would need to give it some push to keep it from being lost in the pile of other things.

This I am writing to you as a friend and I know you will use this information judiciously.

"I do not know whether you are reading 'Not Regina' by Christmas Carol Kauffman or not," wrote J. C. Wenger in a letter sent to Brother A. J. Metzler and to Carol. "If so, I think you will agree that it is one of her finest productions from a literary and a church point of view. It would seem to me that if this book is to be published, it would be fine to do so before the serial comes to an end in the YCC."

Carol wrote this concerning the story:

The plot: Regina, daughter of a prominent weaver in Weisslingen, in the Zurich canton of Switzerland, is greatly disturbed when she finds herself in the thick of the Anabaptist Movement of the Reformation (1525). Although she herself cannot read, she is alert and intelligent and in spite of religious tradition and family ties and beliefs, she is determined to find a clear, undeniable answer of her own conscience to the questions always tormenting her: "Why do learned religious scholars like Grebel, Manz and others differ with Zwingli and why do more and more peace loving people choose to disobey civil authority in spite of severe punishment?"

In the home of the pastor of the state church at Kyburg, her parents feel certain that she can find the answer. She does, but the answer means she is convinced too, to obey God rather than civil authority, regardless of family ties, teaching or punishment ahead. Her sincerity convinces even the Lord's horseman that her faith is real and brings peace; he, too, becomes an Anabaptist and helps her escape death.

Basic Conflict: Are the Anabaptists taking the wrong attitude when they deliberately choose to be disloyal to civil authority? What impels them to take such a stand when they know they will have to give up everything and that severe punishment is inevitable?

Moral: Peace of Soul is to be found only by obeying Truth, regardless of the cost--and peace of the soul is everything.

Weisslingen is a real town. Every place mentioned in the story can be located and I used a map constantly while writing. I visited a good many of these places. In company with Mrs. Paul Peachy, I spent a week in and around Langnau, visited the cheese factory, the barn where the secret meetings were held, saw the trap door and hole in the wall, copied Swiss names from an ancient family tree, and from old tombstones. I spent a week in the Zurich canton, spent half a day at Kyburg, and visited the cave, etc, with Paul Peachey as my guide.

On October 6, 1954, Carol was sent her first copy of *Not Regina*. "To our own beloved Ma Donna Lee," Carol dedicated the book, "who mothered our three younger children, Stanlee De Von, James Milton and Marcia Marie while Nelson and I were abroad, trusting they will each live in the triumphant faith of Regina."

Carol's preface reads:

Several years ago John C. Wenger, church historian and professor at Goshen College Biblical Seminary, suggested that I write a historical story setting forth the faith, life, and persecutions of our Anabaptist ancestors. In the summer of 1952, when the way opened for me to accompany my husband to the Mennonite World Conference at Basel, Switzerland, I determined to take advantage of the opportunity to gather firsthand information for such a story.

At this time Paul Peachy was a graduate student of Anabaptist life at the University of Zurich. I am greatly indebted to him and to his wife Ellen, who served as my guide to many places of interest, and who also acted as my interpreter. Ellen spent a week with me at Langnau in the Emmental Valley. We lived in the home of a Swiss family who had a daughter named Regina. Regina was suggested as a character name as a result of this visit, but the "Regina" of this story is a character of the author's creation and not the Regina of this Swiss family.

Among the many places of interest in that area we visited was a cheese factory and the farmstead where the Anabaptists held secret meetings in the barn. We saw the space in the wall between the house and barn where the Anabaptists hid during persecutions.

I also lived one week in Zurich. We stood where Felix Manz's mother stood on the bank of the Limmat River where her son was executed for his faith. We spent several hours in and around Kyburg Castle, studying the prison tower, Lord Engelhard's courtroom, the torture chamber, and the long steep hill which the Anabaptists had to climb on the way to the castle. We also visited the cave where many Anabaptists found refuge from their pursuers. During a period of prayer in this cave, I received fresh inspiration from the Lord to write this story.

Among the actual historical characters in the story are Ulrich Zwingli, Conrad Grebel, Felix Manz, George Blaurock, Lord Engel-hard, Felix Manz' mother and brother. Most of the other characters are creations of my own, based on stories of Anabaptist life I gathered while in Switzerland.

Never have I worked at any writing that has proved such enrich-ment to my own spiritual life and faith. My sincere prayer is that many who read these pages will receive a similar blessing.

C. Carol Kauffman August 1, 1954

Chapter 19

"Talent to Write"

Carol received the following letter from Brother C. F. Yake, written on September 21, 1954:

I had the privilege of examining the jacket which is to publicize your book "Not Regina," in a beautiful binding, and of course, with an unusual story. This reminded me of the splendid service you have given me to the "Youths Christian Companion" for many years. I recall our first acquaintance with you, and the interesting times along the way. Your product has helped me make the "Youths Christian Companion" a valuable periodical to the young people. Constantly we get words of appreciation for "Not Regina," and trust that it will sell widely as a book, and the sales will amount to many thousands. I praise the Lord for opening the door for this book publication.

The chief purpose for this letter, however is to encourage you to use your pen in the writing of short stories, or other contributions, which may be of special interest to you. In view of the fact that you are the only contributor over a long number of years, and are still doing it, I would very much like a special contribution from you for the last issue of 1954. This is the concluding issue of thirty-five volumes, and with the completion of that issue my responsibilities as editor terminate.

May I invite you to write for me presently, an article or story for that particular issue. It might not be a bad idea for you to write a short article, if you wish, and express yourself about your relationship with the "Youth's Christian Companion" and this office over these years. Then, if you could do so, a good short story for that issue would certainly be appreciated. . . .

Then, I would encourage you to continue your short story work. If you should send in a second story at your earliest convenience, following submission of the aforementioned manuscripts, that would be fine. The editor-elect, Urie A. Bender, will be glad to have you continue your valued service as the Lord leads. A special letter is going out to our contributors, and you will be getting one of these. However, this letter takes priority over all others.

May the Lord richly bless and continue to make you a blessing in your services to the "Youth's Christian Companion."

On September 22, 1954, Carol received a letter from Urie A. Bender:

Although I met you only once at the first Writers' Conference held at Laurelville in 1950, I feel that we are well acquainted. Your continued stories have meant much to me, and I am sure that they have been used of God for the advancement of His kingdom. Only eternity will reveal the results, which have come to individuals because you have been faithful in the exercise of your gift.

Recently you received from Brother Yake, present editor of the "Youth's Christian Companion," an expression of appreciation for your support of our youth paper in the past. He also solicited your contributions in the coming weeks and months. I would like to underline everything that Brother Yake wrote, and add my encouragement to his for the frequent submission of manuscripts from your pen.

I believe that God has given you a talent and He has given you a message that our young people in the Mennonite Church need to have. Presently we are making up a list of contributors for 1955 to appear under the heading, "Who's Who for 1955," in the first issue of the "Youth's Christian Companion" for the New Year. We would be happy to have your name appear in this list, along with any ideas or plans you may have for writing in the near future.

It is my hope that we will be receiving from you, many manuscripts in a steady flow, whether in single story form, or in continued story form. If you have any questions regarding planning for story scheduling for the coming year, or if you would like to discuss ideas with us, please write.

May the Lord richly bless you as you use your pen for His glory.

In the Goshen College archives is a file folder containing Carol's correspondence between 1941 and 1957. In that folder is a carbon copy of a page written by Carol. At the top is hand written "September 1954." It must be shared. It could have possibly been Carol's response to Brother Yake's request for another short story and was printed in the final 1954 *Youth's Christian Companion* issue—the last issue Brother Yake edited:

Twenty-seven years ago I received my first letter from Brother C. F. Yake informing me that a short story, which I had written for a class assignment in literature, while a student at Hesston College, was accepted for publication in the YCC.

To be sure, I was pleased. But the next line nearly took me off my feet, for it told me I had talent to write, which should be developed and dedicated to God and to the Church.

Talent to write? Stories? Me? Surely the letter had been miss-sent. Looking at the envelope once more I began all over. I held my breath, for the concluding paragraph asked if I would agree to send him a story a month!

Something inside me quivered. It unfolded slowly, came alive, grew, and grew from Kansas to Pennsylvania, to a place I had visited once as a child.

From that day to this, Brother Yake has been a friend, a special friend, and a brother, a Church Father of inestimable inspiration to me. He made me feel somehow that we must be workers together in one great printed effort to save our growing people, from the world for God and the Church. Without such a relationship between editor and contributor, writing stories, at least for me, would have ceased long ago.

So I wish to take this opportunity to thank Brother Yake personally for his many kindnesses, considerations, encouragements, corrections and counseling with Christian loyalties in all circumstances down through these twenty-seven years.

It has been a pleasure to work with a man whose retiring prayer from his office is that God will bless the new editor and continue to enrich the lives of our youth in the pages of the Youth's Christian Companion. The many letters in my files from his pen indicate that his heart and soul has been in his work. My own heart-felt prayer is that God will use me to help carry out Brother Yake's hopes and desires in this means of witnessing for the Master.

The Compass, a bulletin of the Christian Authors' Guild, published the following information in their February 1955 issue: "Among "Who's Who" for 1955 in the 'Youth's Christian Companion,' Clayton F. Yake closed 34 years as editor. Urie Bender is his successor. In this issue Mr. Yake states that Christmas Carol Kauffman, a Guild graduate, has been the longest continuing contributor to the 'Youth's Christian Companion' for 27 years. She has written more and has produced for the editor, more book length manuscripts than any other writer."

Despite her accomplishments and many accolades, Carol had a very human side, vulnerable to the fears and thoughts that every woman faces. In about 1955, Carol became concerned about her appearance. So much so, that she decided she needed to look younger. Of special concern was her hair, which was not as thick as it used to be due to the numerous surgeries that she had gone through. With each surgery her hair became even thinner.

"Nelson, what in the world shall I do?" Carol said. "I am getting so thin. Do you think it would be too vain to apply something dark to my scalp so it won't appear so thin, especially when I go out to speak in front of big congregations?"

"Now Mother, you look just fine to me," said Nelson. "No one will notice your scalp, because they will be looking into your eyes, just like I am doing right now. Your beauty comes from the inside anyway, not the outside."

"Well, I might have a good inside but my outside scares me when I look in the mirror!" Carol responded.

For some reason Carol also had fear of rejection. She was continually worried that others would make fun of her. While attending Hesston College, she mentioned in a letter to her parents that she was grateful that her roommate, Mary Histand, did not make fun of her. Carol did not want any one to perceive her as being proud. Both Nelson and Carol were so well known within the church that Carol was always introduced as Nelson Kauffmans wife, and Nelson was always introduced as Christmas Carols husband.

On November 10, 1954, Carol received a letter from Aaron M. Shank of Myerstown, Pennsylvania. This letter related the life stories that would become her next writing project:

Our official board for the Meckville Mennonite Church comprised of Brothers Simon G. Bucher (bishop), Cletus Doutrich (minister), Steve Olesh (deacon) and myself, recently agreed that I should contact you to see if your services would be available to write the life story of our Deacon's parents, John and Annie Olesh.

The members of the Olesh family were natives of Europe and members of the Catholic Church. Protestant missionaries came into their country, and they were led to turn from Catholicism through faith in Christ. Their departure from Catholicism at the time of their marriage carries with it some very thrilling and exciting experiences. The economic situation in their land and a growing family brought them to a condition of deep poverty; and so John, having heard of the prosperity in America, made his way to the States, and returned again to Europe with his savings to help provide for the family. He came to America a second and third time, and while here on his third trip, World War I broke out, and for a period of three years they had no communication with each other.

During these years, about seven in all, Sister Olesh struggled along providing for herself and five or six children, and at times was forced to feed the soldiers from her meager supply. Other exciting and trying experiences came her way before she finally made her way alone with the children to this country to join her husband. During this last absence of her husband she also buried one of her children, and Brother John had never seen this one.

Through all these trying years, Sister Olesh kept a firm hold on God, and witnessed to many, especially to the young folks and children who would gather in her home to hear the Gospel.

Their life in America was one of hardship through much sickness and poverty and spiritual unrest. After living in the west for a while, they finally moved east. They eventually bought one of the largest farms in the community of Meckville.

Four children were born in this country. The first two, twins named Adam and Eve, died soon after birth. The youngest of the children is our Deacon.

One day in the fall of 1932, while John was working in the field, he saw a group of men standing on a little hill not far away. As he walked toward this group of men he heard them sing a song, then bow their heads and pray. He approached the men and learned that the Mennonites (of whom he had never heard) were going to erect a place of worship there. John was convinced by the countenance of these men and their religious service and peculiar garb, that they were the true servants of God. My father was with this group of brethren.

Not long after the building was erected and mission work organized on this little hill about one-half mile from the Olesh home, John and Annie became some of the first fruits of the work there.

Poverty still threatened, and finally the date was set for the Sheriff's sale. On the morning of the sale, John committed it to the Lord and went to the field to work as usual. Before time for the sale, he was notified that they had decided to give him another chance! From then on he began to prosper. Later, on two occasions, they suffered the loss of both house and barn by fire. New buildings have replaced both, and though John is not a rich man, he became perhaps the most prosperous farmer in the community. (The community is one of the poorer type.)

Brother and Sister Olesh have made a real spiritual contribution to the Meckville Church. Some of their children and grandchildren are members of the Mennonite Church. Steve and his wife were converted a few weeks prior to their marriage about five years ago and less than two years later, he was ordained by lot to the office as deacon, which office he is faithfully filling. Joe, who was a heavy drinker and smoker, was gloriously changed about six years ago, and continues faithful. Niclolas Ninkovich, a son-in-law, who was a Greek Catholic and drunkard, was won for Christ and the Church, along with his wife and their daughter Annie.

After a number of years of illness, accompanied by intense physical suffering for many months, Sister Olesh passed away last year, two days before Christmas. During her illness she maintained a peace that was a source of inspiration to all who knew her. In her sickness, she looked forward to death with a desire to depart and be with Christ. Her body is buried in the Meckville Cemetery.

Bro Olesh is now retired and living with his daughter Annie. He is in good health, can converse in five languages and his mind is still keen and alert. We believe that he, with the older children of the family could give you enough of their history for you to write an interesting volume on it.

We would like to hear from you as to whether you would be interested in meeting with the family and securing information for the purpose of putting it in book form.

"We are waiting to consider your manuscripts as often as the Lord gives you ideas and you find the time to develop them," wrote Urie Bender in November. "Have you given any thought to writing another continued story? We would be particularly happy to receive word that you are contemplating such a project."

A month later, she responded to Urie, telling him: "During the past several months, I have received a number of offers from various places for story material. Two of these I am enclosing for you to read. The letter from [Aaron Shank of] Myerstown, Pennsylvania appeals to me above any of the others."

Carol traveled to Bethel, Pennsylvania, and spent several days gathering information for a story that she first named *The Afterglow*. She later changed the title to *Hidden Rainbow*.

On February 14, 1955, Carol received a letter from Anna Ninkovich, daughter of John and Anna Olesh, who lived in Myerstown, Pennsylvania. Anna Ninkovich mentioned the following regarding her parents' story: "There was no Catholic Priest. We had to go to Djnlovac every time for a priest, but many did not go. The priest would come to bless the homes—that is the Catholic homes—and the custom was that each home he went in to bless had to give him some money. He would also come to take charge of a funeral, but some one had to get him and pay him plenty."

A full year later, in February 11, 1956, Carol wrote the following letter to Mr. and Mrs. Aaron Shenk:

At last I am sending you the story, which I started over a year ago. For practically three months during Bible School, Tent meetings, conferences and etc, I did not try to work on it.

Before starting on the story, I did considerable research work on Yugoslavian geography, customs, and the Catholic religion. Of course you and the family agreed that parts of the story would necessarily have to be of my own creation, particularly the details.

Since John talked very broken, the daughter Anna [Ninkovich] was of great help to me. I will leave it entirely to your judgment as to how many of the church board members and the Olesh family should read this. I would like you to feel free in your evaluation, criticisms or suggestions. I hope I have not failed in your expectations. I have done my best and while writing it, the story proved a blessing to my own life.

Carol received a reply from Sister Shenk on March 26, which included some needed changes to the story as well as the following praise:

Through the months that you have been working on the story, we have been praying and waiting. We have also been doing a lot of anticipating and perhaps wondering more than just a little, what form the story would take. . . .

No one was disappointed. All enjoyed the story very much. We learned things that we never knew before, and have enjoyed talking about it all over again. We all had this in common I think; when we started to read, we could hardly stop. Characteristic of a good story, Not?!! . . .

We feel you concluded the story in a unique and very satisfactory manner, especially so, since the family is living, and it would have been difficult to carry the story farther without involving those living to a greater degree than would be desirable.

Through the years quite a number of people in adjoining areas heard of and became interested in the Olesh family, and those who have been told of your efforts in writing the story, seem eager to read it. And we feel that it might help to create more interest in the story if the folks know that Sister Olesh was a very real person who lived among us, right on the map in Pa! And much more appreciated by all who learned to know her during her thirty-odd years. . . .

We do so much appreciate your interest and efforts and trust that God will bless you much, and use your work on "Hidden Rainbow" to encourage and challenge all who read it.

Carol spent a lot of time making revisions and corrections with the manuscript. With all of her responsibilities she had to make every minute count. Because everyone was so busy, she had four different people typing for her. Carol wrote: "I have tried to comply throughout the story with the wishes of the Olesh family and the Meckville Church Board."

Two months later, Urie Bender sent these words to Carol regarding *Hidden Rainbow*: "I have read through your manuscript once and at this point want to express my personal appreciation for the story. It gripped me, especially in the latter half of the manuscript when the conflict of religious allegiance becomes intense."

In August 1956, Nelson and Carol and their two youngest children, James and Marcia, left their beloved Hannibal, Missouri, and moved to Elkhart, Indiana. After twenty-two years of devoted service as leader of the Hannibal Mission, Nelson was asked to serve as the Secretary of Home Missions at the Mennonite Mission Board. Harold Kreider, who was the assistant pastor for many years took over as pastor, and he and his wife, Roberta, and three daughters moved into the parsonage.

Nelson served for years in the presidency of the Board of Education. First as vice president, second as president, and last as vice president, again. This move to Elkhart was a total change for Carol. Her duties as a pastor's wife had come to an end. This new chapter in her life gave her more time to possibly write another story. Nelson traveled extensively with his new church assignment.

With extra time on her hands, Carol took a course in Invisible Reweaving and began a business out of her home doing reweaving and alterations. She contacted several dry cleaning businesses in town, and they kept her continually supplied with almost more business than she could handle. Both James and Marcia were attending Bethany Christian High School in Goshen, Indiana.

Nelson and Carol decided to transfer their church memberships to the Belmont Mennonite Congregation in Elkhart. They found sweet fellowship with the members there. It was also wonderful being just a few blocks away from Carol's father and sisters. Since Hannibal was not that many miles away, the family took many weekend trips to visit Ma Donna and her family who lived on the farm just outside Hannibal.

Nelson and Carol made sure they kept in contact with the hundreds of friends that they had found over the years. They both loved to entertain guests and began inviting foreign exchange students over for meals.

Included in a "Miscellaneous Collection" file is the following written by Carol in 1957:

I was born and raised here in Elkhart, Indiana. After graduating from the local High School, I clerked in a local department store, was advanced to the cashier job; worked in a doctor's office and for one year I worked as a hemstitcher and designer at the Singer Sewing

Machine Center. I helped to work my way through three and a half years of college by sewing for students and faculty. One summer I was floor-walker and time keeper in a Montgomery Ward Store.

I am married and 55 years old, have four children, two married and two at home attending High School.

We just moved back to Elkhart August 7, 1956 after spending 22 years as missionaries in Hannibal, Missouri.

I decided to take up "reweaving" as a part-time job, to help in paying the cost of educating our children, and because I like this business. Since my husband travels a great deal for the Board of Education and the Mission Board of our church, I like to keep busy and busy I am.

I opened my shop in the basement of our own home on September 19, 1956 and to date have turned out over 300 jobs. Occasionally I do alterations and those "extra" things.

Following college, I started writing and have over 100 short stories published, several serials and at the present my fifth book of Christian fiction is about to be released.

If I am not busy at one hobby, I am busy with another. Occasionally I accompany my husband for a speaking engagement. There are no dull or idle moments for me.

Urie Bender notified Carol by letter on November 20, 1956, that the first installment of *Hidden Rainbow* would appear in the *Youth's Christian Companion*'s first issue of 1957. "'Hidden Rainbow' is a story almost impossible to comprehend," said Carol of her new story. "The fortitude of the father of this family, to persevere and to reach his ultimate goal of having his family safe in the United States was truly inspiring."

By April 12, 1957, Carol received notice that the book-approving group at the Mennonite Publishing House favorably passed the publication of her new titled book, *Hidden Rainbow*. Carol dedicated the book "to John and Anna's children who greatly helped in furnishing material for this story."

Carol's Preface reads:

This is not a story dug out of the long ago, nor is it one of my own creation. Should anyone doubt the reality of any part of it, he may make inquiry of John Olesh (Papa), who lives with his daughter Anna and husband Nick Ninkovich, at Bethel, Pennsylvania.

Clustered around John Olesh in beautiful Berks County, below the Blue Mountains, you may locate his devoted children, each of whom contributed material for this story. John, now in his climbing seventies, is active in personal witnessing for Christ, particularly to prison inmates in nearby cities. He can converse in five languages.

The invitation came to me from the official board of the Meckville congregation near Myerstown, Pennsylvania, to come to Bethel and meet personally the Olesh family and hear this remarkable story. For a number of days, I lived in the home of John, Nick, and Anna. As long as I live, God will receive my thanks for this privilege.

Born in Yugoslavia to Catholic parents, John and Anna were led to truth, light, and true happiness through the ministry of a Protestant missionary. Their courage, faith, and suffering for the sake of soul peace will put many of us to shame for ever thinking our way was difficult.

Mother Anna, whose life story on earth has just closed, was considered by all who knew her, nothing less than a miracle. Many drove fifteen miles just to hear her offer prayer, not eloquent, not wordy, but one that described her Christian life of quiet, unwavering courage, serenity, and passionate love for those still in darkness.

Her afterglow is an enduring challenge and inspiration to her church, her children, and her many friends.

My one desire and prayer, like that of the Olesh family and the official church board, is that many, both young and old, who read this story will come to find their own rainbow arching from bended knee heavenward. —Christmas Carol Kauffman

The jacket cover reads:

Long before Yugoslavia had tasted democracy, the small farming village of Milentenac was touched by a freedom that even the most tyrannical religious leaders could not forestall.

Carol and Nelson at their home in Elkhart, Indiana, ca. 1957.

John and Anna Olesh led a simple life in their rented, baked clay home. The young couple was well liked by all the villagers. John, who wanted to provide more for his family, became a local hero after working in America for a few years. The women of the village admired Anna for her struggles during John's absence. But the villagers' respect quickly turned into suspicion and hatred when the Oleshes allowed a hungry traveler into their home.

How could this couple have known that this simple act of kindness would lead to turmoil and hardship? And how could they have imagined that they would have peace in spite of the terrifying circumstances they faced?

The Oleshes and their family learned that when God moves, no government, no organized religion, could stand in His way.

On October 15, 1957, Weaver Book Stores sponsored an evening program in Lancaster, Pennsylvania. The Olesh Family was present and spoke to a huge crowd of interested readers. The program included the family members giving reminiscences of the past. Then Carol spoke about writing the story and three people spoke on what the story has meant to them.

Hi Lights, a publication sheet of the Mennonite Publishing House, had this report in its October 18, 1957 paper:

B. Cutrell brought us a glowing report of the tremendous success of Lancaster publication day autographing party for *Hidden Rainbow*. Weavers, Lancaster and New Holland, are to be complimented for a tremendous job of publicity that so effectively brought more than 2,000 people to the YMCA auditorium during the evening. Quick rescheduling resulted in packing in 800 persons to each of two programs instead of one. It is now estimated that enough to fill the auditorium a third time were unhappily turned away. Many have asked to have it again.

The program included: devotions, tribute to "Mother" and reminiscences by Olesh family members, history of birth and development of book by Pastor Aaron Shank and Author Christmas Carol Kauffman, singing of "Mother's" favorite song by the Weaver Bookstore quartet, responses by four persons who read the book, and B. Cutrell's publisher's response and presentation of complimentary copies to members of the Olesh family and author. Store personnel were able to sell 171 books at the meetings because entrances and exits were mass movements. But author Kauffman was at the store on Tuesday afternoon to autograph copies. Fifteen to eighteen books per day have been sold since the party.

Chapter 20

An Important Contribution

By December 1958, Carol was gathering materials for her sixth full-length story, which would become *For One Moment*. She wrote the following to John Hartzler:

Through the courtesy and approval of Brother Freeman Eschelman, Pastor of the church at Toledo, Ohio, Nelson and I had a two-day interview with Fritz Linhart, a former Nazi, who has been in America for four years; two in Canada and two in Toledo, now being a member of the Mennonite Church at Toledo.

Bro Linhart has had a wonderful conversion story, which he is willing to have published. I would like to have your reaction and evaluation of this possibility; I will give you a synopsis of the story.

He was born in Dresden in 1913 to Lutheran parents. His father was a secretary in the Austrian Consulate. He had a happy home until his father went to war. He was the fifth and last child. His mother worked out. His father in 1918 divorced his wife and took the four youngest children to Koln with his second wife. She never wanted children. Fritz had an unwanted childhood experience. At ten he was put into a German Catholic school in Czechoslovakia where the father was assigned as a Secretary of the consulate in Prague. The Stepmother hoped Fritz would become a priest. He was baptized Catholic. He learned Latin and Greek, and was an altar boy for several years. He despised the corrupt practices of the priests, and wrote home that he wanted to leave school.

He was interested in cutting glass as a trade. His father put him in an apprentice school under a glazing master for three years. His faith in the Catholic Church was shattered. He got his masters degree in glazing. At the age of seventeen, he became a German citizen, and became a nationalist. He walked 80 miles to see Hitler take over Reichstag and became a worshiper of Hitler and believed in all his programs. He looked up his real mother after 13 years of absence from her.

He became engaged to a girl who died of pneumonia. Broken-hearted, he joined the army and fought on the Russian front. He was one of the 150 out of seven million soldiers who got a Gold Medal from Himmler for being 50 times close enough to the enemy to see the whites of their eyes. He was wounded eight times and he surrendered to the Americans. He lost all hope and desire to live with the fall of Hitler. He became a prisoner and was accused of being a spy and was lined up to be shot. He miraculously escaped and met a Christian who tried to help him. He rebelled against God and tried to enter the Russian zone.

He almost lost his life. He went to church in appreciation for deliverance and took a Bible home. He became really converted. He turned against war. He felt that Christians should be as devoted to Christ as he was to Hitler. He volunteered for missionary work but was refused in a school. He met a good Christian girl and got married. He had five years of hardship in Kiel during the reconstruction time. Five years later he came to Winnipeg. He has had definite experiences with God's leading and experiences that convinced him that non-resistance will work.

It would be the purpose of this story to show young people how men can be deceived by promises of the world, the agony of soul that comes when all hope in one's leader of the world system is lost, and the struggles of reorienting life and of gaining faith in God and Christ. The experience of conversion would be prominent. The reasons for losing faith in war and believing in the way of love would be the emphasis at the end.

He is willing to have real names or fictitious. Will this emphasis meet a need today? Let us hear from you.

Just twenty-two days later, Carol received a response from John Hostetler regarding the Fritz Linhart story:

Many of our fiction titles deal with unfortunate war, other ethnic backgrounds, or Catholic characters which have both good and bad features from a publishing standpoint.

Sometimes we have questions about the political or religious implications of such stories. However, we believe we would be interested in seeing a manuscript of your proposal if you can highlight the personal faith and search for truth without dealing too much with the intensity of relations with Nazism, Communism, or Catholicism.

There are several books of this kind on the general market too. If you can report these relations, and overshadow the story with personal faith in God as the triumphant theme, I think we should be interested in seeing you develop it. This, I realize is much easier said than done, but I shall be pleased to help you with counsel as I can.

It took Carol seven months to write this newfound story of courage and faith, in which she changed Fritz Linhart's name to Herbe Engelhardt. She sent the transcript to Fritz and his wife to read. They responded in July 1959:

We are glad to say that our hearts were touched, which leads to a new consecration to Him. We believe that many readers will start to think of their spiritual condition. We feel you have the gift of describing in a very precise way, the inner emotions of the souls of young and adult people.

I was surprised how you could know so many of the thoughts of a boy, which I myself did not realize until I read it and remembered. It was in fact so.

But I may say that Fritz Linhart is not Herbe Engelhardt. I wish I would be as good as Herbe. This brings me to a point that bothers me a little.

The story is in some ways different than it really was. Many people know us. They may have the impression that we did not tell the truth and then ask—What is now in the book? What is the truth and what is not?

The main theme is true without question; only some secondary details were different. We are glad that you changed all personal names.

Please forgive me, I will not criticize the heavy work you have done, but don't you think you were a little bit too sharp against the Catholics? Many believe very sincerely and may feel offended. Maybe I am wrong.

I know the main purpose of the book is to tell the "Happy News" to people in trouble and helping to show the way to get out of it.

We pray that the Lord may help, that this purpose may come true in the hearts of many readers so they may draw the only solution for the problems of their lives, to submit themselves to the loving care of the Savior.

May the Lord give His blessings in the future development of this work. We send the carbon at the same time. In His love united.

Fritz and Kaethe Linhart

By the middle of July 1959, John Hostetler sent an acknowledgment of the *For One Moment* manuscript, which was circulating among the book-approving committee. He suggested a possible schedule for the coming year since it was too late to have a book finished by the fall market.

"*For One Moment* is one of the greatest stories of courage and faith," Carol said. "It is so wonderful to have a personal friendship with the characters of all my stories. They blessed my life even more than I could have ever blessed theirs; to have the opportunity to feel as they felt and to have almost experienced what they experienced."

About that same time, A. J. Metzler wrote a surprise letter to Carol. He enclosed a thermo-fax copy of a letter sent to him with an inquiry concerning the translation of parts or all of her books into Japanese. Mitsuo Ikeda from the University of Rochester in New York had sent the following to Brother Metzler:

I have recently read the books *But Not Forsaken*, by H. G. Brenneman, and *Not Regina*, by C. C. Kauffman, published by you. I am very much impressed by these two books and I am wondering if you have published some other books, which are similar to those. I would appreciate it if you send me a catalogue of the books published by you.

I have a strong emotion that I would like to translate some of them into Japanese, either partly or whole book, depending on the permission by the author and on my ability. I have several reasons why I would like to translate them.

"I think this would be a good opportunity to make a contribution to a much needed literature program in Japan," Brother Metzler wrote in his cover letter, which accompanied Mr. Ikeda's letter. "Would you be willing to grant free publishing rights there?"

As soon as September 17, Carol got word from Paul Erb that *For One Moment* was approved for publication and would be printed first in the *Youth's Christian Companion*, beginning in early 1960, followed by a book published in the fall.

For One Moment was published in September 1960. "To my father Abraham R. Miller," Carol dedicated the book, "whose Christian faith has always been a source of great inspiration to me and whose consistent Christian life has always been worthy of my confidence."

Carol's forward reads:

Guilt, fear, failure, hurts…young Herbe Engelhardt is sucked into the swirling vortex of emotional confusion when his father divorces his mother, takes Herbe and his brother off to another home in a different city, and naively thinks everything will be better.

Thereafter, Herbe is driven by insecurity and hunger for something solid, for something he cannot name or understand. He longs for something conspicuously missing in his disrupted childhood, missing in his pseudo-religious training, missing in his work as a glazier, missing, he discovers, even in Hitler's promising regime.

Is life a mindless progression of disappointments? Is it a wasteland of pain and dashed hopes? Must it be empty of purpose and meaning?

Bitter, frustrated, fighting a God he doesn't know or understand, Herbe comes to a moment of crisis. In that one moment, that eternity against the wall, Herbe's destiny is determined.

This moving story is based on the real struggles of a boy who grew up in the emotional turmoil of a broken home and the political turmoil of Nazi Germany.

Don't be surprised if you find it nearly impossible to lay this book down until you have read the final page. It will indelibly impress you with the importance of love, the emptiness of the world, and the goodness of God that leads to repentance.

The following is from the original book cover:

To know God for one moment is the prayer on Herbe's lips as he awaits death at the hands of a ruthless communist guard. Both body and soul cry out for deliverance. But the sudden answer to his prayer belies the fact that, until then, the story of Herbe is actually a thirsting agony of unuttered prayer that issues finally in words at this wall of death.

Herbe began trudging toward this wall as a child. The account of these wanderings is not his alone, however. *For One Moment* is the story of many boys and girls. Taken from real life, Herbe stands as the symbol of countless children whose tender lives have been roughly torn—children whose dreams have been ruthlessly shattered and young people whose desperate searching's have taken them through the torturous twisting of an unguided, or worse, misguided adolescence.

The story of Herbe's life points a stark finger at some of the evil forces that play upon society. It shows the foundations of a home weakened by war, and then broken by divorce. It pictures the frustrated anger and consternation of a five-year-old when a mother and sister are left behind and a pseudo parent substituted. It reveals the terrible emptiness in a youthful heart when false ideologies crumble.

You'll live this story with Herbe. And in living it you'll grope for reasons why. You'll feel heartache, you'll face death and, if you're seeking, you'll find answers—the one answer.

The Gospel Book Store in Goshen, Indiana, had a special autographing party for Carol on Saturday, October 1, 1960, at Bethany

Christian High School with "Herbe" and his wife for all to meet. Then on October 14, the Weaver Book Store, in Lancaster, planned a meeting like the one Carol had with the Olesh family for *Hidden Rainbow*. Only this time they decided to have it in the local high school auditorium in Highland, Ohio. Carol gave the talk "How I Was Led to Write *For One Moment*." One thousand people were present. One person drove more than one hundred miles to attend.

Ten days later Paul Erb sent this letter to Carol:

Congratulations on the publication of your new book. The big turnout at your autographing party at Goshen is an evidence of the secure audience which you have found among our people.

I am wondering whether you have another book in process. I would like to encourage you to proceed on your next assignment, whatever it is. Our people will continue buying your books, we are convinced. If you have no other full-length book in mind, I think we once talked about the possibility of collecting and publishing a volume of short stories you have written, with probably some new ones added. Would this appeal to you? Please let me know what your plans are.

Carol sent this reply to Brother Erb:

Your kind words in the letter addressed to me on October 11, are appreciated very much. The turn out at the Berlin Ohio autographing party was twice as large as the one at Goshen. Herbe and I both were overwhelmed. Our prayer is that God will get all the glory through this experience.

The most rewarding and thrilling experience of my entire writing career came to me on October 5, when my youngest sister Helena, who has been living in sin for 35 years, called me on the phone and said, "I just finished reading *For One Moment*, and I want to tell you that it has brought me to my senses and I am going to live a different life from this day on. The other books you wrote convicted me, but this is the one that brought me to this position. Next Christmas I plan to be home with the family." You can hardly imagine the joy in our family over this victory, after all these years of praying over her!

It was my privilege to be to be at the bedside of Lucy Winchester the night before she passed away. I was glad I could tell her that I learned of one soul, a woman in Virginia who attributed her accepting Jesus Christ, through the reading of her story.

At the present, I am not working on a story because I can't decide which one to accept. I have had so many offered to me since I finished *For One Moment;* I hardly know which direction to go. I am praying for the Lord to lead me this time as definitely as he did for me before.

On October 29, Carol and "Herbe" appeared at a program held at the Conestoga Valley High School in Lancaster County, Pennsylvania. Event coordinators planned two separate programs, one at 6:30 and another at 8:30, to accommodate all the people that they anticipated would attend, with autographing sessions directly after each meeting. In the end, four separate evening programs were given—at 4:00, 6:30, 8:30, and 10:00.

"Six thousand persons saw and heard 'Herbe Engelhardt' (Fritz Linhart) at the Conestoga High School on Saturday afternoon and evening October 29," reported the *Gospel Herald* on November 8, 1960. "The police turned away another two thousand for lack of accommodations. It is not known how many returned home before reaching the meetings because of traffic congestion."

Chapter 21

Well Received

During the last week of November 1960, Carol spoke on story writing to a group of Elkhart High School students, the same school she and Norman once attended. During the same month, she received requests from Iowa, Illinois, and again in Pennsylvania for her and "Herbe" to give meetings similar to those they held in October. So on Friday December 9, 1960, Carol and Herbe gave programs at Penn Manor High School, sponsored by the Weaver Book store of Lancaster County, Pennsylvania. A large number of Amish came in horse and buggy to this meeting, requiring special accommodations.

The next morning, Saturday, December 10, she and Herbe gave two programs at the Peguea Valley High School. The same night, massive crowds attended three separate meetings at the Souderton Area Joint High School, sponsored by the Herald Book Store of Souderton, Pennsylvania. On Sunday morning, December 11, Carol spoke at the Towamencin Mennonite Church on the "Values of Life."

In the third weekend of December, Carol had quite an experience. On Friday and Saturday, she and Herbe gave seven programs to crowds totaling 3,300. Sunday morning they were snowbound and couldn't reach the airport. (Upon calling the airport, they were informed that all the flights have been cancelled anyway.) Monday was the same story. Tuesday their reservations were transferred from Allentown to the Philadelphia airport, as the street where they were staying had been blown shut with drifts of snow during the night. After flying to Toledo, they found that their train was nine and a half hours late from New York and covered with snow.

The whirlwind of traveling continued for Carol and Herbe. On December 17, they found themselves speaking at the same type of meeting in Kalona, Iowa.

On January 2, 1961, Herald Press was surprised to receive a letter from Halvor Hjertvik, manager of a Publishing House in Norway, requesting Norwegian rights to publish Carol's books. Just twenty-eight days later, A. J. Metzler sent a letter to Gerhard Reimer from Basel, Switzerland, which shared the following news:

While attending the Mennonite Central Committees annual meeting in Chicago recently, Irene Bishop reported a conversation she had with Mr. and Mrs. Nelson Kauffman. Irene quoted someone (at the moment I forgot who) who felt that Christmas Carol Kauffman's new book For One Moment, would have good possibilities if translated and published into German.

A month later Ellrose Zook from the publishing house sent the wonderful news to Mr. Hjertvik in Norway granting any rights for a translation that would be agreeable with the author, since she holds all translation rights to her works.

We are therefore forwarding this letter to Christmas Carol Kauffman. She will likely reply to you regarding translation rights for the book For One Moment. Inquiries regarding other books should be sent to her.

Carol responded in a letter to Mr. Hjertvik on February 20. Part of that letter gives a very positive response: "I will be very happy for the prospect of For One Moment serving an audience in your country. There seems to be a real appreciation for it in Christian circles here. Several book clubs have used it as their first selection.

Under separate cover, I am sending you two other titles which have European background, and which are still in print here, *Not Regina* and *Hidden Rainbow*. I will be happy if you could use either of these also. The other books I have written have totally American settings, but are now out of print. One, *Light From Heaven* is now being reprinted. If you would like copies of these, I could send them to you.

"The fact is," wrote Nomi Forlag from Norway, "that we have read *For One Moment* and were so enthusiastic for the book, that we want permission to print it in Norway. We also have interest in the publishing right for your other books too. We can tell you that Det Norske Misjonsselskaap, which is the greatest evangelical mission society on the continent, owns our publishing and today it is the greatest religious publishing house in Norway. I am looking forward to receiving a positive reply."

On April 20, 1961, Carol signed a contract/royalty agreement with Nomi Forlag to have her books translated and published in Norway. The publisher suggested that the book also be translated in Swedish and Danish. This publisher sold to five hundred stores.

In late February 1961, Carol sent a letter to Paul Erb—she'd found her next story:

While at the Lancaster meeting with Herbe the first time, a minister in the area informed me he could direct me to a man who had an interesting story, if and when I would be interested.

While Nelson and I were in Christopher Dock in January, we drove to Lancaster twice, and had these interviews with the character, who is Reverend Robert Turner, pastor of the Salunga Church of the Brethren.

This man, who is well known in the area, and whose wife works at the Weaver Book Store, was ready and willing to share his experiences and so was his wife and Mr. and Mrs. Harnish, his foster parents, who we interviewed in Lititz.

The story is different from any other that has been given me. It appeals to me in a number of respects, but before I would attempt to start working on it, I would like your reaction and evaluation.

My purpose in writing this story would be to try to portray some of the struggles of an adolescent and teenager living under such circumstances. The tremendous heartaches and longings of this boy in his struggle of loyalty to his foster parents, who he dearly loved and respected, and his compelling desire to get even with what he thought were fates against him, set the stage for his conflict. Furthermore, I would endeavor to show what a great influence for good Christian foster parents have on homeless children, as well as what a blessing a foster son can be.

Since Nelson and I were responsible for placing five such infants into Christian homes and since we have kept in contact with each of these cases for the past fifteen years, I feel somewhat familiar with such circumstances.

Briefly this is the story: Not until after Robert Turner was married, did he learn the mystery of his life. This is a story filled with mystery. Sarah Wood, a young hotel worker in Glasgow, Scotland, started for America to learn our methods for the same kind of work and to visit her two older sisters, who were married, one in Georgia, the other in Philadelphia.

On the same boat, she and a salesman of hotel accessories from England, made love. On arriving in New York they married. Six months later Sarah's wealthy sister in Georgia informed her that this man had another wife living in England. Sarah demanded an answer from him. He admitted. She refused to live with him unless he returned to England and got a divorce.

While in England, World War I came. He enlisted to avoid being drafted and was soon killed. Sarah, pregnant, went to Philadelphia to live with her sister until her delivery. While in the hospital her sister from Georgia came to see her and took command, saying this was a disgrace to the family and persuaded her to give the baby away and resume her maiden name. Sarah was heartbroken and wanted to die, and gave in to her sister's commands.

The sister started down the street with the baby and noticed a Mennonite Mission and gave the baby to a stranger, a girl, with orders to take it to the mission. People there said they were not a fondling home, but took the baby anyway. Visitors at the Mission agreed to take the baby by trolley to Millersville Children's Home. The baby's only identification was a slip of paper that Sarah secretly slipped inside the blanket, Robert Turner, May 24, 1913. Mother Sarah.

The Souders and Sister Mae, workers at the Home, fell in love with this baby. Souder's had a son slightly older. These two boys grew up like brothers. The Harnish's who lived on a farm two miles away had already taken a girl, now fourteen and a boy now eleven, from the home. They wanted another boy about nine years old. They visited the Children's home with that intent. They saw Bobby and could not forget him. Weeks later they returned to the Children's Home, when he was three years old, and asked for the baby. Sister Mae could hardly stand to see him leave. The Harnish's furnished a wonderful home and although he was very happy there, he could not forget Sister Mae.

Once in school, problems started with greater intensity because his name was Turner and his parents name was Harnish. Who was he? Where did he come from? Did he belong to anyone? No one could tell him. Each year these questions plagued him more. He and the Souder boy together determined to find out. In secret he searched the files in the Home Office. He found his name and that his mother's name was Sarah. He traced the name on paper and carried it in his shoe until it was worn out. He dreamed about his mother and cried for her. He feared he might be illegitimate. He had many inward conflicts.

He accepted Christ as a young man and was baptized beside G. Irvin Lehman. He was a good student and made excellent grades. He was obedient in the home, yet he was determined to find out where he came from.

Over his teenage years he had conflicts of hate with various experiences. The Harnish's sold the farm and moved to town. He got different jobs and saved up his money to take a trip to Philadelphia. At seventeen he took the trip with a neighbor boy. He looked in the city directory and found Sarah Turner listed. He walked many blocks to find out she was a colored woman. He had new fears. He called on many other Turners and no one heard of Sarah.

In the meantime Sarah had remarried. Before her marriage the fact that she had given up her baby always haunted her. She told her sad story to this man and promised to marry him only if he would help her locate her son and bring him back to her. He traced him to the children's home but Souders fearing what this strange man wanted, said only that he was in a good home. He went back and told her that the baby had died in infancy.

Bob, as a young man, took a trip to California with three other boys and there he had an experience with an atheist that confused him, but the consistent life at the Harnish's home kept him steadfast.

He went to Eastern Mennonite College, and a school in Philadelphia and Millersville. He married in 1937. Through the influence of his wife, together they persisted, until one day he located his mother, now a widow, and he learned the mystery surrounding his early life.

The Harnish's still treat him as their son and he honors them as his parents, although they never adopted him. He now testifies that if his mother's second husband had taken him home, it would have been to his ruination for he was very well to do.

He says that one of the outstanding influences in his early life was this Sister Mae. For years he so longed to have someone to call his own sister that he lied about it and told people that Sister Mae was his own sister.

One of the dominant hungers is to belong. In his frustrations he thought he would get satisfaction from joining the army. He went through a stage when he tried to find satisfaction making boats and airplanes and rafts that would belong to him.

This would be the thread through the story, *I Must Belong*. But, I will not use any of the real names

Paul Erb's reply came one month later:

I have just read your letter of February 22, in which you tell me of your leads on a new story about Robert Turner. This sounds interesting and should be a helpful theme, for there are many adopted and foster in our church. The story could be a help both to them and to their foster parents. Certainly the story you have outlined is loaded with emotion, but also with opportunities to set forth great principles.

Shetler and I agree that we do not have a story on this subject. In fact, I do not know one, and if you can handle this well, it ought to be a good one. I would encourage you to go ahead.

More than a year later, on March 31, 1962, Carol completed the manuscript for *Search to Belong*, Robert Turner's story. Carol sent the following letter to Brother and Sister Robert Turner:

At last I have the story finished and am sending you a carbon copy. Please return it at your earliest convenience. Usually it takes me about eleven months to write a story of this length. However, many other duties have delayed my working on this. In fact, in early January I went with Nelson to Florida specifically to write.

When I sent "Herbe" the story *For One Moment* to read, before it went to press to Scottsdale, he said he could say that ninety percent of it was fact. I am not sure that you can give that percent testimony to this story; however, I am safe in saying that I added to this one. In every instance where I have departed from the truth, I did so for the sake of developing the plot.

In February, Paul Erb, book editor at Scottsdale, was here and read what I had finished and was typed, then about 25 chapters. He said he was very pleased with it and was anxious for me to get it completed.

When I gathered material for *Hidden Rainbow* and *Dannie of Cedar Cliffs*, I spent a week with the family in each case, for I used real names in both, so I worked for accuracy. However, even in those stories, parts were also my own creation. In most of my stories I was given permission to omit some characters. It would make a story too long and too complicated to use everyone.

My wholehearted desire is that I have honestly, rightly, and fairly developed your own character personally. Please don't say I made you too idealistic. I purposely tried not to make you a goodie goodie. My family helped pray with me about this project. My sincere prayer is that it will accomplish what I have prayed it will. I had interviews with schoolteachers and parents who had experiences with orphaned children.

"I read it and I feel it is a good piece of work," replied Robert Turner. "I would like to sit down with you, and go over it in detail, but that seems impossible; therefore, the only thing for me to do is to write a detailed letter. This I want to do as soon as possible."

By May 24, Carol received this welcome announcement from Ben Cutrell, Publishing Agent: "Congratulations, Sister Kauffman, on the completion of another excellent manuscript. We are happy to become its publisher with the anticipation that its message will be well received. We think that this theme will make an important contribution to the current religious book-publishing world. You have done a very good job."

A day later, on May 25, 1962, Carol wrote to Brother Paul Erb:

Needless to say, I am delighted with the report of the book-approving group that *Search To Belong* has been accepted for book publication. I am also glad you think it is an improvement over my previous writings.

At the moment, I am not enthused over any of the stories which have been offered to me in the past. I am still waiting and hoping that something unexpected will come to my attention like this last one did. At this moment I do not have another story that appeals to me, but I will be on the lookout for one. As soon as I get the feel on a story, I will send you the gist.

Carol dedicated *Search to Belong* "to the fond memory of Sister Laura Umstattd" who was a faithful member of the Hannibal Mission Church. Carol's Preface reads:

Search to Belong is based on an actual experience and has been written by permission. All the names are fictitious. The author has created some details. This story has been written with the hope that it will:

1. Encourage foster children to respect and honor their foster parents.
2. Encourage foster parents to understand, love and respect the adopted child.
3. Assure children of unfortunate circumstances, that they can

overcome every obstacle, and make a fine contribution to society.

4. Remind workers in children's homes of the lasting impression they make on the children they work with.

5. Help the general reader to understand the needs of the foster child.

The book jacket states:

When little David Grant came to live in their home, the Aaron Loomases didn't know who he really was, or where his real parents were. Neither did Melvin Kolb or the workers at the Millersville Children's Home, where David spent the first three years of his life.

This biographical novel by Christmas Carol Kauffman will let its readers feel the emotions of David Grant as he grows to manhood. They will realize what it means for a child not to know who he really is; what it is like to face the possibility of being "illegitimate"; how difficult it is to be convinced that his foster parents really care, even when they are the kindest people in all the world.

Besides David, there are some people worth meeting: Sister Lora, first to teach David the meaning of love and acceptance; Miss Ranger, the teacher who understands; and somewhere--a lonely mother who wonders what has happened to her baby boy.

Mrs. Kauffman helps the reader view with new sympathy those who have been the victims of broken relationships and impossible circumstances—and those who have tried to do something about it.

Carol sent a copy of *Search to Belong* to Art Linkletter with the note: "Many times I heard you say on the radio or T.V. that you were adopted. I feel led to send you a copy of my latest book, which deals with one phase of the placed child situation. It is a biographical novel, based on the life story of a young man, now a minister in Pennsylvania. If you find the time to read this book, I would love to hear from you."

Carol got a reply that read: "Thank you most sincerely for the copy of *Search to Belong*. It appears most interesting, and I am look-

ing forward to finding the time to read it. Gratefully, Art Linkletter."

On June 1, 1963, Carol and "David Grant" participated in an
autographing Book Party at the Souderton, Pennsylvania, Herald
Book Store. There was a formal program with Carol and "David"
both speaking. It was very well attended.

On June 13, 1963, Carol received the following letter from Joyce
Snader, a teenage girl living in New Holland, Pennsylvania. Carol
received many hundreds of letters; she saved them all. This precious
one stood out from the crowd:

Greetings from Lancaster County, Pennsylvania! Perhaps you have
received many letters from a lot of people who you have never met.
Well, now you are receiving a letter from a typical teenager in Lancaster County.

I have read several of your books and I thought they were the best
books that I have ever read! I simply had to write and express myself
on paper, what I thought of some very fine Christian fiction books
written by a talented author. You!

Some time ago you made an appearance with Herbe from *One
Moment* at Conestoga High School. I enjoyed that tremendously! I
just got done reading *Search to Belong*. I am a very fast reader and I
read that book in exactly nine hours. After I was finished reading that
book I thanked God for my real Christian parents. In many books, you
are given the setting of the story, but to the reader it's an imaginary
place. But in this book, I was familiar with the setting of the story,
which made it twice as interesting.

I am quite a bookworm. Last week I was complaining to my mother that I read all the Christian fiction in our church library and how
I wished for a new book to read. The next Sunday my sister bought
home *Search to Belong*. I started reading it at 5:00 p.m. and finished
it the next morning at 10:00 a.m.

That was only one of the good books that I read, written by you. I
can plainly remember when I read *Lucy Winchester*. How that book
touched my heart!

I really haven't told you about myself except that I am a teenager. I am fifteen and go to Garden Spot High School. I am a member of the Weaverland Mennonite Church. I am so happy for you, Christmas Carol. I truly wish that more people would use their talents to please God. I know that you are a very busy woman. But, won't you please write back to me so I won't think that this letter ended up nowhere. I can't thank God enough for giving you the talent to write books. And, I can't thank you enough for using your talent to please God. May God richly bless you!

Yours in God's Love, Joyce Snader.

Chapter 22

Illness Strikes Again

As she entered 1964, Carol found herself without a writing project for the first time since she began *Lucy Winchester,* twenty-four years before. "It regrets me to say I have no story in the making and can give you no idea when I will be starting one," Carol wrote to Elsose Zook at Herald Press. "At least ten persons have offered me stories since *Search to Belong* was released, but for one reason or several, not one appealed to me enough to take it seriously. If God wants me to write another story I am ready and willing to be used as in the past. Some one gave me a suggestion for a story of my own creation, but that too does not appeal to me. You may hear from me some day."

Carol received a letter from Urie Bender telling her that a publisher wanted to translate *Hidden Rainbow* into the French language, as readers of Carol's books in Quebec, Canada, expressed a desire to have them translated into French. Moody Press out of Chicago, Illinois, began publishing Carol's books.

The Mennonite Mission Board's newsletter printed the following news on January 24, 1964: "C. Carol Kauffman received notice this week that *Marquis Who's Who Inc.*, will print a short biography of her and a list of her books in the 1964 edition of "Who's Who of America Women.""

Library Lines printed the following in their January, February, and March 1965 issue:

Permit me to digress a wee bit and share an intensely fascinating book with my fellow librarians, I've grown to love the folk from whose recipe books many savory dishes appear. Mary Emma Showalter brings quaint "Bulbs" of molasses of Grandma's kitchen up-to-date. I cherish a fond hope that someday I may visit *Mennonite Community Cookbook* areas. A warm spiritual welcome awaits one, I'm sure. I am grateful to my friend, the Herald Press manager, Maynard Shetler, for giving me this bewitching book.

By special request he obtained from their outstanding author, Christmas Carol Kauffman, (yes she was born on December 25th) a favorite family recipe and I tempt each (male and female) with Grandmother Miller's Chocolate Cake:

Cream 2 cups sugar with 2/3 c butter; add 5 egg yolks; beat 3 minutes. Dissolve ½ tsp soda in 1-cup sour milk. Alternately add this with 2 cups sifted all-purpose flour to first mixture. Beat 5 minutes. Add 2 squares melted chocolate. Fold in stiffly beaten egg whites. Put in three round wax paper lined pans. Grease sides. Bake 30 minutes in a 350° oven. Write me at 148 W. 16th St., Holland, Michigan for the Fudge Frosting notes. Eva Schakelaar

Another of Selena Belle Miller's recipes that was a favorite of Carol and her children were apple fritters:

Apple Fritters
2/3 cup milk or buttermilk
1 beaten egg
1/3 cup sugar
1 tsp cinnamon
2 tsp baking powder
1 1/3 cup flour
Mix well and add
2 or 3 peeled diced apples

Drop by spoon fulls into hot oil When golden turn over. Drain on paper bag. When cooled down roll in powdered or cinnamon sugar.

The Sound of Music was released in the local theaters in March 1965. Carol has a passion to go see the movie, especially since she had visited Switzerland to gather first-hand information to write *Not Regina* thirteen years earlier. She was very concerned that she not be recognized going into a theater in town. So one evening, of course after dark and wearing a scarf tied over her head, she and Marcia drove fifteen miles to the neighboring town to attempt to calm Carol's fears.

"Oh dear," Carol said to Marcia on the way to the theater, "My mother and father would roll over in their graves if they knew I was doing something like this tonight!"

Luckily she was never found out about this hidden adventure until readers like yourself see it printed right here on the pages of her life story!

The *Elkhart Truth* newspaper featured an article about Carol in their May 20, 1965, issue:

"I have to know what the last sentence is going to be before I write the first," says the Elkhart novelist Christmas Carol Miller Kauffman.

The author will not write just anyone's story. As she explained, the prospective character must have been "someone in emotional conflict who resolved it with a satisfactory conclusion based on religious faith." The complete work has to tell "a lesson in life," she says.

Although Mrs. Kauffman confesses she has told her own life story fifty times, she has never written it. Beginning with her birth in Elkhart on Christmas Day, Christmas Carol feels her life carries the "new found hope" which her name implies; namely, her marriage to the Rev. Mr. Kauffman when she was a young widow and their resulting religious work.

Besides her "stand up" writing career, she often pencils her work while standing up because she can think faster in that position. This mother, grandmother and busy homemaker finds time for invisible reweaving which she turned into a successful business. "I need something to occupy my time at home," she said.

Local residents who have not met this active woman will have the opportunity to do so Saturday. Mrs. Kauffman will be hostess at an autograph party beginning at 1 p.m. in the Bethel Bookstore. She will be introducing her latest book, *Search To Belong*, which relates the experiences of a foster child.

In January 1966, Nelson and Carol sent out the following letter to many lifetime friends who knew of Ma Donna's first grave illness in 1947 with rheumatic fever and then her three repeated attacks. She was married, and through the miracles of prayer in her behalf was blessed to give birth to three wonderful children. But because her heart was so severely damaged from the rheumatic fever attacks, the doctors would not proceed with open-heart surgery until they could at least predict a fifty-fifty chance of her survival. Nelson and Carol sent the following letter requesting fervent prayer in her behalf:

On January 25, our daughter MaDonna, Mrs. Ben Eberly, now living in Rocky Ford, Colorado, is scheduled to have open-heart surgery at the General Rose Memorial Hospital in Denver, Colorado.

Since you are aware, with us, of the seriousness of such surgery, we are inviting you to share with us in prayer for her and her family during this time. She will spend five days in intensive care following the surgery and will be in the hospital at least two weeks after that.

It is a real comfort to have the assurance of your fellowship in prayer in this experience.

Nelson and Carol Kauffman

In all things, in all circumstances and in all ways, our Heavenly Father is ready and willing to answer our prayer of faith if and when it is His divine will to do so. He will answer our requests when He knows that it is what we need. This was a time of great spiritual growth and faith. The prayers of Nelson, Carol, Ma Donna, and the entire family's prayers were justified.

Proverbs 30:5 says: "Every word of God is pure: he is a shield unto them that put their trust in him."

Psalms 1:6 states: "For the Lord knoweth the way of the righteous."

Psalms 11:5 declares: "The Lord trieth the righteous."

Nelson and Carol had been tried time and time again in their test of faith regarding their "Sweet Little Dolly." They knew the Lord understood their hearts. They trusted in His shield.

The most important thing in their entire lives was to be obedient to His divine will, follow the guidance of the still small whisper of the Holy Ghost, and be an instrument in the Lord's hands for good.

James 5:15 states: "And the prayer of faith shall save the sick, and the Lord shall raise him up."

Ma Donna recovered from this major surgery with wonderful miracles from heaven. One valve was too large, so they used a gathering stitch to make it smaller. A second valve was too small, and it was fitted with a new plastic valve the correct size for her very enlarged heart.

Before this miracle surgery she was too weak to care for her home and family. After the surgery she could run up a full flight of stairs and even go mountain climbing!

In summer 1967, Marcia, who was now married and living only twelve miles from her parents, visited Carol one afternoon, as she often did. Carol had a yellow-gray look about her. The whites of her eyes were almost as yellow as a manila file folder.

"Mother, you absolutely MUST go see a doctor today!" Marcia said, knowing something was horribly wrong. "I know that you are very ill. Not only are the whites of your eyes yellow, but your skin also. If you won't go yourself, I will take you right away."

"I hate doctors. I DO NOT WANT TO GO!" Carol boldly declared. "I will be okay. I am afraid they will just put me in the hospital. I have had enough of that in my life. I will just have Daddy come home and pray with me. I'll call him right away and all will be okay."

Carol knew better. Her fears were burning inside. She just would not let herself accept the truth. "I'm going to be all right, I have to be all right! I have grandchildren to love and care for."

Marcia knew that her mother would not go to the doctor on her own. Years before when they still lived in Hannibal, Carol traveled to the Missouri State Prison in Jefferson City with Nelson. She slipped and fell on a broken sidewalk and crushed her left elbow. She refused to see a doctor and spent weeks sitting in the bedroom with her elbow in a sling, almost unable to move because of the horrible pain. Her arm was bright purple, and then slowly changed to different shades of purple and gray, until it was completely healed. It took months. Thank the Lord it was her left arm so she could still write!

"See," Carol had insisted, "I didn't need any doctor at all. It's a lot cheaper that way too. Too many doctor bills keep me from doing what I want to do for others."

Nelson was out of town, so Marcia phoned and asked her father to come home as soon as possible. But Marcia did not wait for Nelson's return; she took Carol to the doctor immediately. Carol knew inside that this needed to be done, even though she insisted otherwise. She had experienced enough sickness, pain, and operations throughout her lifetime. She didn't want the doctor's bad news, but he confirmed her inward fear. She was placed in the hospital within the hour, critically ill with infectious hepatitis.

Nelson canceled all his church-related travels and spent days and nights at the hospital at Carol's bedside. The immediate family was ordered to take Gamma Globulin shots because her condition was so infectious. Only those with the shots could visit her. Even so, the family members, along with all the nurses and doctors had to wear gloves, masks, and hospital robes each time they entered the room.

Carol received literally hundreds of cards and letters as news of her grave illness spread through out the church. Thousands prayed for her recovery.

Nelson and Carol loved to go out to eat together when he came home from his frequent Mission Board travels. Both wondered if she could have possibly contacted this devastating illness from a waitress who carried the infection.

After Carol spent weeks in Elkhart General Hospital, the family thought she would soon die. Carol wondered if her time on earth was up too. She was so weak she could barely speak. She couldn't even lift her head from the pillow. Finally she was strong enough to return home.

Carol spent the first few months battling with utter exhaustion. Friends from the Belmont Mennonite Church brought in daily meals. They had such a love for Nelson and Carol that bringing in meals was one way they could show how much they cared. All food that was brought into the home had to be eaten with disposable spoons, forks, and plates because Nelson was not to eat with any thing Carol would have used. Carol felt helpless because she could not help others. After a lifetime of devout service, it was now Carol's turn to receive the love and caring that she so graciously gave to others over the years. Nelson was very attentive to her every need. Hundreds prayed for her recovery. It finally came after a long convalescence at home.

Carol loved to teach Sunday School. At the Belmont Mennonite Church in Elkhart, Indiana, Carol had a class of active thirteen- and fourteen-year-olds. They loved her dearly, not only as a teacher, but also as a friend. Carol was in her sixties! Most young teenagers don't have an "old lady" as a friend unless it is their own grandma, but there was no generation gap with these young people. Carol couldn't wait until she was feeling well enough to get back to one of the things she loved the most—teaching the youth and sharing her testimony of the Lord and Savior. She desired to plant seeds of faith and commitment in each individual class member.

Carol always made their class time extra special. She suggested that the class have ongoing missionary projects. Charity work was a natural with Carol. She wanted the same feelings to grow within each individual member of her class. She inspired them to have a desire to bless the less fortunate. Carol loved parties, too, and found time and special reasons to have her Sunday School class meet often for fun and laughter.

Robert Baker wrote the following article for the April 12, 1968, Mennonite Board of Missions Newsletter:

INVASION OF 216 TOWELS

Picture 20 boys and girls, age 13 and 14, smilingly marching up to the front of your church some Sunday morning, each of those intermediates carrying a sack of 10 or 11 large bath towels in their arms. One sits there in amazement, wondering what this unorthodox procession means.

There is nothing in the traditions of the Mennonite Church that supports this, there is nothing in our conference regulations that remotely suggests such behavior would be in order. This hardly fits in with the two hymns, 15 verses of scripture, and three-pointed Mennonite sermon that is standard fare at so many churches.

Whence cometh these invaders, these smiling, happy young people? What meaneth such actions, these splashes of worldly color amidst the quiet brown and gray hues of the sanctuary?

One squirms a bit in his comfortable pew, glances uneasily at his neighbor. Is this legal?

But relax, it's all right! Really, You should have been there at the Belmont Mennonite Church, Elkhart, Indiana, on April 7, 1968. You would have felt like those two brethren felt after Jesus had walked with them to Emmaus and there broken bread with them.

There are many Sunday School classes at the Belmont Church, many teachers, but there is only one Intermediate Class, there is only one Christmas Carol Kauffman. They are in a class by themselves. Every boy and girl at Belmont looks forward to being in this class.

The teacher has the magic touch. She holds them in the hollow of her hand. She may be a grandmother, but she understands the young set. One would hardly think that she could cope with this vivacious, vibrant, vitality-laded teenage mass of protoplasm, but she never loses her cool.

You may think of Carol as an author, as a bishop's wife, but now you must add teaching to her accomplishments. This is year number five with that age group. She loves them and they love her. She is motivated by one desire in her teaching—that of winning her pupils to Jesus Christ.

She desperately wants each of them to meet the Master. And toward this goal each class experience is directed. It has been her joyful experiences to have nineteen of her pupils accept Jesus as Lord of their life.

The "towel invasion" began as Carol was beginning with a new batch of intermediates. And she suggested that they might want to have a mission project. The class was told to think about it. Bob Rumfelt, a mere lad of thirteen, was in the class that day and suggested that they start as of then, now.

Bob whipped a worn dollar bill out of his pocket to start it off. Carol passed around an open Bible and each pupil who cared to do so, placed his "sacrifice" on the "altar." Suggestions as to where it should go came from the class. The Arabs in Jordan and the Faith Rescue Mission in Elkhart were mentioned.

Mennonite Central Committee wanted sixty-five-thousand bath towels for ten different countries. Fine. Bath towels it would be, stacks of bath towels, armloads of them. This class would do it. No sweat.

And the money began to roll in, Sunday after Sunday. It came from baby-sitting jobs, paper routes, allowances, and surrendered milk shakes. Before it would be done the sum raised would represent eleven-hundred McDonald hamburgers or four-thousand nickel candy bars.

It was not the widow's mite; it was the intermediate's mite that began dropping like gentle rain into the offering basket that slipped around each Sunday. Some saved for several weeks and shocked the class with folding money as it splashed among gentle coins.

Then disaster struck. Infectious hepatitis smote Carol Kauffman and she took up residence at the Elkhart General Hospital. For twelve long weeks, for thirteen Sundays she was absent from the class. Would the project fold up?

Nonsense! Nothing folds up in this class. Carrie Chupp took over the teaching of the class and money continued to pour in. It was squirreled away by class members as if their life depended upon it.

They were relentless in the pursuit of their goal. They chiseled and collected, sweated and scraped without mercy or restraint. From adolescent tithing cans came even two five-dollar bills, but coins continued to dominate the scene.

When Carol came back after that long convalescence, the money in the towel treasury was nearly one hundred dollars. Carol was shocked by the accumulation and rejoiced at the Lord working among them.

The intermediates should have been satisfied, but they were not. They continued to prime and pump the fund. Come spring they raked a large yard of a Prairie Street Mennonite Church brother and in sifted a ten-dollar bill. Randy Boyts, the class treasurer, felt like Silas Marner as he gleefully counted the accumulation several times a week.

The teacher was commissioned to begin getting "towel prices." When she coat tailed the manager at Grant's Department Store in Elkhart and asked him how many towels she could get for one-hundred dollars, he, of course, wanted to know more. Not many customers buy towels in such volume.

When she explained that it was her Sunday School class that wanted to buy them for relief, he was flabbergasted. He didn't know that there were children of such nature in Elkhart. When Carol calmly affirmed that there were, he immediately declared a ten percent discount to such a "wonderful class of boys and girls."

And later when Carol Kauffman went back to that same store manager and said that because of continued giving, she wanted to raise the order to two-hundred dollars, the man, according to Carol Kauffman, "about flipped." But for the teacher of the intermediates, nothing is surprising.

When the two-hundred-sixteen towels were wheeled up to the counter at the department store, waiting customers gaped and stretched their necks, "oohing" and "ahing." Carol is a little woman, pert and alert. There's lots of volume in this little package.

While the towels were being checked out at the register, she testified to the onlookers about this "wonderful" Sunday School class of hers. And the audience shook their heads. Did she mean twenty-two boys and girls saved two hundred dollars for relief?

And Carol, as pleased as a mother hen with her new hatched chicks, said there at Grants as she has said many times at Belmont, "There was never a Sunday School class like this Sunday School class." Only former members of the class that were there at Belmont shared their secret project with the entire congregation. Each Sunday we try to have what we call a "Focus on Missions." It is given just before the offering is lifted. Carol gave the "Focus on Missions" that morning.

She marched to the front and told the story as given above. Then her troops marched into the main auditorium through a side door. They spread themselves across the front of the sanctuary, each one carrying a stack of gaily-colored bath towels. And there before the congregation they dedicated two-hundred-sixteen towels to the Lord. It was pretty moving.

When they were done, Carol turned to us for response. We could only say what we felt so deep within us. From the congregation went up a grateful, "Amen, Amen." On April 7, 1968, every intermediate pupil stood six feet tall. The teacher stood six-foot one.

Nelson wrote a letter to Elsose Zook for Carol in November 1967:

Recently Carol received a letter from an official of Moody Press suggesting that she rewrite *Lucy Winchester,* and if she would do this, they would be interested in publishing it. She is seriously considering this now. She will not be able to do other work for some time because she has hepatitis.

Would you be interested in the manuscript? Mrs. Kauffman has been in the hospital twice since November 6 and may come home tomorrow or the next day. She will not be able to work at her normal rate for some time, but may want to do some writing.

By December Carol felt well enough to start rewriting *Lucy Winchester,* adding some chapters and including Lucy's passing.

Carol wrote a letter to Ristin Voitto Publishers in Helsinki, Finland. They requested a photograph of her in their last correspondence. Carol wrote:

It might be interesting to you to know that I am a small woman, not quite five feet in height and weigh one hundred ten pounds. I was forty years old when I wrote my first book. Now I am a grandmother of seven and will be sixty-six on Christmas day. My name is listed in "Who's Who of American Women."

If God so leads I hope to write another story based on real life experiences. Right now by request, I am rewriting my first book *Lucy Winchester* for a new publication. It has been out of print for over ten years, and since I wrote it I was given a scholarship by Herald Press to take an advanced writers course. That is how I became a member of the Christian Author's Guild. I am at liberty to give you publishing rights. Herald Press holds publishing rights to *Search to Belong* so you would need to contact Mr. Ben Cutrel the publishing agent and negotiate with him.

Carol was asked to speak to a group meeting of the Christian Business and Professional Women of America in Chicago, Illinois, in November. "I am not able to give you a definite answer," she responded. "Although I have gained considerable strength, my blood test shows my liver is not functioning properly yet. My doctor told me I had to cancel all speaking engagements for a year. I would like very much to be able to, but in all fairness to you, do not hold this date open for me."

Pathway Publishing House in Aylmer, Ontario, requested the opportunity of publishing Carol's stories. Her reply was:

Over the years I have had numerous requests to have *Unspoken Love* [her only full-length story still unpublished] published in book form, but the answer I got from Scottsdale was that it is outdated because there was nothing like CCC camp today, but the story is true and a number of the characters in the story were greatly disappointed when it was not published, after the house promised that it would be.

I will leave it entirely to your judgment, what to do about that publication. I can say that because of repeated requests, *Light from Heaven* was republished and has been selling very well. Moody has put it in soft back. Also, Moody suggested I re-write *Lucy Winchester* which has been out of print for a number of years, and at the present the Publishing House is having it republished.

I have material on a new true story, which I hope I can start working on before too long.

The publishing house in Finland wrote that sales were going well for Carol's book *For One Moment* and asked for publishing rights for all of her other books.

Chapter 23

A Life Fulfilled

Carol received a recognition certificate signed by C. Maxwell Stewart, which reads:

The National Register of Prominent Americans
Through the Board Of Trustees has elected
Christmas Carol Kauffman
A member of Prominent Distinction of The National Register Of Prominent Americans
With full recognition of such affiliation, attested to by the Seal of the Register
and the signature affixed hereto.

Carol's father, Abraham Rohrer Miller, passed away on December 31, 1968. He lived one hundred years, three months, twenty-three days. His mind was active and alert up to one week before his passing. He died of old age. When Abraham was ninety-five, the DMV would not renew his driver's license. He was devastated because for many years he spent Sunday afternoons visiting invalid friends, many of who were twenty years younger. At age ninety-seven, he walked a granddaughter up the aisle when she was married. His furnace repair business came to a halt when he could no longer drive on his own.

At his funeral the first week of January 1969, Carol was very ill with what she assumed was a bad case of the flu. At the conclusion of the memorial meal at the church, she went to see the doctor who gave her some medicine and sent her home to recover.

After a few days she was feeling much worse. The doctor immediately had her admitted to the hospital on January 6. After further examination, the doctor determined that Carol needed her gallbladder removed. No, not a ninth major surgery! But there was no getting out of this one. It had to be done.

The surgeon confirmed after removing her gallbladder that her spleen, pancreas, and liver were barely functioning. One doctor gave a welcomed diagnosis that she would gradually get better with proper medication and antibiotics and that she would soon be well enough to go home. A second doctor determined that her body would gradually decline and death was certain to occur, possibly before the end of the month. Nelson, of course, clung to the hope of the first diagnosis.

Nelson spent day and night at her side, giving words of comfort and reminiscing about their precious years together. He went home only to bathe, shave, change clothes, and get the mail.

On January 18, Nelson wrote to the extended family:

Dear Ones in the Family,

A letter came to our house about the time Carol went to the hospital, and ordinarily I suppose she would write, but I will this time since I discovered the letter on the stand here. By all signs the doctor seems well pleased. This noon she ate her first solid foods and I am hoping that she will be able to take it. Her liver was in very bad shape and the doctor was uncertain about her at first, but it seems that many prayers are being answered for her. I have been in the hospital most of the time since January 6. Esther stayed with her for four nights also, for which we are so thankful.

Things are different now also since Grandpa is gone. He was with us a long time and left a great testimony, which I hope we can all learn from. I am not sure when Carol will be able to come home and what the future holds, but I hope that she can get back to fairly normal living again. She will no doubt need to take Cortisone a long time, for that seems to be the only thing that reduces swelling of the liver.

This changes my schedule also, but I am glad to be in the office more and around home. I so hope also that she will get well.

God bless you all and thanks for your prayers. We thank God for the good health of all of you. Love to all, Daddy

Hundreds of cards and letters of love, get-well wishes, and appreciation arrived in postal bags at the house and hospital. Nelson read each one for Carol. She felt tremendous love and support from every one, both near and far.

Carol was more concerned about her family than her own severe illness. She sure loved her grandchildren! One granddaughter was just born two days before Carol's sixty-seventh birthday, not even a month previous. She couldn't wait to hold precious little Melissa! She reminded Nelson that two of the grandchildren had birthdays in January. Yvonne was going to be three on January 11, and Bradley would turn ten on January 12. Carol had already purchased their birthday gifts. Nothing pleased her more than to shower her grandchildren with gifts of love. "Nelson be sure to get each grandchild little valentine gifts and candy," she kept reminding her husband, as Valentine's Day was just the next month. "I want them to remember me and remember how deeply I loved them. How much I will miss them." She continually asked Nelson about her church friends who were ill.

Flowers lined the room. After two weeks, her condition was declining instead of improving. Nelson called Ma Donna, Stanlee, and James (all three of whom lived out of state) and asked them to come as soon as possible. He knew that they wanted time to visit with their mother before the Lord took her home to be with Him. After Carol's condition became more life threatening, the doctors would allow only the immediate family in her room.

Carol's four children, along with Nelson, spent hours in the hospital. They passed the time in the lounge reminiscing and putting puzzles together in between personal visits with Carol. The most difficult experience for them was to witness Carol suffer with excruciating pain in spite of the medication.

Carol knew her time was near at hand. Tears were shed, until there seemed to be no more, not because there was no hope of eternal life but because of the separation that was soon to come. Her last week was spent in and out of consciousness.

All four children took turns spending one-on-one time with their loving mother. Before Carol lost consciousness Marcia told her the names she had chosen for her soon-to-be-born baby. The special name if it was a boy and the specific name chosen for a girl.

"Mother, how am I going to make it without you?" Marcia cried. "I can't believe this is happening to you. The Lord must love you so much he wants you home to be with Him. It's way too soon for you to go, but I can't bear seeing you suffer any more. It rips my heart to see you like this."

They both shed tears. Both for gratitude of being mother and daughter and gratitude for experiencing love that binds, love that endures, and love that brings greatest joy in this life and the life awaiting the faithful.

"Marcia, will you make sure my hands look okay in my casket?" Carol requested. "The veins in my hands look so awful. And please make sure my hair looks okay. It's your turn to take care of me now dear little one."

More tears were shed.

"Oh, dear, I was so much hoping to finish at least the story that I have started about the precious lady in Chicago," Carol remembered. "I guess it will have to wait. I'm so sorry that I couldn't finish just one more story. It must be written. It must be told!"

She slipped into an hour of labored breathing. Then came back to and spoke again.

"Marcia, I was so hoping to have a gift to give to Robert Baker even though it is long before his birthday. If I wait too long, then I won't be able to give him anything. We have always had such a fondness for each other because of our writing interest. Would you go and find him a really beautiful pen and tell him it is especially from me?"

"Yes, Mother," agreed Marcia. "Is there anything else?"

"Yes, make sure you choose my navy dress for them to bury me in. I like that one because it has long sleeves and will cover up my arms. They are all blue from the I.V.'s. Also, it is cold outside too and I would be wearing it to church Sunday if I would be going."

"Oh dear me, my hands, my hands they are even worse than my arms!" Carol pleaded, "I am not a proud woman, I never wanted to be proud in the Lords eyes, but . . ." She slipped away for what seemed like an hour then woke up enough to ask again, "Could you help Daddy, and decide what to do about my hands, they look so ugly?"

"Yes," Marcia promised. "Daddy and I will make you happy. Is there anything else?"

"One more thing, I told Daddy to make sure my Sunday School class all be there and recognized when they speak of me at my funeral. They are so important to me. I love them so. I hope they know that for sure."

Carol slipped away again, this time for many hours.

This shouldn't be happening! There were still too many unwritten stories to be found, grandchildren and great-grandchildren to see born, and lifelong friends to visit. More tears flowed.

Just before Marcia left that evening, Carol regained consciousness enough to mention one more thing, "There are so many people out in the hall all dressed in white, please don't let them come take me before I am ready to go."

Marcia pleaded with the Lord to take Carol home soon; she could not stand to see her mother suffer more. Carol was finally ready to go the following morning.

There was a bright, beautiful, clear winter sky on the morning of January 30, 1969. At age sixty-seven years, one month, five days, Carol peacefully passed away at nine-twenty.

She was survived by her husband, Nelson; two sons, Stanlee of Chicago, Illinois, and James of Lawrence, Kansas; two daughters, Ma Donna Eberly of Amarillo, Texas, and Marcia Miller of Goshen, Indiana. Also three sisters, Mary Esther Bigler and Helen Myer of Elkhart, Indiana, and Nellie Mann of Naples, Idaho.

News of Carol's death spread very quickly. She was buried on Saturday, February 1, in the Prairie Street Cemetery, in Elkhart, Indiana. A memorial service was held at the Prairie Street Mennonite Church on Sunday, February 2.

"She died as she wrote, herself in the middle of the story, deeply immersed in every action," stated Carol's friend and well-known author Robert Baker in an article that appeared in the November 1969 issue of *Christian Living*, a Mennonite Church monthly publication:

ON THE DEATH OF CHRISTMAS CAROL KAUFFMAN

Christmas Carol Kauffman was a small woman. Christmas Carol Kauffman was a large woman. She was small in stature; she was large in spirit. She was the wife of Nelson Kauffman, Mennonite educator, writer, bishop, minister, and evangelist. She stood beside him, perhaps a step behind him, the mother of his children, the keeper of his home, content to serve him, their family, and their church.

And yet she found time to be a prolific Mennonite novelist, the author of eight novels and over a hundred short stories. She wrote out of her 22 years of mission experience at Hannibal, Missouri, her travels to Europe, her active life in the church. She did not write for the scholar; she wrote for common people, and many loved her. Youth's Christian Companion serialized several of her novels, captivating the readers, and unfortunately, this resulted in some youth papers being read behind Bibles and hymnbooks as sermons were preached and songs were sung.

Over a dozen years ago the Nelson Kauffmans moved to Elkhart, Indiana, and we all at the Belmont Mennonite Church were thankful they chose us over a multitude of other churches in the Mennonite ghetto of northern Indiana. They became an integral part of our fellowship.

My vocation is teaching; Carol's was homemaking. Our avocations, writing, were the same. And it gave us common ground for conversation. When one knew her, she was willing to share her loves and fears. Her loves were Nelson, her family, the Mennonite Church. One of her fears was that which is common to many of us, the fear of rejection. It was a needless fear. To know her was to accept her.

Besides being a wife, a mother, a writer, she taught a Sunday school class, served on the Missions Committee at the Belmont Mennonite Church, and was in much demand as a speaker for various churches and writing organizations throughout the country.

She lived a full life, rich, vibrant. And Christmas Carol Kauffman died like she lived, zestfully, with full anticipation. She moved from life to death with complete freedom. For her, death was a new story, one like those she wrote, truthful, real. As she lay upon her hospital bed and the plot of that story began to unfold before her, she threw herself into the mystery of death and became intensely involved with it. She died like she wrote, herself in the middle of the story, deeply immersed in every action—doctors, nurses, and family playing minor roles; she the leading character. It was a thrilling story, it should be told.

When I visited her in the hospital, I realized I never saw her defeated. She did apologize for her cries when the pain became too great to hold within her frail body. But, I never heard her question her condition, no words of protest to God, no begging, just acceptance with complete abandonment and assurance that she was in the hands of the One she loved.

On those visits to that antiseptic hospital room, Carol would make two requests of me. She would ask me to sign the little visitor's book and she would ask me to pray for her. And when I prayed, she always held my hand, firmly, resolutely, and unashamedly. Her firm clasp seemed to be an attempt to comfort me. For Carol cared for more for others than herself.

Part of the time at the hospital she was in a double room. She worried about the patient in the bed beside her. Was that woman getting the proper care? Were people being kind to her? Carol would not live without caring for others. Her room companion recovered; Carol did not. But that was all right with Carol. She was more interested in others than herself.

When Christmas Carol Kauffman first went to the hospital, she expected to regain her health. But God decided otherwise. Her earlier bout with hepatitis had taken its toll. A laboratory report after gall bladder surgery revealed "persistent hepatitis, severe." Her liver, scarred and hardened, could not keep up with the driving demands of the tiny woman. And Carol soon realized that God was planning that she should make her abode with Him.

So Carol, several days before her death on January 30, 1969, told her husband, Nelson, to jot down the things she wanted at her funeral and at her memorial service. The funeral service would be simple, private, only the family and relatives. But for the memorial service she had many plans. And Nelson took an envelope from his pocket and wrote down her wishes for that public memorial service. Elaine Nand, from the Belmont congregation, should sing "O Holy Night." Barbara Stowell of the Engelwood Church in Chicago where her son Stanlee is pastor should also sing. And would it not be nice if her Intermediate Sunday School class from Belmont ushered at the memorial service? And some of the talented class should provide pre-service music, and softly play their stringed instruments in the balcony of the Prairie Street Mennonite Church. Perhaps her friend Johnny Allison should have the devotional, and, of course, Ray Bair, her pastor, would preach the sermon.

I was present at the memorial service. It was beautiful. By then she was buried; yet she was present. She was there when Elaine Nand cried at the end of her song, the notes wavering, quivering. Carol was there in spirit to pat her on the hand to say, "There, there, it's all right, it's all right." Carol was there when members of her Sunday school class wiped tears that spilled from their eyes, swallowed the emotion that rose in their throats. And she comforted them.

Carol cared. Proof? Listen. The last time I stopped at the hospital to see her it was not possible to visit with her. The physical condition was deteriorating, as spiritual concepts seemed to sharpen. I did speak to Nelson. His face was tired, drawn. And I felt I must do something for him. What could I do for this man who has done so much for the church? So I asked him, "Is there anything I can do?" At first he shook his head, but then he said, "Yes there is something you can do. Will you deliver this card to the Hartzler-Gutermuth Funeral Home?" I took it. It was a tiny card authorizing that Carol's eyes go to the eye bank. It was her wish. As she was dying, she thought of others. I delivered the card, heart full, eyes brimming.

Can death be the highlight of one's life? Is death a triumph or a disaster? For Carol it was a triumph. The last afternoon of her conscious life was January 29, 1969. She was in a private room at the Elkhart General Hospital. In her room at the time was husband Nelson, daughter Ma Donna, son James, long-time friend Johnny Allison. It was three-thirty. Carol knew that this was the time to say things she felt and was experiencing, thoughts that lay upon her heart. Only a writer would understand this fully, to sense the pregnant words inside that must be born.

Carol looked around and within a matter of thirty minutes said a number of things that could only be said by someone like Carol. She said, *"It is real bright."* Of course, it would be bright. Heaven was just over the horizon, Jesus was the light. A doctor stepped into the room. Carol included him in her next statement, "I wish you could all go along." Carol wanted to share her anticipated joys. Her loved ones heard her say clearly, "The gate is open." Yes, Jesus opened that gate two thousand years ago. Her face lit up as she murmured, "I am the happiest woman in the world." And why not? In a few hours she would leave her pain-wracked body and slip into one of unlimited spiritual dimensions, perfectly designed for her. Moments later Carol found comfort in the Work as she whispered, "Jesus said I am the way." That's right, Carol, He is the Way, the Truth and the Life. You found it so, you found it so.

After this she said nothing more until six that evening. Then came her last words, that great line from Tennyson: "May there be no moaning of the bar when I am put out to sea." I'm sorry, Carol, we did mix grief with our joy when we heard your frail craft had sailed. We have to. We must weep for those we love.

At 7:00 that evening she was given a sedative. At 9:20 the next morning her soul fled. God welcomed her into heaven, and probably some angelic choral group sang a carol for Carol.

Carol had a little book entitled *A Diary of Private Prayer* by John Baillie. It contains a month of prayers for private worship experiences. Beside each one is a blank page for the participant to write one's own prayer. I've read the prayers she penned in that book. They are written in blue ink, in black ink, small words, large words. And as I read them, I hear Carol talking to God.

The first night I opened that little book of prayers by Christmas Carol, the first one I saw was:

"My emotions are big and I thank thee for emotions. Someday I will adore Thee to my heart's fullness and praise Thee for all You have done for me and with me here on earth. Let the glory of Thy goodness fill my being, mind, soul, and body, that those who come to this house will know I am a happy, radiant living Christian because of Your unspeakable love."

"Your prayer is answered, Carol."

The woman of whom I write was not perfect. She would have been the first to admit her imperfections. I write not to eulogize her but to share her glorious departure, for in her triumphal dying she told me and all who have eyes to see, ears to hear, that our God is real, alive, close, tenderly involved with His children.

Some people come to death with whining and regrets, dragging their feet, rebellious at the summons. They protest leaving this earth, for they fear the unknown, they are in terror. Not Carol Kauffman. When you know God in life, you don't fear Him in death.

Nelson made sure that her wishes were fulfilled in every way. The Prairie Street Mennonite Church was filled to capacity. Friends traveled hundreds of miles to support the family and express their love.

Mel Lapp, a worker who spent three years in Hannibal, gave the opening prayer. Harold Kreider, the man who helped so much with the Hannibal Mission as assistant pastor and then pastor when Nelson and Carol moved to Elkhart, gave her life history.

Pastor Ray Bair gave the sermon. Following are some of his selected remarks as he shared Carol's handwritten prayers:

It was a never-ending source of amazement to us at Belmont over the years, and especially these last two years in particular, to sense the love and bonds and understanding that existed between Carol and her intermediate class. We never knew what to expect when the class would come up with some kind of project and experience together. It was always a source of joy within the congregation to sense this kind of relationship. Carol will be deeply missed in that class. There will be faithful teachers that will come and serve, but there will not be another Carol in their midst. We all know this.

Every year there was an annual trip that the intermediate class took to Chicago. Those of us who knew what happened on those trips, always looked forward to the intermediates going, because we knew that something was going to happen with the Spirit while they were gone, and it did. And again and again lives would be blessed in that experience as they went from place to place, from spiritual experience to spiritual experience. Some of the young people found Christ as Savior on these trips. They had times of great joy and fun; good times together.

One of the stops on their annual trip to Chicago was always at the Englewood Mennonite Church where Brother Kauffman's son Stanlee serves as pastor, and it is most fitting that today the Englewood Church Cherub Choir will share with us in song.

This is a hand-picked service; a heart-picked one. It isn't very difficult to find out what Carol is trying to say to us. It is her last way of saying it. The text that she requested to use is Psalms 4:3. It says: "But know that the Lord has set apart the godly for himself; the Lord will hear when I call him."

I am going to be using a good book this afternoon, "A Diary of Private Prayer," which is really a collection of poems by John Baillie. In a great deal of this book, Carol had written her own prayers and I want to use parts of some of these and the total of some of them; they are not long. Often in these prayers she would be remembering her husband and children and grandchildren. I will read those parts that apply to all of us and from which out of this we can gain some encouragement, some instruction and some further insight into what it was that caused her to be the kind of God's daughter that she was.

In an introductory way, because it seems to be the spirit of the afternoon, I would like to read one of them in which she prayed:

Dear God, I know you often dig our wells of joy with your spade of sorrow. Thank you for each trial that has drawn me closer to your blessed side, in prayer and confiding. The greater the sorrow, the greater the joy. You move in mysterious ways, your wonders to perform.

I am sure you can well imagine, that after my reading again and again, which I have, these prayers in the days since her death, that I feel like I know Carol better that I ever did before. Perhaps in a new way, and I am sure, I know Christ in a new way as well. And, we would hope that this is what would happen to us all in these moments of meditation now.

One of the things that Carol has said many times, I understand, and I heard her say it in the hospital. She said she felt so cleansed, washed, so clean and the first time I heard her say it, I felt like my first impulse to say, "Carol, you don't need to be cleansed, you are such a good woman already; such a deep Christian." But yet this was the cry of her heart. She wrote as she prayed and said:

Purge me dear Heavenly Father, from sin through thine own precious blood. Wash me and I shall be whiter than the driven snow. I must confess, I have neglected the study of thy most glorious word that has and will alone keep me from sins, both great and small.

Another time she wrote:

My sins, my sins, they take such hold on me, dear Lord, that I marvel at thy mercy on my soul and at the multitude of thy forgiveness. Great is thy graciousness and marvelous thy love. Help me today to learn what you mean when you say, "Thy faith hath made thee whole." Forgive me for faithlessness and eyes that have not seen; ears that have not heard. A heart that hath not known compassion for the lost about me. I have fainted too often and staggered at your promises. Give me thy power to cast out every fear in my own heart and to go boldly out to witness that, "love casts out fear."

Another prayer of Carol's:

Christ Jesus, who has promised to baptize us with the Holy Ghost and with fire, help me today, not to break one of the least of your holy commandments or to speak lightly to another about the sacredness of them. For to thy kingdom are we one.

Dear Lord and Father of us all, help me now to serve you with my entire being in love and patience, remembering it is our faithfulness you want, not our success.

Another went this way:

Dear Lord, I thank thee for a warm house and solid floors and a roof that does not leak; for windows to look out and let daylight in, for bread and eggs and a stove to cook on.

. . . God's goodness is revealed in many ordinary ways. But, there is a stretch from this point to the other end, to the other extreme, and it is that there is faith that God can do the unordinary; that the ordinary things of life do not bind him.

And Carol prayed:

Dear Lord, I realize that when you do something great, you start with a great problem and when you do something astounding, you start with impossibility. Thank you, my dear Lord.

Another prayer:

Dear Father, should anyone stop today at my door for a cup of water, I will give it in thy name. Teach me the blessings of joyful giving. Most precious Jesus, fill me today with thy Holy Spirit and turn my heart to those in soul distress.

Let my lips speak today of the things of eternity. Let my only desire be to bring more glory to thy ever-holy name. For each time I have failed to exactly forgive. Now, for these young souls from unhappy homes, give me an extra compassion and an understanding sympathy. Amen

She prayed yet another:

Because you made me you understand my ways. Today I am determined to love thee more, trust thee more, serve thee more and witness for thee in an unusual way. I am very ordinary, but you are extremely extraordinary. Therefore, since I am yours you can do great things through me.

One more prayer:

> Dear Lord, my Savior, to be a more effective Christian woman, wife, mother, teacher, neighbor— this I long to be, and I need your divine help. For each lack of intense interest in my calling, do forgive me. This life is short—tomorrow may be too late to speak that certain right word to that certain person. Give me wisdom, love, patience, tact, and above all, sincerity of heart and purpose. Remember those of our family who are facing hard decisions and perplexing trials. Hold us together so we can demonstrate to the world our blessings, handed down to us from praying parents, Amen.

Set apart for God. I'm sure there could be no greater thing that could happen as far as Carol would be concerned. Today, may we come to have a deeper closer relationship with the Savior.

On September 9, 1970, Nelson signed a contract with Pathway Publishing Corporation of Aylmer, Ontario, Canada, to publish *One Boy's Battle*, the story that Carol finished writing in 1951 but was never published. *One Boy's Battle* is the same story of Millard Grinstead as *Unspoken Love*, but it omitted the first twenty-seven chapters and began with his youth. It was released in book form on March 1, 1971. On a carbon-copy paper in the folder from the archives is Carol's dedication, hand-written in pencil:

> To the two sons God has given us,
> Stanlee De Von 16
> James Milton 11
> and to
> my aged father
> whose daily Christian life
> has always been an example
> of
> patience, piety, and purity.

By 1975, sixty-six thousand copies of Carol's stories that Moody Press published had been sold. Moody Press filled circular bookracks in restaurants, grocery stores, and many other businesses though out the United States with Christian literature such as Carol's.

In 1976, Carolyn Mullet from Hartsville, Ohio, wrote and directed a dramatization of *Light from Heaven*. *Little Pete and Other Stories* and *Unspoken Love* were published by the Conestoga Valley Book Bindery in 1972.

Carols books continued to be published in several foreign languages, including Japanese, providing readers in many different countries, wholesome life changing, uplifting stories.

Carol's son Stanlee wrote the foreword for the 1971 edition of *One Boy's Battle* (*Unspoken Love*):

You have in your grasp a life-changing story. It's been over 20 years since my mother laid down her pen and said her last words. Yet, I continue to receive letters like these:

From Mission Kansas: "I grew up with two alcoholic parents. I have been in six mental hospitals. In desperation I went to a book-store. I don't know why, but I bought one of your mother's books. Until that day I had never heard of Christmas Carol Kauffman. During the next two weeks I devoured all of her books that I could buy or borrow. Her books helped me see what real life is all about. I now have an understanding of true Christianity. I can face hurt and trial with new assurance that God will see me through."

From Paden, Oklahoma: I would like at least fifty copies of each of your mother's books. I want to give them to Christian schools and young friends. Christmas Carol Kauffman's writings are so helpful to Christian living. Please tell me where I can buy her books."

Mother became ill with hepatitis as she was writing her [ninth] book. She was unable to complete it before she passed away. It was the story of a black woman who lived in a small second story flat on the south side of Chicago.

This woman had enough love to mother over thirty children, none of them her own.

In such true stories, real life and true Christianity have spoken to many persons around the world. Mother's books have been printed in several languages.

Some of her books are out of print. Fortunately one of her stories has come alive again in the edition you now hold. I pray you will be blessed as you read "One Boy's Battle."

Myra, the main character's mother, wrote to the author of this story: "It will make me very happy if just one boy like our Millard will be drawn to Christ by reading this story. This is my prayer."

Nine of Christmas Carol Kauffman's books are still being published today by Christian Light Publications in Harrisonburg, Virginia.

In chapter twenty-five of *Not Regina*, Carol wrote and shared her lifetime belief and personal commitment to Jesus Christ:

"The Bible also teaches true discipleship, which means that our entire way of life must be patterned after Christ. That means we can't hide our identity, for everything we say and think and do will be an outward expression of our inner experience with Christ. "Whosoever will come after me, let him deny himself, and take up his cross, and follow after me." It is not attending church every Sunday. It's far more than that. It's living with Christ and for Christ every moment of every day. We are no longer our own, but Christ's, for he has purchased us with His own precious blood, and put His Spirit within us to guide us and make us want to follow Him."

"Do you understand that Regina?"

"Yes," she said, "Tell me more."

"Regina, you must know that God does not promise an easy life to those who follow Him. He promises His children misunderstandings, sufferings, trials, hardships, but He tells them to count it all joy when they fall into many kinds of temptations, knowing that the trying of faith worketh patience.

"When our minds are stayed on Christ, we can have perfect peace. And even though you may have to stand against your parents, Regina, you can know that Christ stands with you. The Bible asks children to obey their parents, but when parents ask children to do something contrary to God's will, God's higher law that we should obey Him rather than man must be our guide. 'He that loveth father or mother more than me,' Jesus said, 'is not worthy of me.'"

"And that would mean a friend, too?" asked Regina.

"It would mean any person or anything that could keep us from serving God with all our hearts. Unless we love Him above everything else, we do not really love Him."

***

In spite of the pains of our world of experiences, we must keep our focus on the things of eternal benefit. All of us have a chance to choose righteousness over evil, truth over falsehoods, and hope over mediocrity.

Each character in my mother's stories chose to reign triumphant in the midst of enormous hardships and stumbling blocks.

Stumbling blocks become stepping-stones, not only to help us individually, but also to bless the lives of others in the example set. The choice is ours, how and what we do with our own personal trials in life.

Mother chose stories that would uplift and inspire and motivate others to change. In the fifth chapter of Matthew, Jesus said:

"Ye are the light of the world. A city that is set on a hill cannot be hid.

"Neither do men light a candle and put it under a bushel, but on a candlestick; and it giveth light to all that are in the house.

"Let your light so shine before men that they may see your good works and glorify your Father which is in Heaven.

"For verily I say unto you, till heaven and earth pass, one jot or one tittle shall in no wise pass from the law, till it all be fulfilled. [A jot is a very small amount. A tittle is absolutely nothing at all.]

"Whosoever therefore shall break one of these least commandments and shall teach men so, he shall be called the least in the kingdom of heaven: but whosoever shall do and teach them, the same shall be called great in the kingdom of heaven."

Romans 5:19 declares: "By the obedience of one shall many be made righteous." This refers to Our Savior Jesus Christ's obedience, but it can also be interpreted to include Mother's obedience to the

Lord. Her books have taught and inspired thousands to desire to live a Christ-like life. That was her sole purpose in life—to share the gospel light and the gospel life through her story writing. Now her life has become an open book. She taught us well through sharing her own personal gospel light through the life she lived.

It has been my privilege as her daughter, to write her life story, and share the testimony of my mother's life with others; that her sixty-seven short years were well spent. She taught us well through her example, and she can indeed be called "great" for her service on earth as she entered the kingdom of heaven.

In John 14:6, Jesus said, "I am the way, the truth and the life." Jesus Christ is truth. Truth alone sets us free. Truth is sure and steadfast. Truth rings strong. There is no doubt. There is no wondering. There is no fear. Truth brings courage, courage to stand firm. Jesus Christ will provide courage and strength beyond any and all things. The early Anabaptist leaders fought a fight for truth, no matter what the consequence. Even torture. Even death. Without doubt. Without hesitation. Jesus Christ is our sure anchor in any storm, the light for every dark path. Jesus Christ is our personal Savior, who invites us to come and find His way, His truth, and His life.

As one strives for faithfulness in serving our Lord and Savior Jesus Christ, and by earnestly seeking His divine will, we are all partakers of His infinite atonement (see Romans 5:11). He gave His life that we all might live again. It is a sacrifice beyond our mortal understanding because of our Savior's great love for each and every one of us. "With his stripes we are healed" (Isaiah 53:5). Because of His atoning sacrifice, we are saved from eternal death. With His love, we can begin to understand the depth of His atoning sacrifice. We all must seek to accept this greatest gift to mankind.

—Marcia Kauffman Clark

References

M any sources used in this book are found in the Mennonite
Church USA Archives–Goshen, located at 1700 S. Main
Street, Goshen, Indiana 46526. Goshen Archive sources include:

"The Story of Carol Miller and Norman Hostetler," told by Nellie
Mann, transcribed by Dorothy Jean Horst (Nellie's daughter),
sent to Marcia Clark, January 26, 2003.

"Story of early years of growing up," by Nellie Mann as told in a letter, October 24, 1968, to Ma Donna Eberly, 6 pages, originals and
photocopies.

Information about Christmas Carol from niece Dorothy Jean Horst.

Letters from Nelson E. Kauffman to Carol Hostetler, 1929–1930,
1942, photocopies.

Letters from Carol to Nelson, no dates given, during courtship, originals.

Letters from Nelson to Carol, no dates given, during courtship, originals.

Letters from Christmas Carol Kauffman to Mary Histand, 1931–
1932, photocopies.

Letter from Nelson Kauffman to Abram and Selena Miller, 1949–
1950.

Materials collected by and originating from Ma Donna Eberly. Ma Donna collected this material while she was taking a writing course and wrote a short story about her mother Christmas Carol Kauffman

Ma Donna Eberly, "Christmas Carol," unpublished manuscript, 33 pages plus table of contents, Amarillo, Texas.

Compositions of Christmas Carol Kauffman, 1912–1913, originals.

Letters from Carol Hostetler to Abram Miller, 1928–1929, originals.

Letter from Carol Kauffman to Abram and Selena Miller, 1931.

Letter from Carol Hostetler to her parents, undated, while she was attending Hesston College Hesston, Kansas (1926–29).

Twenty letters from Carol Kauffman to Abram and Selena Miller, 1930–1934. Includes short story "Comin' Home Soon," written ca. 1932, originals.

Letters written from Abram and Selena Miller to Carol Kauffman, 1930–33, originals.

Letter from Carol Kauffman to Nelson Kauffman, September 19, 1942.

Letter from Nelson Kauffman to Carol Hostetler, 1929, La Junta, Colorado.

Newspaper clipping, "Hostetler-Kauffman Marriage," June 10, 1929.

Church Record of Carol and Nelson E Kauffman and family, "Hannibal Mennonite Gospel Mission," Hannibal, Missouri, 1934–1957.

"Life Story of Christmas Carol," Carol speaking on cassette tape, 1960,

Cassette tape of Christmas Carol Kauffman's funeral service, 1969.

File folders including correspondence between Carol Kauffman and various editors and publishers for each published book.

Robert Baker, "On the Death of Christmas Carol Kauffman," Christian Living, November 1969.

Robert Baker, "Invasion of 216 Towels," Mennonite Board of Missions Newsletter, April 12, 1968.

Sources used in this book and currently in the author's possession include:

Mennonite church hymnals: "Life Songs" and "Church Hymnal."

The entire collection of Christmas Carol Kauffman's books.

James Whitcomb Riley, "Riley Love Lyrics," (Brooklyn, N.Y.: 1883, Braunworth, 1883; reprinted, 1921), includes original photos.

Family History booklet prepared by David Mann, includes letters written by Abraham Rohrer Miller and Selena Belle Wade between December 12, 1894 and March 12, 1896.

Cassette tape of Abraham Rohrer Miller and interview by Dorothy Jean Horst.

Russell Krabill, "Christmas Carol, Beloved Writer," Mennonite Quarterly Review, August 23, 1990.

Books by Christmas Carol Kauffman

Lucy Winchester

Lucy Winchester stumbled through years of spiritual ignorance, doubt, disappointment, and despair until she eventually found peace again in Christ. This true account reflects the goodness of God patiently leading those who are thirsty to the fountain of living water.

Light from Heaven

Joseph Armstrong suffered cruel scorn, rejection, and deprivation at the hands of his father. But the faith of his devout mother taught Joseph to trust his kind heavenly Father who helped him love and forgive and rise above his circumstances to a life of purpose and peace.

Dannie of Cedar Cliffs

The life story of Daniel Martin illustrates early Mennonite life and shows what part a layman can have in the progress and up building of the church.

Not Regina

When Regina Strahm finds herself caught in the religious tumult of 1500s Switzerland, she is warned against the Anabaptist heresy. But why then does the official religion fail to satisfy her spiritual emptiness? Have the heretics found a quality of life worth dying for?

Hidden Rainbow

When a forbidden New Testament shatters the calm of their Yugoslavian village, John and Anna Olesh learn that when God moves, no government, no organized religion, can stand in His way.

For One Moment

For One Moment portrays a home weakened by war, then broken by divorce, the terror and tragedy of battle, the emptiness of a life without God, but ultimately reveals the reality, personal interest, and love of the Saviour.

Search to Belong

When little David Grant comes to live with the Loomases, they didn't know who he is or where his real parents are. This biographical novel explores what it means for David not to know who he really is and how difficult it is to be convinced that his foster parents really care.

Little Pete and Other Stories

"Little Pete," "The Pink Plate," and "Trusie Kohl" are just three of thirteen stories that will bring tears to your eye and offer a deep concern for others. Each story contains a lesson for readers of all ages.

One Boy's Battle

The true account of a young man who was almost persuaded to become a Christian but turned his back on his mother's and church's teaching to join the army. In the thick of the battle, he turns to the Lord in repentance.

M arcia Kauffman Clark is the youngest of Nelson Edward and Christmas Carol Kauffman's four children. She moved with her parents and brother James Milton, to Elkhart, Indiana in August 1956. Marcia sang in a sextet with the same six girls all four years while attending Bethany Christian High School in Goshen, Indiana. She attended Hesston College in Hesston Kansas for two years and graduated with a Secondary Education Degree in Home Economics in 1965 from Goshen College, Goshen, Indiana. The greatest highlight of her high school and college years was singing and especially with the traveling choirs while in college. Marcia moved to Phoenix, Arizona, in 1969. She has enjoyed teaching, singing, sewing, and creative writing. She sang first alto in a ladies quartette for twenty-one years. She had the opportunity of traveling in Europe twice as a ten-year member of the Sonoran Desert Chorale. She and her husband, Stephen, live in Tempe, Arizona, and have eight children, twenty-two grandchildren, and one great-grandson.

Marcia Kauffman Clark can be reached by mail at:
1026 East Alameda Drive
Tempe, Arizona 85282